Macmillan Books for Teachers

Beyond The Sentence

Introducing discourse analysis

Scott Thornbury

MACMILLAN

Macmillan Education
4 Crinan Street
London N1 9XW
A division of Macmillan Publishers Limited
Companies and representatives throughout the world

ISBN 978-1-4050-6407-1

Note to Teachers
Photocopies may be made, for classroom use, of pages 164–175
without the prior written permission of Macmillan Publishers
Limited. However, please note that the copyright law, which does not
normally permit multiple copying of published material, applies to the
rest of this book.

Series design by Mike Brain
Page layout by Sharon Ryan
Illustrated by Janos Jantner
Cover design by Andrew Oliver
Cover photograph by © Robert Morris / Alamy

The authors and publishers would like to thank the following for
permission to reproduce their material:

Extract from *Introducing Egyptian Hieroglyphs* by B Watterson (Scottish
Academic Press, 1993), reprinted by permission of the publisher; Extract from
'Police dog sacked after biting innocent man' taken from www.ananova.com
16.09.03, reprinted by permission of the publisher; 'HAVE YOU forgotten the
way to my hut' from *One Rose, One Bowl: The Zen Poetry of Ryokan* translated
by John Stevens (Weatherhill Publishers, 1977), copyright © Weatherhill Inc
1977 reprinted by arrangement with Weatherhill Inc, an imprint of Shambhala
Publications Inc, Boston (www.shambhala.com); 'I EXPECTED to see only
one pink blossoms' from *One Rose, One Bowl: The Zen Poetry of Ryokan*
translated by John Stevens (Weatherhill Publishers, 1977), copyright ©
Weatherhill Inc 1977 reprinted by arrangement with Weatherhill Inc, an
imprint of Shambhala Publications Inc, Boston (www.shambhala.com);
Extracts from *Reward Pre-Intermediate Student Book* by S Greenall
(Heinemann, 1994), reprinted by permission of the publishers; and from
English File Student's Book 1 by C Oxenden and P Seligson (Oxford University
Press, 1996), copyright © Oxford University Press 1996, reprinted by
permission of the publishers and 'Go Slow' from *The Switch* by Murray
Edmond (Auckland University Press, 1994), reprinted by permission of the
publisher on behalf of the author; Extract from *Johnson's Clean and Clear*
Advert, reprinted by permission of Johnson & Johnson Ltd; Extract from
'Seiko Advert' taken from *Jack Magazine* April 2004, reprinted by permission
of SEIKO UK Ltd; Extract from 'Martian Mettle' by Govert Schilling taken
from *New Scientist* vol.180 Issue 2426 20.12.03, reprinted by permission of the
publisher; Extracts from *Kingfisher Pocket Encyclopedia* (Kingfisher
Publications Plc, 1983), copyright © Kingfisher Publications Plc 1983,
reprinted by permission of the publisher; Extracts from *Great Little
Encyclopedia* edited by Nicola Sail and Amanda Learmonth (Miles Kelly
Publishing Ltd, 2000), reprinted by permission of the publisher; Extract from
Arab Folk Tales by I Bushnaq (Penguin Books, 1986), reprinted by permission
of Random House Inc; Extract from *The Penguin Book of Australian Jokes* by
Phillip Adams and Patrice Newell (Penguin Group Australia Limited,1994),
reprinted by permission of the author; Extract from 'Why dogs chase
rabbits' by Danny Evanishen taken from www.ethnic.bc.ca/sampledurak.html,
reprinted by permission of the author; Extract from *OAL: Defining Issues in
English Language Teaching* by H Widdowson (Oxford University Press,2003),
copyright © Oxford University Press 2003, reprinted by permission of the
publisher; Extract from *Learning To Write First Language/Second Language*
edited by A Freedman, I Pringle and J Yalden (Longman, 1983), reprinted by
permission of the publisher; Extract from 'The Habit'by F Spufford from
Granta 77 2002; Extract from *OAL: Teaching Language As Communication* by
H Widdowson (Oxford University Press, 1978), copyright © Oxford
University Press 1978, reprinted by permission of the publisher; 'Death of the
Poet' by Dorothy Porter copyright © Dorothy Porter from *Heat 3* 1991,
reprinted by permission of David Higham Associates; Extract from *Collins
DIY Manual* by Albert Jackson and David Day (HarperCollins, 1993),
copyright © Albert Jackson/David Day 1993, reprinted by permission of the
publisher; Extracts from *Aussietalk: Macquarie/UTS Australian English Corpus*,
reprinted by permission of the publisher; Extracts from *The Royle Family: The
Complete Scripts* by C Aherne and C Cash (Granada Media, an imprint of
Andre Deutsch Limited, 2002), reprinted by permission of the publisher;
Extract from www.fury.com, reprinted by permission of the publisher; Extracts
from *English File Students Book 1* by Clive Oxenden and Paul Seligson (Oxford

University Press, 1996), copyright © Oxford University Press 1996, reprinted
by permission of the publisher; Extract from *Men Talk: Stories in the Making of
Masculinities* by J Coates (Blackwell Publishers, 2003), reprinted by
permission of the publisher; Extracts from *Oxford Progressive English Course for
Adult Learners, Book One* by Albert Sydney Hornby (Oxford University Press,
1954), copyright © Albert Sydney Hornby 1954, reprinted by permission of
the author; and from *The Bald Prima Donna: A Pseudo-Play in Act One Act* by
E Ionesco translated by D Watson (John Calder Publishers, 1958), reprinted
by permission of the publisher; Extract from 'The Pop Star and the Footballer'
from *New Headway Pre-Intermediate Student Book* by Liz and John Soars
(Oxford University Press, 2000), copyright © Oxford University Press 2000,
reprinted by permission of the publisher; Extracts from *Sugar* Magazine
March 2000, reprinted by permission of the publisher; and from 'Column 8'
first published in *Sydney Morning Herald* 08.09.92, reprinted by permission of
the publishers; 'How to recycle a goat',copyright © Christian Aid, reprinted by
permission of the publisher; 'Leave-taking' by Susan Bamforth taken from
Mini Sagas edited by Brian Aldiss (Enitharmon Press, 2001), reprinted by
permission of the publisher; 'Grass' first published in *Cornhuskers* (Harcourt
Inc, 1918), copyright © Holt, Rinehart and Winston 1918, renewed 1946 by
Carl Sandburg, reprinted by permission of the publisher; Six lines from
'America' by Allen Ginsberg copyright © Allen Ginsberg 1984 taken from
Journals Mid-Fifties 1954-1958 (Penguin Books, 1996), reprinted by
permission of The Wylie Agency Inc; Extract from *Mr Norris Changes Trains*
by C Isherwood (Chatto & Windus, 1935), copyright © The Estate of
Christopher Isherwood 1935, reprinted by permission of Curtis Brown Ltd,
London on behalf of the Estate; Extract from 'British Government' first
published in *The Independent on Sunday* 21.09.03, copyright © Independent
Newspapers 2003, reprinted by permission of the publisher; Extract from
'Unit 42, Listening to Notice' from *Impact Grammar* by Rod Ellis and Stephen
Gaies (Addison Wesley Longman China Limited, 1999), copyright ©
Addison Wesley Longman China Limited 1999), reprinted by permission of
the publisher; Extract from *Framework 2* by B Goldstein (Richmond
Publishing, 2003), copyright © Richmond Publishing 2003, reprinted by
permission of the publisher; Extract from 'Stratford settles for draw after top
hockey start' from www.stuff.co.nz/stuff/dailynews 29.06.04, reprinted by
permission of Taranaki Daily News; 'Millions of snowflakes in the blue sky'
and 'Your body is as beautiful as the sea' both poems were supplied to
Francesca Verd but we have been unable to trace the students who wrote them;
Extract from *Innovation in English Language Teaching* by D Hall (Routledge,
2001), reprinted by permission of the publisher; 'A Dream So Real' by Patrick
Forsyth taken from *Mini Sagas* edited by Brian Aldiss; foword by Joanna
Lumley (Enitharmon Press, 2001), reprinted by permission of the publisher;
Extracts from adverts for 'Wrinkle Free' and 'Easy Shoe Shine' both from
Kleeneze Catalogue, reprinted by permission of Kleeneze; Extracts from 'The
Girl Who Stayed in the Fork of a Tree' and 'Keep Your Secrets' both taken
from *The Virago Book of Fairy Tales* edited by A Carter (Virago, 1990); Extract
from advert for 'RetarDEX' taken from *Men's Health* Magazine December
2003, reprinted by permission of the publisher; Extract from 'A comparison of
textbook and authentic interactions' taken from *ELT Journal* 58/4 October
2004, copyright Oxford University Press 2004, reprinted by permission of the
publisher; Extract from *Upper Intermediate Matters* Student Book by J Bell and
R Gower (Longman, 1992), reprinted by permission of the publisher; Extract
from 'Top of the food chain' by Emily Colston first published in
www.tntmagazine.com March 2004, reprinted by permission of the author and
publisher; Extracts from *An Unsuitable Attachment* by Barbara Pym (Grafton
Books, 1983), reprinted by permission of The Executors of Barbara Pym; and
How To Be Good by Nick Hornby (Viking, 2001), copyright © Nick Hornby
2001, reprinted by permission of Penguin Books Ltd; and *Whale Rider* by Witi
Ihimaera (Reed Books New Zealand, 1987); 'A Dream So Real' by Patrick
Forsyth taken from *Mini Sagas* edited by Brian Aldiss; foword by Joanna
Lumley (Enitharmon Press, 2001), reprinted by permission of the publisher;
Extracts from adverts for 'Wrinkle Free' and 'Easy Shoe Shine' both from
Kleeneze Catalogue, reprinted by permission of Kleeneze); Extract from
'A comparison of textbook and authentic interactions' taken from *ELT Journal*
58/4 October 2004, copyright Oxford University Press 2004, reprinted by
permission of the publisher; Extract from *Upper Intermediate Matters* Student
Book by J Bell and R Gower (Longman, 1992), reprinted by permission of the
publisher; Extract from 'Top of the food chain' by Emily Colston first
published in www.tntmagazine.com March 2004, reprinted by permission of
the author and publisher.

The authors and publishers would like to thank the following for
permission to reproduce their photographic material:

Haddon Davies p122(bl); Piet Luthi p185; Pippa McNee p122 (br);
Photodisc p149.

Although every effort has been made to contact copyright holders before
publication, this has not always been possible. If notified, the publisher
undertakes to rectify any errors or omissions at the earliest opportunity.

Printed and bound in Thailand

2018 2017 2016 2015 2014
16 15 14 13 12 11 10 9 8

Contents

About the author   4

About the series   5

Introduction   6

Part 1   **Beyond the sentence**
1 Unlocking text   8
2 What makes a text?   17
3 What makes a text make sense?   35
4 Spoken texts   63
5 Texts in context   84
6 Classroom texts   103
7 Literary texts and loaded texts   133
8 Learner texts   153

Part 2   **Classroom activities**
Photocopiable task sheets   163

Reading list and References   186
Index   190

About the author

My teaching and training experience has been mainly in Egypt and Spain, with stints in the UK and my native New Zealand. Now I divide my time between running short courses, conference presentations, and writing.

I have an MA in TEFL from the University of Reading, as well as the RSA/UCLES Diploma. I have written a number of books for teachers on the teaching of language systems and skills, as well as a lexically-based grammar for students. I am presently writing a dictionary of ELT.

Thanks...

to my informants (Catriona Akana, Anna Tsevekidou, Dennis Newson), my text sources (Rob Haines, Peter Coles, Sandra MacKay, the ETAS conference speakers, and Tessa); also to readers Matt Jones and Felicity O'Dell for their useful reports, and to Ben Goldstein for his helpful feedback on Chapter 7. Special thanks to my (unwitting) mentors, whose presentations, articles, and books have been a constant source of inspiration, particularly Ron Carter, Guy Cook, Michael Hoey, Mike McCarthy, John Sinclair, and Henry Widdowson. (The usual caveats and waivers apply.) And enormous thanks, finally, to David Riley, Jill Florent and Adrian Underhill, whose joint guidance and unflagging enthusiasm kept me on track, and to Alyson Maskell, whose editorship, once again, has been exemplary.

Dedication

To Murray – for all the texts we have shared. Arohanui.

About the series

Macmillan Books for Teachers

Welcome to the Macmillan Books for Teachers series. These books are for you if you are a trainee teacher, practising teacher or teacher trainer. They help you to:

- develop your skills and confidence
- reflect on what you do and why you do it
- inform your practice with theory
- improve your practice
- become the best teacher you can be

The handbooks are written from a humanistic and student-centred perspective. They offer:

- practical techniques and ideas for classroom activities
- key insights into relevant background theory
- ways to apply techniques and insights in your work

The authors are teachers and trainers. We take a 'learning as you go' approach in sharing our experience with you. We help you reflect on ways you can facilitate learning, and bring your personal strengths to your work. We offer you insights from research into language and language learning and suggest ways of using these insights in your classroom. You can also go to http://www.onestopenglish.com and ask the authors for advice.

We encourage you to experiment and to develop variety and choice, so that you can understand the how and why of your work. We hope you will develop confidence in your own teaching and in your ability to respond creatively to new situations.

Adrian Underhill

Titles in the Series

An A–Z of ELT	Scott Thornbury
Beyond the Sentence	Scott Thornbury
Blended Learning	Barney Barrett and Pete Sharma
Children Learning English	Jayne Moon
Discover English	Rod Bolitho & Brian Tomlinson
Learning Teaching	Jim Scrivener
Sound Foundations	Adrian Underhill
Teaching Practice	Roger Gower, Diane Phillips & Steve Walters
Teaching Reading Skills	Christine Nuttall
Uncovering Grammar	Scott Thornbury
500 Activities for the Primary Classroom	Carol Read
700 Classroom Activities	David Seymour & Maria Popova

Introduction to *Beyond The Sentence*

text, n.   *A continuous piece of spoken or written language,*
especially one with a recognizable beginning and ending. [1]

Language is realized, first and foremost, as text. Not as isolated sounds, or words, or sentences, but as whole texts. And users of language have to cope with texts. They have to make sense of them and they have to produce them. This is as true for second language users as it is for first language users. As teachers of second language users, therefore, our top priority is to help our learners engage with texts. This book sets out to show how this can be done.

We live in a world of text. We are surrounded by text: in our homes, in the streets, at work and at school. If you are like me, you wake up in the morning listening to radio text, you glance idly at the cereal packet text as you skim the morning paper, your fridge is festooned with reminders and messages, you go on-line and check your e-mail, you read the ads on the bus on the way to work and work itself is a veritable deluge of texts: spoken and written, handwritten and electronic, formal and informal. Apparently the average American is targeted by 3000 messages per day. That includes phone calls, e-mail, meetings and conversations. [2] According to some estimates, typical workers send and receive some 200 messages and documents a day. On average we are exposed to anything from 600 to 1600 advertising messages a day, depending on which source you consult. And these figures pre-date the advent of text messaging. By 2003, in one day alone people in Britain were sending 56 million text messages to each other, a figure that had doubled in just a year. By the end of that year they had sent 20 billion messages. In fact, so accustomed are we to text that it's hard to imagine what life must have been like in the pre-electronic, let alone the pre-Gutenberg, era.

This steady exposure to language in the form of texts is a boon, of course, to language learners – assuming, that is, that the texts are in the language that the learner is learning. In the case of English, this is often so, even in places where English is not the first language. You'd be hard put to find anywhere on earth that is beyond the reach of an English language pop song, website, movie, or even T-shirt. For better or worse, English-language text is ubiquitous. This, in turn, is good news for the teacher of English. Or should be. But with so much English language text available, it's not always easy to know what to select for teaching purposes, or how to use it. Moreover, language teaching has traditionally been more concerned with individual sentences rather than texts, as such. Even in this supposedly communicative era, a lot of the language presentation and practice material available in published coursebooks is sentence-based. There is good reason for this: sentences, after all, are key building blocks of language and have a relatively fixed and describable grammar. But language, in its natural state, is not isolated sentences: it is text. As one linguist put it, 'Language always happens as text and not as isolated words and sentences. From an aesthetic, social or educational perspective it is the text which is the significant unit of language.' [3]

Going 'beyond the sentence' in order to explore the structure and the purposes of whole texts falls within the orbit of what is called *discourse analysis*. Put simply, *discourse* is the way that language – either spoken or written – is used for communicative effect in a real-world situation. Discourse analysis is the study of such language, and the analysis of the features and uses of texts – or *text analysis* – is an integral component of discourse analysis. One way of looking at the distinction between *discourse* and *text* is to think of discourse as the *process*, and the text as the *product*. That is, speakers (or writers) engage in a communicative process that involves language – such as a shopping exchange, or the expression of birthday greetings – and the record of the language that is used in this discourse is called its text.

Recognition of the primacy of text has meant that texts have started to play a more prominent role in teaching materials and have even penetrated into the public examinations: the Cambridge First Certificate in English (FCE) examination, for example, is now almost entirely text-based. Nevertheless, many teachers are still unsure as to how to exploit texts in their teaching. Often texts are used simply as a vehicle for teaching a pre-selected item of sentence grammar. Or they are used to develop the skills and subskills of listening and reading, without much attention being given to the text-specific features of their composition. The texts themselves are often somewhat bland and are typically inauthentic – that is, they have been especially written for teaching purposes. Literary texts are often treated with suspicion by teachers, as presenting too many problems of both a linguistic and cultural kind.

This book aims to address these issues. By the end, you should have a better idea of

- what a text is and what its characteristic features are
- how to categorize and describe texts, eg according to their genre, function, organization and style
- how to find, select and adapt texts
- how to exploit texts for language teaching and skills development purposes
- how to unpack the hidden messages of texts
- how to use literary texts in the classroom and
- how to evaluate and use learners' texts.

More generally, it is hoped that you will come away convinced of the value of text-based language teaching and be motivated to go 'beyond the sentence' and explore this rich resource with your learners.

The book has been written with both novice and experienced teachers in mind. While some linguistic terminology is inevitable, this has been kept to a minimum, as have references to academic and theoretical literature. For those interested in following up some of the themes of the book, a reading list of selected books and articles can be found at the back.

Chapter 1 **Unlocking texts**

Discovery activity 1.1 *Unlocking texts*

Put yourself in the position of a *beginner*, a complete beginner. Here is a text – it comes from the tomb of an Egyptian noble who lived several thousand years ago.[4] I'm assuming you can neither read hieroglyphs nor speak Ancient Egyptian. But study it closely. Can you make any sense of it? Can you at least spot some patterns or regularities?

1.1

Commentary ■■■

The urge to make sense of text – even of the text of a language that we neither speak nor read – is such that we are quite capable of inventing meanings on the basis of the flimsiest of evidence. It's possible, for example, that you took a guess that the text is about birds, since figures of birds occur frequently. This, in fact, was the strategy adopted by those scholars who first attempted to decipher hieroglyphs: 'They all looked for a symbolic meaning for each hieroglyphic sign. They expected a picture of three wavy lines to mean water and only water; a picture of a head to mean a head, that of an owl to mean an owl and so on. They made no allowance for the fact that such pictures may, in fact, be phonograms (sound signs), or, indeed, letters of an alphabet rather than pictographs.'[5] It took some time before this very literal and 'bottom-up' approach to decipherment was abandoned. Nevertheless, some of the symbols in the text are pictographs, as we shall see, so the strategy is not entirely unproductive.

On the other hand, knowing that the text was found in a tomb, you may have guessed that it had a religious significance, that it was a sacred text, or a biography of the deceased, for example. This 'top-down' strategy, using contextual clues, would have put you on the right track. You may also have noticed some repetition of elements – the four owls and their associated plant-like symbols, for example. Or the four sets of three vertical bars. Putting two-and-two together and using your background knowledge of text types and funerary culture, you might have guessed that these reiterations indicate a ritualistic discourse style, as befits a funerary text, such as a prayer or incantation.

If you turn to page 185, you'll find a transcription, transliteration and translation of the text and you'll see that the interpretation we have reached is not far from the mark. Some of the signs *do* in fact mean what they resemble, such as *bread, oxen* and *geese*. The repeated plant-like object and owl combination seem to form the meaning *a thousand of*, which does form a kind of refrain and the whole text does have a ritual function: the offering of funerary gifts.

So, our 'reading' of the text, while in no way profound, is amazingly accurate, given our zero knowledge of the 'code'. What we have done is 'read between the lines' – or between the glyphs – exploiting different clues in order to access different types of knowledge. There are at least three different types of clue we used: the signs themselves, the patterns of signs, and the context. These clues in turn triggered inferences at the level of word meaning, text type, and the overall purpose of the text.

At the same time, by studying the translation, we are already in the position of making some tentative deductions about Ancient Egyptian – its writing system (eg that the three vertical bars are possibly some kind of plural marker) and possibly its grammar and even the culture which the language gave voice to. This one text is starting to reveal the secrets of a whole language and society. ■

 Learners of English are faced with similar – if not quite such daunting – challenges when confronted with English-language texts. They too must mobilize a variety of 'text attack' strategies in order to glean some kind of sense from the text. And, through texts, they have access to 'insider knowledge' – about the language and the culture, of which the text is a realization.

Discovery activity 1.2   *What makes texts difficult?*

Take, for example, the following text[6]. What would you expect learners to find difficult about it?

1.2

Police dog sacked after biting innocent man

A police dog in Basel, Switzerland, has got the sack for biting an innocent bystander at the scene of a burglary.

Shep, a six-year-old German Shepherd, was taken off duty after the incident. The man had to be taken to hospital in an ambulance for treatment to a leg injury.

Shep's handler, who had been called to a burglary at a city boutique, was told the suspect was still in the building. But as officers carried out a search, the dog wandered outside to where a group of people were watching events. He then allegedly bit a 20-year-old man.

Shep was one of eight dogs serving with Basel police. A spokesman said this was the first such incident to have occurred in the city.

Commentary ■ ■ ■

Here, in fact, is what some learners – all of roughly the same level of proficiency – had to say, on being asked to rate the text for difficulty:

1 'Difficult. Because I don't understand some vocabulary and for this I need a dictionary.'
2 'The vocabulary is difficult but the text is easy to understand.'
3 'A little easy. Because it's a little history.'
4 'Difficult, not because vocabulary but for the content.'
5 'Not difficult. It's easy to understand some word by its context.'
6 'Difficult because it uses more complex constructions and more unknown vocabulary.'

Note how a variety of factors seem to interact in terms of the learners' perceptions of the difficulty of the text. There are the more obvious ground-level language factors, such as vocabulary and grammar ('complex constructions'), but also the higher-level features, such as the context (which helps the deduction of unfamiliar vocabulary) and the text type itself: 'a little history', ie a story or anecdote. For this learner, the fact that it is a recognizable text type seems to off-set the ground-level difficulties of vocabulary and grammar, perhaps. And then there is the 'content' difficulty, which, to the fourth respondent, is something quite apart from the vocabulary. What does he mean by this? Perhaps the text failed to activate a coherent mental picture (or *schema*) of the events. This may in part be due to the fact that the events are recounted not in their chronological order, but in an order favoured by news reporting, where the outcome of the situation is summarized before the events themselves are detailed.

All this suggests that learners approach texts from different directions and with different expectations. This, of course, has implications for the way teachers deal with texts in the classroom. At the very least, we need to bear in mind that a text on the page may 'generate' very different texts in the minds of the learners. ■

So far we have been discussing the way learners respond to texts. But, of course, they also have problems creating texts. Here, for example, is the reconstruction from memory by one learner of the text we have just read:

1.3

> *A police dog has been sacked for biting an innocent 20-years-old-man at the scene of a burglary. The dog is from Switzerland and it has bitten the man in the leg. The fact is that the policeman that hand the dog - there are 8 police dogs in Basel - had been told that a man, accused of burglary was still in the shop. When the police were in the building where the facts had taken place, the dog wandered in the street and bit the man, who had been taken to the hospital in an ambulance. Police said it is the first time that occurred.*

The learner has succeeded in including all the main facts and events into the account and has done so using language that is generally well-formed (apart from the verb *hand* instead of *handle*). To a reader unfamiliar with the story, though, it may not be that easy to reconstruct the events and participants from this account. Some of the information, such as the fact that the dog is from Switzerland, is incorporated rather randomly into the text and might be distracting. Nor is it entirely clear which man – the burglar or someone else? – was bitten by the dog (*the dog wandered in the street and bit the man*). The use of narrative tenses helps give a generally accurate idea of the order of events, but only our knowledge of the order in which such things happen in real life helps us make sense of the use of the past perfect in the phrase *the man… had been taken to the hospital*. And the use of the phrase *the fact is* in the third sentence sends a slightly misleading signal as to how this sentence connects to what has preceded it: it suggests that what we have been told so far is in fact a fiction! Finally, the word *that* in the last sentence clearly refers to something further back in the text – but what exactly? And does the writer, by choosing *that* rather than *this*, really intend to put some distance between herself and the events? (Compare this with the last line of the original text, for example.)

All this suggests that the ability to write connected and intelligible text is – like the ability to interpret text – a complex interaction of a variety of skills. It is clearly not simply a matter of stringing sentences together.

Why texts?

The above discussion reinforces the view that learning a language is more than the learning of its grammar, vocabulary and pronunciation. And that the ability to handle texts does not necessarily result from the ability simply to read and produce sentences. There is nothing new, of course, about this. Over a hundred years ago, a leading writer on second language learning, Henry Sweet, had this to say: 'When the sounds of a language have once been mastered, the main foundation of its study will be connected texts.'[7] Not words, nor sentences, note, but connected texts. Sweet added that 'it is only in connected texts that the language itself can be given with each word in a natural and adequate context'.

Nor was the idea that you can learn a language through detailed analysis of texts new even in Henry Sweet's time. In 1850 a certain T. Robertson published an English language textbook for French speakers (subsequently re-edited for Spanish speakers) that was based entirely on the study of a single text, spread over 20 units. The first unit of the first course starts with the first sentence of the text (apparently a story from the Arabian Nights):

1.4

> We are told that the Sultan Mahmoud, by his perpetual wars abroad and his tyranny at home, had filled the dominions of his forefathers with ruin and desolation and had unpeopled the Persian empire.

The text is first translated word by word and phrase by phrase and this forms the basis of exercises that involve translating the text back and forth. At this point, children and women and anyone else who simply wants to get to grips with the language as soon as possible, are advised to skip the next section, which 'is written specifically for those laborious persons who wish to know exactly what it is they are committing to memory'.

For those laborious persons, the one-sentence text is then subject to rigorous analysis at the level of pronunciation, vocabulary (every word is translated into

French) and grammar. For example, the word *unpeopled* is analysed into its component parts and each part is commented on, including the prefix *un-* and the suffix *-ed*, with other examples of similar compounds being supplied. In the grammar section, the first phrase, *We are told*, is analysed as an instance of the passive; *his perpetual wars* and *the Persian empire* are broken down into their components to demonstrate the formation of noun phrases in English. Further exercises of deconstruction and reconstruction follow. And the pattern is repeated for the next 19 units, that is, until the end of the story.

The problem with this approach is that, as Robertson himself acknowledged, it can become very pedantic and hence very boring. Also, unless the texts that are chosen for study bear some resemblance to the language needs of the learners, all this analysis is somewhat academic. It is hard to imagine there being much need, even in 1850, for the verb *to unpeople*, however good an example of English word formation it might be.

Nevertheless, the idea that texts – even very short ones – can 'deliver' a great deal of information about the language, is suggestive. Updating Robertson's method somewhat, let's have a look at a relatively modern text. Here is the 20th century translation of a Japanese haiku-like poem by the hermit-monk Ryokān (born c. 1758)[8]. As you read it, consider what features of language it embodies that might be of use to a learner:

1.5

> *Have you forgotten the way to my hut?*
> *Every evening I wait for the sound of your footsteps,*
> *But you do not appear.*

Short as it is, the poem is a complete text. It consists of 21 words (of which two are repeated twice, to make 23 in all) and these are organized into two sentences, the second of which consists of two clauses, making it a compound sentence. All but seven of the 26 letters of the written alphabet appear in the text. Of the 24 consonant sounds in English, 16 are represented, along with 15 of the 20 (British English) vowel sounds.

The text shows a typical distribution between grammar words (or *function* words) and *content* words. Function words include *have, to, of* and *not*, and content words are the ones that carry the burden of meaning, such as *forgotten, way, hut* and *footsteps*. Of the 21 words in the text, 15 are in the top 200 words in English according to frequency counts, and seven (ie a third of all the words) are in the top 20. Again, this is a fairly typical distribution.

Turning our attention to the grammar, what does the text tell us about the way English sentences are organized? First of all, all the eight different parts of speech are represented, apart from adjectives (unless you classify *my* and *your* as adjectives rather than determiners). So, we have nouns (eg *hut*), pronouns (eg *you*), verbs (eg *forgotten*), determiners (eg *the, every*), prepositions (eg *to*), a conjunction (*but*) and an adverb (*not*). Of the nouns, one has the plural suffix *-s*. Of the verbs, one is in the form of the past participle (*forgotten*); there are two auxiliary verbs (*have, do*) and two finite verbs (*wait* and *appear*).

These word types are in turn organized into three of the most common phrasal combinations in English. So, we have noun phrases (*my hut, every evening*), verb phrases (*have forgotten*) and prepositional phrases (*to my hut*). The noun phrases show instances of pre-modification with determiners (as in <u>my</u> hut, <u>the</u> sound) and post-modification using either a prepositional phrase (*the way <u>to my hut</u>*) or an *of* construction (*the sound <u>of your footsteps</u>*). These are all very common ways of grouping words in English.

These words and groups of words in turn realize the main functions typically found in combination in sentences, such as subjects (*I*), objects (*the way to my hut*), verbs (*appear*) and adverbials (*every evening*). The three clauses each demonstrate three common verb patterns, respectively: verb + object (ie a transitive verb pattern); verb + preposition (*for*) + object ; and a verb with no object (ie an intransitive verb). As well as the basic statement form of subject + verb (*I wait…*) there is an example each of (1) the inversion of subject and verb to make questions (*Have you forgotten..?*) and (2) the use of a 'dummy operator' + *not* to form negative statements (*you do not appear*). The way English verbs are marked for tense and aspect is also exemplified, with two verbs in the present tense unmarked for aspect (*wait, appear*) and one example of a present perfect construction (*have… forgotten*). Finally, at the level of connected discourse, the conjunction *but* connects the two parts of the second sentence, signalling that what follows contrasts in some way with what went before. And the repetition of *you* across the two sentences helps connect them.

This rather detailed analysis of one very short text is simply intended to demonstrate how much 'language' there is in a text and, therefore, how much potential texts have for the purposes of exemplifying features of language – of phonology, orthography (ie the writing system), vocabulary, grammar and discourse – for teaching purposes. Stuck on a desert island with only a book of haikus at hand, a resourceful teacher has the means to teach a great many facts about the language. (This is not meant to imply, of course, that teaching facts about the language is all that is involved in language teaching. For a start, it ignores the possibility of using texts to trigger language production on the part of the learners.)

Discovery activity 1.3   *Unpacking a text*

Here is another poem by Ryokan[9]. Can you 'unpack' its grammar? That is to say, what further features of English grammar does it display that might usefully be highlighted for learners?

1.6

> *I expected to see only pink blossoms*
> *but a gentle spring snow has fallen*
> *and the cherry trees are wearing a white coat.*

Commentary ■ ■ ■

Like the first Ryokān poem we looked at, this one has a representative range of high frequency features of English, including all the parts of speech (except for prepositions, if you discount the infinitive marker *to*). Unlike the first poem, however, this one is particularly rich in adjectives (*pink, gentle, white*). It also includes another form of noun pre-modification which is very common in English: the use of nouns to modify other nouns, as in <u>*spring*</u> *snow* and <u>*cherry*</u> *trees*. Also of interest is the verb + *to*-infinitive pattern, extremely common in English, represented by *expected to see*. Here, too, is an example of an infinitive (*to see*), as well as a regular past tense verb (*expected*) and examples of each of the two aspects in English: the perfect (*has fallen*) and the continuous (*are wearing*). These, incidentally, demonstrate agreement (or *concord*) in English, ie the way singular subjects take singular verb forms (*has*) and plural take plural (*are*). Another feature that is well represented in this text is the article system, including both the definite and indefinite articles (*the, a*) and the 'zero article', ie the absence of any determiner in front of a noun phrase, as in *pink blossoms*. ■

Incidentally, between the two texts (1.5 and 1.6), only three letters of the alphabet (*j, q, z*), plus three each of the consonant and vowel sounds in English, remain unrepresented. Eleven of the 25 most frequent words in English occur, some of them more than once. Grammar coverage across the two texts includes:

- all the parts of speech
- the basic article system
- common ways of forming noun phrases and preposition phrases
- first and second person subject pronouns and possessive adjectives
- transitive and intransitive verb constructions
- the infinitive
- affirmative and negative statements and question forms
- present and past simple tenses
- continuous and perfect aspect
- sentence-initial and sentence-medial adverbials, and
- additive and contrastive connectors.

In short, a good deal of the traditional elementary syllabus is locked up in these two poems – 'a world in a grain of sand', as William Blake put it.

I should stress, at this point, that I didn't have to look hard to find texts that have such rich seams of grammar running through them. *All* texts have grammar and – especially if they are authentic texts, but not too specialized – the grammar that is embedded in them is bound to be fairly representative of English grammar as a whole. In this sense, language shares a feature of other complex systems: its smallest self-standing components (ie texts) are miniature representations of the system as a whole (ie lexico-grammar).

I said that a good deal of grammar is 'locked up' in the two poems and I chose the (phrasal) verb 'locked up' deliberately. The fact that the texts contain examples of X, Y and Z features of English grammar is not of much use to language learners a) if they don't notice these features, and b) if they don't know how representative, typical, frequent, generative, etc, these features are. That is where the teacher comes in. It is by means of the teacher's expertise that these features are 'unlocked'. The process is not dissimilar to the way the secret of the hieroglyphs was unlocked by Champollion using the Rosetta Stone.

Classroom applications

At strategic points in each chapter we will be looking in more detail at ways of exploiting texts for language work. But here are a few basic text-unlocking techniques to get you going.

1 Dictate a short text – such as one of the haikus by Ryokān – and allow learners to compare and correct their texts, before asking them to:
   • count how many sentences there are
   • count how many words there are and how many words are repeated
   • identify the word classes (noun, adjective, etc)
   • say how many countable nouns there are
   • say how many uncountable nouns there are
   • say how many adjectives, determiners, adverbs, etc, there are
   • underline all the verbs
   • identify the tense, aspect and voice of each verb phrase
   • find any collocations, ie words that you think might co-occur frequently (learners can check their intuitions against a good learners' dictionary)
   • find any figurative or idiomatic use of language, including phrasal verbs
   • identify any cohesive devices
   • find any pronouns and identify their referents (ie the words they refer to).

2 After this detailed analysis of the text, ask the learners, working together, to try and re-construct it from memory. It may help to provide some word prompts on the board, eg:
   … pink blossoms
   … gentle spring snow
   cherry trees … white coat.

3 Prepare a 'gap-fill' version of the text for a subsequent lesson. Here is how a colleague of mine used this gap-fill idea with a group of ESL students in Oregon, who are studying the English of Natural Resource Technology (NRT), in order to work in that field once they return to Central America:

> There was a lull in the conversation. I waited, then piped up with how interesting one of the required books for NRT was. The book's all about how to find one's way in the wilderness, read topographical maps and things like that. I said I'd just learned how to determine direction using a non-digital watch. Interest! Well, I said, let me read the short paragraph to you...

> The paragraph became a point of discussion among pairs. [...] Finally, students read the paragraph to themselves, discussed it, then listened to me read it once more as they read along.

> We took a break, during which I wrote up the paragraph on the board. Next, I created gaps in place of the 'grammar' or function words, which I transferred to the other half of the board in random order. If a word occurred more than once, I marked it accordingly, e.g. 'the (x7)'.

> After the break, I asked the students to fill in the blanks then compare with a partner and finally with the original text. [...] Fifteen minutes left... I ask for the difference between function/grammar words and content words by pointing out that we've been finding function words. I talk quickly about how learning grammar might just be learning how to fill in the spaces between the content words or mix them successfully with the grammar words.

How could you do this on your own? Right, find a text, copy it, get rid of the function words and put them back like we did. Problems? How to best get rid of the words. We need to leave the text alone for a while so we're not just working from memory as we did today to some extent (still provided a meaningful challenge to students, I think).

Rob Haines

Rob's lesson is a good example of how even short texts can be used productively to *unlock* language features. After all, *every word* in a text yields a potential language lesson. In any text, therefore, there resides a whole syllabus waiting to be uncovered.

Chapter 2   **What makes a text?**

Think back over your day (assuming you're not reading this at breakfast). How many texts have you engaged with – either receptively or productively? And how many *kinds* of texts have you engaged with? Well, probably so many that it's impossible either to recall them or to list them, especially if you include spoken text. Just to give you an idea, here's how my day started:

- radio news (spoken, receptive)
- two pages of a novel (written, receptive)
- sporadic conversation with partner (spoken, interactive)
- reading and responding to e-mails (written, interactive)
- listening to programme details on radio (spoken, receptive)
- overhearing snatches of partner's phone conversation (spoken, receptive)
- making shopping list (written, productive)
- consulting reference books on discourse analysis (written, receptive)
- writing this paragraph (written, productive)

And that doesn't count the incidental, sometimes accidental, noticing of such domestic trivia as food package labels, the logo on the fridge, the initials on the hot and cold taps, the brand name on the computer keyboard I am using to write this with and so on.

In this chapter we will address these issues:
What distinguishes text from non-text?
What distinguishes one kind of text from another?

Discovery activity 2.1   *Texts or non-texts?*

Look at the following seven extracts. Which, in your opinion, qualify as texts? What are your criteria?

2.1

> **For the perfect cup**, use one tea bag per person and add freshly drawn boiling water. Leave standing for three to five minutes before stirring gently. Can be served with or without milk and sugar.

2.2

> Scott,
> Thanks for sendingme the disk.
> Sandy mckay

2.3

> 1 The university has got a park.
> 2 It has got a modern tram system.
> 3 He has got a swimming pool.
> 4 I have got tickets for the theatre.
> 5 Rio has got some beautiful beaches.
> 6 She has got a good view from the window. [10]

2.4

> Suzy Stressed gets up late and has a shower. She doesn't have breakfast. She goes to work by car. She gets to work at five to nine. She uses the lift. At eleven o'clock she has a cigarette and a black coffee. Suzy has lunch at half past one. She finishes work at six o'clock. Then she goes to an Italian class. She gets home late. After that she watches TV. She has dinner at eleven o'clock. She goes to bed very late. Suzy is very stressed. Do you live like Suzy?[11]

2.5

> *I like a pumpkin.*
> *I like a celery.*
> *Go toward the 21st century.*

2.6

> so   go
> go   so
> sl   ow
> go   oh
> low   ow
> oh[12]

2.7

> YOU ARE NOW
> ENTERING
>
> THE HUMAN HEART

Commentary ■ ■ ■

The fact is that all seven of these 'language events' (I'm avoiding using the word *text* at the moment) actually *happened*. That is to say, they are all attested instances of language in use. In that sense, they have some claim to be considered as texts. Some, however, seem more acceptable as texts than others. The first, for example, is a recognizable text type, ie a set of instructions typical of food packaging (it was, in fact written on a teabag wrapper). The second clearly belongs to the very general category of *letter* and has the obvious purpose of *thanking* someone for something. Moreover, both 2.1 and 2.2, as short as they are, seem to be entire texts (although the second might make more sense if we knew something of the previous correspondence – what *disk* is being referred to, for example?). And both texts are organized in a logical way: at the very least, they both have a beginning, a middle and an end. They also use language in a way that is acceptably well-formed (although the second one contains a spacing error – *sendingme* – suggesting a fairly casual production process, in turn indicating an informal medium: it is in fact an e-mail). Which brings us to the last point: their appropriacy. Each was appropriate in the context in which it originally occurred.

To sum up, both 2.1 and 2.2

- are self-contained
- are well-formed
- hang together (ie they are *cohesive*)
- make sense (ie they are *coherent*)
- have a clear communicative purpose
- are recognizable text types
- were appropriate to their contexts of use.

On all of the above grounds, their status as texts seems unproblematic.

The other five 'texts', however, appear not to fulfil all of these conditions. Text 2.3 doesn't hang together: it's just six unconnected sentences; 2.4 is obviously written to display a feature of grammar, but it is neither identifiable as a genuine text type nor does it have any apparent communicative purpose; the fifth one makes no sense whatsoever and it's difficult to imagine a context in which it would make sense (see Chapter 5 for more on this); the sixth makes slight sense, but seems more playful than communicative and it's not clear that it is self-contained, even as poetry; and 2.7 is difficult to situate – where would such a text be appropriate? In short, texts 2.3 to 2.7 fail a number of 'text' tests. They are either

- not self-contained, or
- not well-formed, or
- not cohesive, or
- not coherent, or
- not communicative, or
- not typical, or
- not appropriate. ■

Over the next two chapters we will look at each of these qualities in turn (although not necessarily in the above order). In this chapter our concern is with cohesion.

Cohesion

Let's take a look at the 'text' 2.3 again:

---

1 The university has got a park.
2 It has got a modern tram system.
3 He has got a swimming pool.
4 I have got tickets for the theatre.
5 Rio has got some beautiful beaches.
6 She has got a good view from the window. [10]

Initially, it looks as if this is setting out to be a connected piece of text. The *it* of sentence 2 looks as if it refers to *the university* of sentence 1. These expectations are dashed, however, by the mention of a *tram system*: universities seldom, if ever, have their own tram systems, modern or otherwise. And by sentence 3 we are in no doubt that what we are reading is a series of isolated sentences, whose only common element is the grammar structure *have got*. The fact that the sentences are numbered is, of course, a dead give-away. In fact, they could be re-arranged in any order without disturbing the integrity of the exercise, in which, by the way, students of English have to convert the uncontracted forms of *has/have got* into contracted forms.

On the other hand, text 2.4, about Suzy Stressed, is clearly not a collection of isolated sentences. Our assumption that the pronoun *she* in the second sentence refers to the subject of the first sentence is not disappointed.

> Suzy Stressed gets up late and has a shower. She doesn't have breakfast. She goes to work by car. She gets to work at five to nine… etc.

In fact, every sentence seems 'tied' in this way to the subject *Suzy Stressed*. Moreover, there are no unexpected *tram systems* to throw us off balance: the word *breakfast*, for example, sits comfortably with *has a shower* in the first sentence and *goes to work* in the third sentence. They belong to the same *lexical set*, and, together with other expressions such as *gets home, has dinner, goes to bed*, and so on, form a kind of *lexical chain* of topically related lexical items. The repeated use of time expressions (*five to nine, eleven o'clock, half past one*, etc) forms another lexical chain. There is also some direct repetition of vocabulary, such as the word *work* in the third and fourth sentences, which also reappears later in the sentence *She finishes work at six o'clock*. Finally, connecting expressions like *then* and *after that* make explicit links across sentences. They serve to bind their respective sentences to the ones that preceded them. Note, also, that it simply wouldn't be possible to rearrange the sentences so that the text started with *Then she goes to an Italian class*, or *After that she watches TV*, for instance. Both *then* and *after that* make sense only by reference to previous text.

To sum up, the text is made cohesive (in the way that example 2.3 is not) by a combination of *lexical* and *grammatical* devices. The lexical connectors include repetition and the lexical chaining of words that share similar meaning. The grammatical connectors are pronouns (*she* and *that*) and linkers (*then*).

Discovery activity 2.2   *Cohesive devices*

Here is another text, in this case, an advertisement. Can you find examples of lexical and grammatical cohesion in it? Are there any other devices that bind it together as a text?

2.8

Being under control is knowing the secret of cleaner, clearer, more beautiful skin.

(And it's not soap.)

Whatever else in your life may be spinning out of control, it doesn't have to be spots.
Rule number one, two and three: clean skin is the secret of clear skin.

•

With a name like Johnson's Clean & Clear,
it's no great secret whose cleansing lotion you should be using.

•

No other cleanser removes more of the dirt, oil and make-up that can lead to spots.
And what's even better it does this without drying.
It actually tingles on your skin to tell you it's working.

•

Not that it needs to. You can see for yourself.
A fresher, clearer complexion that even soap and water can't match.

•

Take it from us. Use Johnson's Clean & Clear as a one-step cleanser,
or an after cleansing astringent, and you'll never get in a lather over spots again.

Commentary ■ ■ ■ *(p3)* Lexical cohesion

Examples of lexical repetition include *skin* (four times), *clear*, *clean*, *secret*, and *spots* (three times each), and *control* and *soap* (twice each). Note also the words belonging to the same word family, ie words that share a common root: *clear* and *clearer; clean, cleaner, cleansing,* and *cleanser.* The fact that these words are prominent is, of course, not accidental, since they carry the main thrust of the advertisement's message (*control* through *cleaner, clearer skin*) and many have positive connotations.

the same word family

There are a number of words that are thematically related and which form chains running through the text (eg *skin, complexion; soap, cleansing lotion, cleanser, water, after-cleansing astringent, lather*) plus a number of synonyms (*fresher, cleaner*), as well as the antonyms *dirt* and *clean,* and *under control, out of control.* There is also a rudimentary list: *dirt, oil* and *make-up.*

Grammatical cohesion is realized by pronouns, which refer the reader back to their *referents* (ie concepts previously introduced into the text), as in *Being under control is knowing the secret of cleaner, clearer, more beautiful skin. (And it's not soap.)* Here, the pronoun *it* in the second sentence refers back to *the secret* in the first. *It* can also refer forward, and to a general idea, rather than to any specific word or clause, as in: *Take it from us. Use Johnson's Clean & Clear as a one-step cleanser […], and you'll never get in a lather over spots again.*

Take it from us also demonstrates how some pronouns do not have referents *in* the text itself, but outside it. Thus, the referent of *us* is not retrievable from the text, either before or after, but refers to the sponsors of the text (ie Johnson). Likewise *your* and *you* in the sentence *It actually tingles on your skin to tell you it's working* refer to the reader. This is also a kind of cohesive device, since it binds the text to its larger context. The technical name for language that makes direct connection to the material world is *deixis* (adjective: *deictic*).

Note, by the way, that the sponsoring authority (sometimes called the *author*) of the text is not necessarily the same individual as the *writer.* In this text, for example, the pronoun *us* does not refer to the actual writer, who was no doubt the anonymous employee of some advertising agency, but to the company itself.

Another form of grammatical cohesion is displayed in the sentence *And what's even better it does this without drying,* where *does this* stands for (or replaces) the proposition expressed in the previous sentence (ie: *removes more of the dirt, oil and make-up that can lead to spots*). The combination of *does* and *this* is unintelligible without reference to the previous sentence, hence it is a feature of the text's cohesion.

The use of *do/does* to substitute for a preceding verb phrase is called *substitution.* Words like *so* and *not* commonly substitute for whole clauses, as in:

> Will it rain? ~ I think so. (= I think it will rain)
> Will it rain? ~ I think not. (= I think it won't rain)

Substitution can operate at the level of individual words too. The pronouns *one* and *ones* commonly stand in for nouns or noun phrases, as in these two sentences from an advert for Beefeater gin (which also displays clause substitution using *so*):

2.9

> Is it important that a gin comes from London? The ones that don't, seem to think so.

The second sentence, unpacked, would read: *The gins that don't come from London seem to think that it is important that a gin does come from London.* This is a good example of how cohesion works to pack elements of previous text into the text that follows.

Another form of substitution is 'substitution-by-zero', as in this example from the cleansing lotion ad:

It actually tingles on your skin to tell you it's working. Not that it needs to.

Needs to *what?* Needs to tingle on your skin, etc. Rather than repeat this, the writer simply leaves a blank, which the reader fills in. The technical name for 'substitution-by-zero' is *ellipsis*, ie the leaving out of elements that can be retrieved from elsewhere. In the gin ad, quoted above, *The ones that don't [...]* is an example of ellipsis, where *come from London*, retrievable from the previous sentence, fills the empty slot.

The term *cohesion* suggests the presence in a text of explicit linking words, such as *however, but, although,* and so on. There is only one explicit linking word in text 2.8: the use of *and* in the second sentence (*And it's not a soap*), and later on in the sentence beginning *And what's even better… And* is an instance of a conjunction. Other conjunctions are *but, so, or* and *because.* These typically have a sentence-internal function – that is, they connect clauses inside sentences. Connectors that link sentences are called *conjuncts.* (They are also commonly called *linkers.*) Common conjuncts are such sequencing expressions as *first, to begin with, lastly,* the reinforcing expressions *what's more, furthermore* and expressions used to make concessions, such as *however, in spite of that, on the other hand.* Note that the absence of conjuncts, apart from *and,* in the Johnson's ad suggests that perhaps the text is so cohesive already that it doesn't need them.

And what's even better displays yet another cohesive device: the use of comparatives to build on, and thus connect to, previous text. The phrase *what's even better* presupposes a previous mention (direct or indirect) of something good.

Another grammatical feature of the text that serves to give it internal consistency and hence acts as a kind of cohesive device is the use of *tense.* Apart from the *will* in the last sentence, all the main verbs are in the present and are unmarked for aspect (ie there are no continuous or perfect forms). Another way of connecting text, which is neither lexical nor strictly grammatical, might be best described as *rhetorical.* For example, in text 2.9, the presence of a question in the text (*Is it important that a gin comes from London?*) raises the expectation of finding an answer in the text that follows. When this expectation is met, we have a further, rhetorical, means by which sentences are connected and the text is made cohesive.

Another form of rhetorical cohesion is what is called *parallelism,* where sentences 'echo' one another. In this ad, for Seiko watches, parallelism is established in the repeated use of *It's not your…*:

It's not your music.
It's not your handshake.
It's not your clothes.
It's your watch that says most about who you are.

Apart from binding the text together, the parallelism serves to highlight the contrast between the first three lines of the text and the 'punchline', where the pattern is subverted. As we will see in Chapter 7, it is a device that is frequently used in literary texts. ■

To sum up, there are a number of ways that texts are made cohesive, and these cohesive devices (also called linking devices) are traditionally classified at the level of lexis, grammar and discourse (or rhetoric). These include:

- lexical cohesion:
  - direct repetition, word families, synonyms and antonyms
  - words from the same semantic field, lexical chains and lists
  - substitution with *one/ones*
- grammatical cohesion
  - reference: pronouns, articles (more on this below)
  - substitution of clause elements using *so*, *not*, *do/does/did*, etc
  - ellipsis of clause elements
  - conjuncts (also called linkers)
  - comparatives
  - tense
- rhetorical cohesion
  - question–answer
  - parallelism

Reference

We have noted the way that elements in a text refer to other elements (their *referents*) both inside and outside the text and how this cross-referencing serves to bind the text together, connecting sentences with other sentences and connecting the text to its context. Reference is such an important aspect of cohesion – and one that causes trouble to learners – that it's worth looking at it in more detail.

Reference, as we have seen, is commonly achieved through the use of pronouns (*he*, *we*, *it*; *this* and *that*, *these* and *those*) and articles. We'll look at each of these in turn.

We have seen how pronouns refer back to previously mentioned referents. Here's another example, from a Ukrainian folk tale.

2.10

> One day a dog left his home and went out into the wide world to get a job. He worked long and hard and finally took his wages and bought a lovely new pair of boots... *anaphoric reference*

The pronoun *he* and the possessive determiner *his* have back-reference to the *dog*. Back-reference is technically called *anaphoric* reference. The words *he* and *his* act like little index fingers, directing us back in the text to these first mentions. (In actual fact, the pronouns are directing our attention not at something back in the *text*, but at a concept that has been introduced into our evolving mental construction of the narrative as a result of our reading of the text. This mental construction is called a *schema*. Only occasionally, when we have 'lost the plot', do we have to physically search the text itself to find the source of a reference. But, normally, it is to the mental schema we refer, not to the text. More on schemas in Chapter 3.)

Less commonly, and for certain stylistic effects, the referring pronoun can anticipate the referent. This kind of reference is called *cataphoric*. The underlined words in the following text[13] point forward to their referent, rather than back:

2.11

> He's played junkies and city slickers, Jedi knights and US rangers. He's at home in Hollywood's boulevards and Glasgow's tenements. He spends his life in the arms of beautiful women and is happily married … . It seems Ewan McGregor can do anything he wants.

The pronouns *it, this* and *that* can all refer back (ie anaphorically) to whole topics (rather than single nouns) that have been mentioned previously. For example, in the last sentence of the following extract from a book review[14], the pronoun *it* refers to the complete proposition expressed in the preceding sentence:

2.12

> 'HARD work, no pay, eternal glory,' ran the internet ad for volunteers for a couple of weeks in a simulated Mars base at Devon Island in the high Arctic, or in the Utah desert. More than 400 applied. In Mars on Earth, Mars Society president and astronautical engineer Robert Zubrin relates the checkered history of the project, as well as his experiences as a crew member. Zubrin describes himself as mercurial, optimistic and romantic. It shows.

What shows? Not Zubrin, obviously. Here *it* refers to the whole idea of Zubrin being mercurial, optimistic and romantic.

As a rule, *it* is used to continue referring to the same topic, *this* draws attention to new or important topics and *that* has the effect of distancing the writer (or speaker) from the topic. For example:

2.13

> **SOUND**
> … When the sound wave strikes our ears, it causes our eardrums to vibrate and nerves send signals to the brain. This is how we hear. If there were no air, there would be nothing to carry the sound. That is why there is no sound in space.[15]

The pronoun *this*, in referring to the whole process described in the sentence that precedes it, serves to bring into sharp focus the point the writer is making. On the other hand, the writer has chosen *that* rather than *this* in the last sentence, perhaps because she is referring to something that is rather peripheral to the main topic, which is SOUND. If the topic had been SPACE, she might have chosen *this* instead. Another difference between *this* and *that* is that the former can refer both back and forward in a text, whereas *that* only ever has back reference.

Pronouns can have referents *outside* the text, as well as inside it. That is to say, the index finger can point beyond the text: we saw this with the pronoun *us* in the Johnson ad: *Take it from us.* Reference outside the text is called *exophoric* reference. The referent may be in the form of visual information on the page, as in this caption to an illustration in a children's reference book[16]:

2.14

> This is a Roman valve that allowed water to be pumped uphill. Water would then come out of fountains such as the one shown here.

Or, as in the case of spoken language, the referent may be in the immediate physical environment. To continue the story of the dog in the Ukrainian folk tale (text 2.10):

> On his way home he met up with a rabbit, who said, 'Those are beautiful boots, indeed. May I try them on, please?'
>
> *environment*

Like pronouns, the definite article *the* can also make connections back, forward and outside the text. Again, to return to the story about the dog, note how each instance of *the* implies a previous mention of the noun that it determines:

> The dog was so proud of the boots that he agreed, and he sat down to take them off. The rabbit sat down next to the dog, pulled on the boots and admired himself.

The function of *the* is to signal knowledge that is *given*, ie knowledge that is shared between writer and reader (or between speaker and listener). It is as if to say: *you know which dog (or boots, or rabbit) I am talking about.* The reason we know, in this case, is because the dog and the boots and the rabbit have been introduced to us previously in the text, using the indefinite article *a* to flag new information: *A dog… a pair of boots… a rabbit.*

A dog… the dog is a clear example of the way new information becomes given information. Often, however, the noun is not repeated verbatim in this way (*dog – dog*), but is expressed differently, eg by a synonym or a more general term, as in the following story opening[17], where the Beduin's son is referred to successively as *son, boy* and *child*, where *the town* is referred to as *the place*, and where the Beduin himself is later called *the father*:

2.15

> A Beduin once had business in the cattle market of a town. He took his young son with him, but in the confusion of the place he lost track of his boy and the child was stolen.
>
> The father hired a crier to shout through the streets that a reward of one thousand piasters was offered for the return of the child. Although the man who held the boy heard the crier, greed had opened his belly and he hoped to earn an even larger sum. So he waited and said nothing.
>
> On the following day the crier was sent through the streets again…

The above text also demonstrates how a noun can be made definite, not by what has already been said about it, but by what is about to be said about it. That is, *the* refers forward in the text, rather than back. The answers to the questions *Which cattle market?* and *Which confusion?* are not located back in the text, but immediately after the noun: *the cattle market of a town; the confusion of the place.* Likewise: *the return of the child.* Other ways of qualifying a noun so as to make it definite include the use of relative clauses, as in *the man who held the boy.* Nouns can also be made definite through the addition, for example, of adjectives, especially adjectives that imply uniqueness, as in *the following day.*

Neither forward nor back reference seems to account for the use of the definite article in *the streets*, however: *The father hired a crier to shout through the streets...*. Which streets? There is no answer to the question that is explicit in the text. In this case, of course, the reader infers which streets are being identified by reference to the previous mention of *a town*; towns have streets (and post offices and bus stations and town halls and mayors, and so on). Once the town 'schema' is activated, therefore, it would be unnecessary, even pedantic, to specify which streets by writing, for instance, *the streets of the town*.

Here is a more contemporary example[18], where, once the basic schema has been triggered, the answers to the question *Which?* can easily be inferred. First of all, here is the first line:

2.16

> In the evening Hamim took me to his movie theater...

How many things and events does the above sentence evoke? Now read on:

> We entered by a side door and stood near the screen, watching the show. It was a steamy Los Angeles mystery dubbed into Arabic. I forget the title and plot ... Hamim told me he had seen the movie before; but I noticed now that he intended to see it again. I wanted to leave, but ... we stayed to the end.

In this text, none of the nouns identified with *the* have been mentioned previously. How do we know, then, which screen, which show, which title, etc, is being referred to? The identity of each is, of course, easily recoverable by reference to the mental schema of the movie theatre. If you substituted just some of these items with others from a different schema, you can easily see how the word *the* no longer fits, since it no longer 'points' to a shared schema:

> In the evening Hamim took me to his movie theatre. We entered by a side door and stood near the aquarium, watching the antelopes...

Definiteness is a quality that is not only inferred from clues in the text, but also conferred by recourse to common knowledge of the world *outside* the text. The underlined references in the opening of the following (Armenian) folk tale[19] are all recoverable from our knowledge of the world. (You should by now be able to explain the other instances of *the*.)

2.17

> There was once a rich man who had a very beautiful wife and a beautiful daughter known as Nourie Hadig (tiny piece of pomegranate). Every month when the moon appeared in the sky, the wife asked, 'New moon, am I the most beautiful, or are you?' And every month the moon replied. 'You are the most beautiful'...

The answers to the questions *Which moon?* and *Which sky?* are not to be found in the text at all, neither explicitly mentioned nor implicitly inferred. The referents are outside the text altogether (ie they are exophoric), in the shared general knowledge of reader and writer, where there is only one moon and only one sky. When there is only one of something, we always know which one is being referred to!

Shared world information can consist of things in the immediate context, like *the cat* or *the corkscrew*, or things in the local context, like *the post office*, *the pub*, or things in the national or global or universal context, like *the Queen* or *the United Nations* or *the sun*.

Exophoric reference means that a lot can be left unsaid when speaking or writing. When, for example, my neighbour buzzes and asks, 'Can I borrow the electric drill?' I understand that she means the electric drill that is part of our shared world, the one she has borrowed a number of times before. Likewise, the referent of *the* in a note pinned up in the office ('Can you switch off the lights when you leave?') is in the shared world of reader and writer. It is this 'insider' knowledge which makes it difficult, often, to understand other people's mail (if you are the kind of person who reads other people's mail!). Take this e-mail I sent to my sister:

2.18

> Dear Trish,
> I picked up the box this morning – thanks so much for the goodies – can't wait to try them. What do you do with the figs I wonder? And the apron will be perfect for Sant Pol barbies. How's the new granddaughter? I e-mailed Lib both to share congratulations and to check if she had got the Amazon voucher – she hadn't. I suspect she may have trashed it, thinking it was spam. Oh well.

The prevalence of the definite article in this text reflects both the close relationship between writer and reader and the fact that the writer is not so much relaying news as responding to, or commenting on, events that are already familiar.

Nominalization

Pronouns and articles are used to refer backwards, forwards or outwards, to specific referents. But we can also make references in a less focused, more general way, using certain nouns, a process called *nominalization*. To return to text 2.11, for example, in the sentence *Robert Zubrin relates the checkered history of the project*, the word *project* has no previous mention in the text, but refers back in a general way to the events described in the first sentence of the text. Nouns that are typically used to 'nominalize' actions and events include *situation*, *process* and *way*. Ideas, too, can be referred to, using words like *idea*, *theory* and *viewpoint*. And, very commonly, words like *explanation*, *criticism*, *proposal*, *suggestion*, etc, are used to refer to what has been said or written. For example, in this extract[20] two writers have just mentioned how they first heard about the 'recovered memory' controversy and how it prompted them to collaborate on a thriller:

2.19

> Since we had come across the idea together we decided to write it together. Much of that process seems vague now, but I remember the day before we started writing…

Here, both *the idea* and *that process* refer back in a general way to previously mentioned thoughts and events.

Classroom applications

It should be fairly obvious that the way reference works can only be properly understood when both referring expression and referent are locatable in the context. The meaning of a word like *the,* for example, is not easily contained in sentence-length examples. The same can be said for *it, this, that* and other referring devices. This suggests that, at the very least, learners need to meet and use these items in contexts beyond the level of the sentence, ie in extended segments of text.

Discovery activity 2.3   *Referents*

One way of raising awareness as to how articles and pronouns work to achieve cohesion in a text is to ask students to identify the referents (ie the things referred to) of each instance of reference in a text. And, in the case of the definite article, to say why the referent is being presented as definite. The referent can be either in the text, or inferable from the text, or in the world outside the text. If it is *in* the text, it could be back in the text (anaphoric reference) or forward in the text (cataphoric reference). If it is outside the text (exophoric reference), it could be in the immediate physical context, or in the general knowledge of the world that the speakers share. Try doing it with this joke[21]:

2.20

> An American, a Frenchman and an Australian were sitting in a bar overlooking Sydney Harbour. 'Do you know why America is the[1] wealthiest country in the[2] world?' asked the[3] American. 'It[4]'s because we[5] build big and we build fast. We put up the[6] Empire State Building in six weeks.'
>
> 'Six weeks, mon dieu, so long!' snapped the[7] Frenchman. 'Ze[8] Eiffel Tower we put up in one month exactement. And you[9],' he continued, turning to the[10] Australian, 'what has Australia done to match that[11]?'
>
> 'Ah, nuthin', mate. Not that I know of.'
>
> The American pointed to the[12] Harbour Bridge. 'What about that[13]?' he[14] asked.
>
> The[15] Australian looked over his[16] shoulder. 'Dunno, mate. [It[17]] Wasn't there yesterday.'

Commentary ■ ■ ■

Here is a suggested answer to the task:

1 The referent (country) is made definite by a superlative adjective, which implies that there is only one such country with this quality and hence the question *Which country?* has only one possible answer, which, in this case, occurs back in the text (*America*).

2 exophoric: in the knowledge that the speakers share: that there is only one world.

3 anaphoric: refers to 'an American' in line 1

4 anaphoric: refers to the whole clause 'why America is the wealthiest country in the world'

5 exophoric: refers to the speaker (and his compatriots)

6 exophoric: only one Empire State Building in the world. It is a characteristic of proper nouns that, by virtue of their uniqueness, they are always definite. This doesn't mean, of course, that all proper nouns take the definite article. Think of your own name, for example.

7 like 3

8 like 6

9 exophoric: refers to the person being addressed

10 like 3

11 anaphoric: refers to the Frenchman's previous claim, ie that the Eiffel Tower was put up in one month

12 like 6

13 exophoric: refers to the actual bridge.

14 anaphoric: 'the American'

15 anaphoric

16 anaphoric

17 exophoric: the actual bridge ■

A slightly easier text for students is the Ukrainian folk tale[22], which you now have in its entirety. It is rich in cross-references:

2.10 (complete)

Why Dogs Chase Rabbits

One day a dog left his home and went out into the wide world to get a job. He worked long and hard and finally took his wages and bought a lovely new pair of boots.

On his way home he met up with a rabbit, who said, 'Those are beautiful boots, indeed. May I try them on, please?'

The dog was so proud of the boots that he agreed and he sat down to take them off. The rabbit sat down next to the dog, pulled on the boots and admired himself. Suddenly he jumped up and ran away.

And that is why dogs still chase rabbits. They are trying to get their boots back.

A logical follow-up to reading the text and identifying the references would be to ask learners to restore the referring words to a 'mutilated' version of the text:

One day (1) _____ dog left (2) _____ home and went out into (3) _____ wide world to get (4) _____ job. (5) _____ worked long and hard and finally took (6) _____ wages and bought (7) _____ lovely new pair of boots.

On (8) _____ way home (9) _____ met up with (10) _____ rabbit who said, '(11) _____ are beautiful boots, indeed. May I try (12) _____ on, please?' etc.

Note that for some of these gaps there may be more than one possible option, eg (1) *a* or *the*, (8) *his* or *the*, according to the intentions of the writer, and therefore learners should be asked to justify their choices, explaining what differences in meaning (if any) are implied.

Conjuncts

We have devoted quite a lot of space to the subject of reference – but what about conjuncts (commonly known as linkers)? Their very name suggests that they play a crucial role in holding a text together. In fact, as we saw in text 2.8, they are not as prevalent as you might think: that particular text was held together more by lexical and referential cohesion than by any explicit linkers – apart from two instances of *and*. Of course, the amount of explicit signposting will depend to a large extent on the type of text we are dealing with. Here, for example, is an extract from a book on applied linguistics[23], with the explicit linkers underlined:

2.21

> <u>As was pointed out earlier</u>, Standard English is generally defined by its lexis and its grammar. <u>In fact</u>, when you come to look for it, standard lexis is very elusive; so elusive that one wonders if it can be said to exist at all. <u>And</u> on reflection it is hard to see how it could exist. <u>To begin with</u>, the notion of standard implies stability, a relatively fixed point of reference. <u>So</u> if I invent a word, for example, it is not, by definition, standard. <u>But</u> people are inventing words all the time to express new ideas and attitudes, to adjust to their changing world.

Note that even in this text, where every sentence is explicitly linked to a previous one, the linkers are all relatively non-academic, apart from the phrase *as was pointed out earlier*. In fact, three of the most common linkers are each represented in this text: *and, but* and *so*. So common are these that there are grounds for arguing that, for the purposes of speaking and writing, most learners need learn only these three (plus a few sequencing linkers), reserving the more obscure or formal linkers, such as *nevertheless* and *furthermore*, for recognition purposes only. It stands to reason that these are best presented to learners in their contexts, ie in connected text. A standard activity type is a combination of identification and categorization.

Discovery activity 2.4   *Conjuncts*

Identify the sentence conjuncts in these short texts and classify them. (Note that, for the purposes of this discussion, we are interested only in ways that sentences are linked one with another, as opposed to internally. Sentence-internal linkers, eg *such as* in text 2.22, can be ignored for the time being.)

2.22

> Cold-blooded creatures, such as reptiles, cannot control their body temperature like we can. This is why they prefer life on land, where it is easier for them to warm up. But there are some reptiles that have adapted to ocean life.[24]

2.23

> Ancient Egyptians were skilled at making mummies. The body's insides were removed, except for the heart. Next, the body was left to dry for 40 days. Then it was washed and filled with linen to keep its shape. Finally, the body was oiled and wrapped in linen bandages.[25]

2.24

> A spider has eight legs. So it is not an insect. It is a type of animal called an arachnid.[26]

2.25

> Plant-eaters must spend much of their time eating in order to get enough nourishment (goodness from food). A zebra, for example, spends at least half its day munching grass. The good side to being a plant-eater, though, is that the animal does not have to chase and fight for its food as hunters do.[27]

2.26

> Roman baths were more than a place to get clean. They were also places to relax, meet friends and get fit.[28]

Commentary ■ ■ ■

Conjuncts can express a number of different categories of logical relation between parts of a text. The main categories (with examples from the above texts in bold) are:

- **additive** – that is, relations of addition, exemplification, similarity, emphasis: *also*, *too*, *as well*, *moreover*, *what's more*, *in addition*, *for example*, *likewise*, *similarly*
- **adversative** – that is, relations of contrast or alternatives: *but*, *though*, *however*, *on the other hand*, *in fact*, *alternatively*
- **causal** – that is, relations of cause and result: *this is why*, *so*, *therefore*, *as a result*
- **temporal** – that is, relations of sequence in time: *next*, *then*, *finally*, *in the meantime*, *ever since*.

Notice that some conjuncts are single words (usually adverbs), such as *nevertheless*, *eventually*, while some are preposition phrases (*as a result*, *in addition*), and there are others that consist of entire clauses, such as *what's more*, *this is because*....

The above categories, too, are very broad categories and it would be misleading to think that the items within a category are interchangeable. For a start, there are different syntactic constraints on where each conjunct can be placed in a sentence. Compare, for example:
  a) The film was slow. But I enjoyed it.
  b) The film was slow. I enjoyed it, though.
and
  a) Jackie's a vegetarian. Karl is a vegetarian, too.
  b) Jackie's a vegetarian. Karl is also a vegetarian.

 There are also stylistic differences, some conjuncts being very formal, even pompous *(notwithstanding, whereupon)* and others being relatively informal and characteristic of spoken language (*still*, *what's more*).

All of these factors create problems for learners, resulting in under-use and over-use (as we shall see below) and misuse, as in these examples (the misused linkers are underlined):

1 *To tell you the truth, I come from a small family. There are four of us in our family: My mother, my father, my sister and I.* *I dare say*, *we also have got a cat. Its name is Mozart.*

2 *Hiccupping can be very irritating if we are together with other people or if we hiccup for a very long time.* *However,* *some people can hiccup for hours or even days.*

3 *Then we were on the road again, but only for half an our. The tyre punctured. I opened the boot and realized we didn't have an extra tyre and the tool to changes it.* *At least* *we pull up in front of the hotel at midnight.*

4 *My surprise was when I arrived at home, there was a police car in front of my door.* *Firstly* *I thought that something wrong had happened.* *However,* *when I came in my home, I could see all my family sat in my sitting room with a policeman and a man.*

5 *I'm quite used not only to speaking English with customers but also dealing with people that have English as a second language.* *For that reason,* *I'd like to practising my English even during my leisure time.*

Probably what the writers meant were, respectively:
1 *I might add…*
2 *In fact…*
3 *At last* (or *Eventually…*)
4 *At first* and (possibly) *Indeed…* (since it is unlikely the sight of a policeman allayed his initial fears!)
5 The choice of *that* rather than *this* has the effect of distancing the reason from the consequence; in fact, *This is why…* might work even better to join the two sentences. ■

Classroom applications

The tendency, especially at beginner and elementary levels, to teach the language through isolated sentences means that many learners are uncertain as to how to weld such sentences into connected text. Here, for example, is a text written by an elementary student in response to the task *Write a paragraph each about your free time, recent activities and future plans*:

2.27

I spend my free time doing my homework.
I spend my free time going to a walk with my friends.
I spend my free time listening music.
Last weekend I stayed at home with my family.
Last holiday I went to Tarragona and I went to the beach.
Last weekend I went to the disco with my friends.
The next few months I'm going to stay at home all the day, studing.
I'm going to a picnic in a week.
I'm going to have a long holydays the next few months.

Essentially the text is nothing more than a list of sentences, or, rather, three sets of lists. The only apparent connecting device is the repetition of the sentence frames (eg *I spend my free time -ing*). This (inadvertent) use of parallelism is perhaps more suitable to a song than a written composition! What would help would be the inclusion of some basic conjuncts, especially those that express *addition,* such as *and* and *also*. Asking learners to identify and categorize the conjuncts in a simple text or texts (as you did with texts 2.22–2.26) is one way of drawing attention to them.

One way of forcing the use of linking devices might be to ask the student who wrote text 2.27 to redraft it using fewer words and fewer sentences. Another problem with cohesion is a tendency of learners to overuse certain sentence-internal linkers, such as *and* and *because*. In the following text the learner incorporates *because* into practically every sentence.

2.28

> *In my free time I like to pass when my family. We go to swimming pool because we like to swimming too much. A lot of times I go to video club and I get a film because we like very much the films too. I can not go to the cinema frecuently because I have two children. The last film that all the family saw was Atlantis because other film they do not will like.*

Showing learners that, in order to express causality, there are alternatives to *because,* such as *so,* might help here. Also, substituting some sentence-internal links with links across sentences, using formulae such as *this is because…* and *this is why…* would also help vary the rather repetitive sentence structure. One way of doing this might be to reformulate the text and ask the learner to note any differences. For example:

> I like to spend my free time with my family. We love going swimming so we often go to the pool. And, because we also like films, I go to the video club a lot. I have two children so I don't go to the cinema very often. The last film that we watched together was Atlantis. This is because there was no other film that they wanted to watch.

A follow-up stage, where learners re-cast sentences using the newly presented linkers, might look like this:

> **Re-write each of the following sentences at least twice, choosing from these patterns:**
> I often go to Chinese restaurants because I like Chinese food.
> → *I like Chinese food so I often go to Chinese restaurants.*
> → *Because I like Chinese food I often go to Chinese restaurants.*
> → *I often go to Chinese restaurants. This is because I like Chinese food.*
> → *I like Chinese food. This is why I often go to Chinese restaurants.*
>
> 1. My flatmate doesn't go out much because he is shy.
> 2. The seas are rising because the Arctic ice is melting.
> 3. etc.

Of course, it is important that learners get beyond this rather mechanical stage and start writing short texts of their own creation. One way of doing this might be to set a task such as:

> Describe some changes that have happened in your town/neighbourhood in the last few years and explain why these changes occurred.

The causal element of the task rubric (*explain why…*) should require the use of at least some of the causal linkers practised previously.

An overemphasis on teaching conjuncts, however, at the expense of a focus on other ways of making texts cohesive, can result in the kind of stilted, over-connected type of text that is parodied by Ann Raimes in her article 'Anguish as a Foreign Language'[29]:

> Louie rushed and got ready for work, but, when he went out the door, he saw the snowstorm was very heavy. Therefore, he decided not to go to work. Then, he sat down to enjoy his newspaper. However, he realized his boss might get angry because he did not go to the office. Finally, he made another decision, that he must go to work. So, he went out the door and walked to the bus stop.

Raimes comments: 'Many of us, at one time or another, have praised a student for such a piece of writing. No grammatical mistakes. I have seen such flat paragraphs as this applauded as excellent and I, too, have assessed similar papers with a check mark and the comment "very good".' Raimes attributes this attitude to a pre-occupation with 'bottom-up' processes, as opposed to 'top-down' ones. Bottom-up processes focus on getting the details right at the expense of the whole: 'We have, I fear, trapped our students within the sentence. They worry about accuracy; they stop after each sentence and go back and check it for inflections, word order, spelling and punctuation, breathe a sigh of relief and go on to attack the looming giant of the next sentence.'

As an antidote to this bottom-up view, one idea might be to ask learners to *remove* conjuncts from a text, leaving only those that are absolutely necessary and making any other adjustments (eg in the ordering of the sentences) that might be required.

Conclusion

In this chapter we have considered how a text can be distinguished from a random collection of sentences and what implications this might have for learners in interpreting texts and in producing their own. We looked principally at the question of cohesion – what is it that binds the parts of a text together? The main teaching implications of this discussion of cohesion can be summarized as:

- expose learners to texts rather than to isolated sentences only
- draw attention to, and categorize, the features that bind texts together
- encourage learners to reproduce these features, where appropriate, in their own texts
- provide feedback not only on sentence-level features of learners' texts, but on the overall cohesiveness as well.

In the next chapter we will address the question of coherence: what is it that makes a text make sense?

Chapter 3   What makes a text make sense?

In the last chapter we looked at the way a text hangs together – how is it is 'made cohesive'. But a text needs to do more than simply hang together. It also needs to make sense. In this chapter we will look at ways that this is achieved and the relation between this sense-making quality (a text's *coherence*) and its internal cohesion. To do this it may help to unravel a text in order to demonstrate that its coherence is more than simply a function of its cohesive ties.

Discovery activity 3.1   *Ordering*

Here, for example, is a short text from a children's encyclopedia[30]. The sentences have been re-arranged and lettered. Can you sort them into their correct order? What linguistic (and non-linguistic) clues did you use to help you do the task?

3.1a

> a) Two years later his father took him to play at concerts in the great cities of Europe.
> b) Mozart wrote church music, opera and nearly 50 symphonies.
> c) The Austrian composer Mozart was a musical genius.
> d) He worked hard but earned little money and died very poor at the age of 35.
> e) He began writing music at the age of five.

Commentary ■ ■ ■

In case you didn't get it, the original text is as follows:

3.1b

> (c) The Austrian composer Mozart was a musical genius. (e) He began writing music at the age of five. (a) Two years later his father took him to play at concerts in the great cities of Europe. (b) Mozart wrote church music, opera and nearly 50 symphonies. (d) He worked hard but earned little money and died very poor at the age of 35.

The point of this exercise is that the correct ordering of the sentences does not depend on cohesive ties alone. The only sentence that is explicitly linked to its predecessor is (a) because of the connector *later*. Neither it, nor sentences (e) and (d) – because of the referring pronoun *he* – could begin the text. But apart from that constraint, they could go anywhere, technically speaking. Nevertheless, our expectation, as readers, is that the text will more or less follow the chronological order of Mozart's life. Moreover, it simply wouldn't make sense to put sentence (a) at the end, for example:

3.1c

> He worked hard but earned little money and died very poor at the age of 35. Two years later his father took him to play at concerts in the great cities of Europe. ■

Coherence

This capacity of a text to 'make sense' is called *coherence*. An incoherent text, such as 3.1c, doesn't make sense: however closely connected its individual sentences might be, it is non-sense. Coherence is a quality that the reader derives from the text: it is not simply a function of its cohesion. Even quite cohesive texts can be nonsense, as in this invented example:

3.2

> The Austrian composer Mozart was a musical genius. He has got a swimming pool. It actually tingles on your skin to tell you it's working. Water would then come out of fountains such as the one shown here. And that is why dogs still chase rabbits.

The text, in case you hadn't noticed, is constructed out of sentences from other texts in this and the previous chapter. Meaningless as it is, it is not without cohesion – the sentences are notionally connected by the use of pronouns, substitutions and conjuncts. But it is incoherent – however hard we try, we can't get it to make sense.

Cohesion, then, is a surface feature of texts, independent of the reader. Coherence, on the other hand, results from the interaction between the reader and the text. This is not to say that cohesion and coherence function independently. Writers intentionally use cohesive devices with the aim of making their texts easier to follow, ie more coherent. But if the text is basically nonsense, no amount of linkers will make it coherent. Unfortunately, a lot of student writing reflects an over-dependence on the cohesive 'trees' at the expense of the coherent 'wood', as we shall see shortly.

First, though, we need to consider what exactly it is that makes a text coherent – or, rather, what *helps* make a text coherent, since coherence, I am arguing, is in the eye of the beholder.

The issue of coherence is usually approached from two perspectives: the *micro-level* and the *macro-level*. At the micro-level, readers have certain expectations of how the proposition (ie the meaning) of a sentence is likely to be developed in the sentence or sentences that follow it. When these expectations are met, the immediate text will seem coherent. At the macro-level, coherence is enhanced if a) the reader can easily discern what the text is about, b) the text is organized in a way that answers the reader's likely questions and c) the text is organized in a way that is familiar to the reader.

Micro-level coherence

We'll start by looking at the micro-, sentence-by-sentence, level.

Discovery activity 3.2   *Logical relationships*

Match the two halves of these short authentic texts. What is the logical relation between the two parts of each text?

1 Shares in Parmalat, the Italian global food group, fell by more than 50% after a three-day suspension.	**A** Pool, brook, stunning views, lush groves, comfort, privacy.[31]
2 Doctor Foster went to Gloucester In a shower of rain.	**B** They may be recovered via the lodge on payment of the current fee.
3 Magical Provence: modernized farmhouse in medieval village.	**C** Add Spice Paste and stir well.
4 Shockingly, 10 passengers on a flight are at risk of DVT.	**D** The company had been plagued by apparent balance sheet discrepancies.[32]
5 Bicycles parked other than in the racks provided are liable to be impounded.	**E** We are blocking the pavement. Thank you.
6 Boil water in a saucepan.	**F** *Scholl* flight socks can help prevent you being one of them.[33]
7 To all smokers: Please cross the road to smoke.	**G** He stepped in a puddle Right up to his middle And never went there again.

Commentary ■ ■ ■

The complete texts are: 1-D, 2-G, 3-A, 4-F, 5-B, 6-C, 7-E. The exercise should have been easy to do: apart from anything else, there are lexical clues that bind the texts together. But, there are also implicit logical connections and it is these that help create the feeling that the (admittedly minimalist) texts make sense. The logical connections are the same as those we looked at when discussing linking devices, but note that there are no explicit conjuncts signalling the relation between the two sentences. We take the relation on trust. Here are the relations:

- **additive,** as in text 3-A. The second sentence gives details about, or *specifies*, the statement in the first sentence. This movement, from general to specific, is one that readers are 'primed' to recognize.
- **adversative,** as in texts 4-F and 5-B. In 4-F the second sentence, in claiming to solve the problem stated in the first, makes a contrast that could have been signalled with *however,* for example. In 5-B (which was a notice in the forecourt of an Oxford college) there is a contrast between *impounded* and *recovered,* which could have been signalled with *but* or *however.*
- **causal,** as in texts 1-D and 7-E, where the second sentence provides a reason for the situation or request mentioned in the first.
- **temporal,** as in texts 2-G and 6-C, where the chronological order of events (*and then…*) is implied, rather than explicitly stated. Note that when two past tense sentences are placed together, and in the absence of any other evidence, we assume that the first happened before the second, as in *John sang a song. Janet told a joke.* ■

The above texts have been chosen to demonstrate how whole (admittedly short) texts cohere because of the kinds of expectations that are both set up and satisfied by their component parts. This happens both at the level of the whole text and also at the local level, from one sentence to the next, such that at any point in a text any one sentence both reflects what has gone before and anticipates what is going to come. The sentence 'represents' the text at that point. Take a sentence randomly chosen from the middle of a text:

> (12) The genes carry all the information needed to make a new plant or animal.

We can fairly safely assume that the previous sentence was about genes, and that the sentence that follows will develop this general statement further by saying something more, and possibly more specific, about either *genes* or *information*. Let's see if this is in fact the case:

> (11) Each part is called a *gene*. (12) The genes carry all the information needed to make a new plant or animal. (13) They decide its sex and also what characteristics it inherits.

Our hypotheses have been confirmed: sentence 11 introduced the term *gene* and sentence 13 specified two sub-sets of information subsumed under *all the information* in sentence 12.

We could repeat the exercise with sentence 11 and sentence 13, reflecting back and projecting forward, and again with sentences 10 and 14, and so on, until, in theory, we had 'guessed' the whole text – or, rather, a limited set of potential whole texts. We are able to do this not only because of cohesive clues like the definite article *the* that goes with *genes* in sentence 12, suggesting a previous mention, but also because the information in sentences is distributed in a predictable way. In English, sentences (and the clauses of which they are composed) have a simple two-way division between what the sentence is about (its *topic*) and what the writer or speaker wants to tell you about that topic (the *comment*). Moreover, the topic of the sentence is often associated with what is already known, or *given*. Given information is information that is retrievable because it has been explicitly mentioned at some prior point in the text, or because it is inferable from the text or from the context, or because it is part of the shared world knowledge of writer and reader (or speaker and listener). Given information normally precedes *new* information in the sentence. The new information is typically placed in the comment position.

Theme and rheme / Topic and comment

The topic and comment are also called the *theme* and the *rheme* of the sentence or clause. The different terms derive from different theoretical viewpoints and also from the need to distinguish the topic of a sentence from the topic of a text (which we will discuss below). In our example sentence the topic is *the genes*:

topic (theme)	comment (rheme)
given information	*new information*
(12) The genes	carry all the information needed to make a new plant or animal.

The topic is the 'launch pad' of the message and is typically – but not always – realized by a noun phrase (the grammatical *subject* of the sentence). The comment is what the writer or speaker considers to be 'newsworthy' about the topic: what you as reader or listener need to pay attention to. (For this reason, the comment typically carries the major word stress when articulated.)

The tendency to place the new information in the latter part of a clause or sentence is called *end-weight*. This new information, in turn, often becomes the given information of the next sentence, as in sentences 11 and 12. Or the same topic is carried over and a new comment is made about it (as in sentences 12 and 13):

topic (theme)	comment (rheme)
given information	*new information*
(11) Each part	is called a *gene*.
(12) The genes	carry all the information needed to make a new plant or animal.
(13) They	decide its sex and also what characteristics it inherits.

Predicting 'backwards' again, we can be fairly sure that the word *part* (in the theme of sentence 11), or one of its synonyms, was either the topic or comment of sentence 10. This is in fact the case:

topic (theme)	comment (rheme)
(10) Different parts of each chromosome	carry different 'coded messages'.
(11) Each part	is called a *gene*.

Going back again, we are not surprised to find that *chromosome* is 'carried over' from sentence 9:

topic (theme)	comment (rheme)
(9) Inside every cell	are tiny *chromosomes*…
(10) Different parts of each chromosome	carry different 'coded messages'.
(11) Each part	is called a *gene*.

The comment may consist of more than one element (as in sentence 13), only one of which may be carried over:

topic (theme)	comment (rheme)
(13) They	decide its sex
	and also what characteristics it inherits.
(14) Some inherited characteristics	are stronger than others.

These patterns of topic and comment can be represented like this (after McCarthy 1991)[34]:

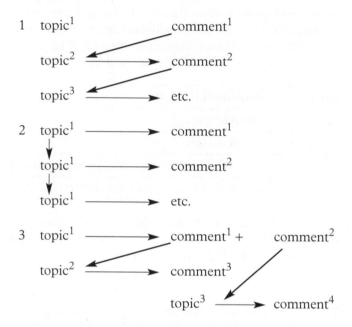

The *Genetics* text demonstrates how writers mix and combine these patterns in order to carry their argument forward in the way they feel is most coherent. (It would be rare to find a longish text that adopted one pattern at the exclusion of others.) As readers, these alternating patterns of topic and comment help us make sense of the writer's argument. Disrupting these patterns, by moving topics to the comment position, for example, would prove very distracting:

> … Different 'coded messages' are carried by different parts of each chromosome. A gene is what each part is called. The information needed to make a new plant or animal is carried by the genes. Its sex and what characteristics it inherits they decide. Stronger than others are some inherited characteristics…

There are other means, as well, for signalling the evolving argument of a text. One is through the use of *nominalization* (see page 27). There are key words, such as *way, problem, answer, situation, process,* and so on, that can either encapsulate what has gone before or set up expectations as to what is to come. Here is another segment from the text on genetics. Note how the underlined words 'gather up' the adjacent sentences, both retrospectively and prospectively:

> (6) Each parent passes on certain characteristics to its offspring. (7) This process is called heredity. (8) Heredity works in an amazing way.

Process encapsulates the entire proposition expressed in sentence 6. *Way,* especially in rheme position, signals that some kind of description will follow. It would be very odd if the sentence that follows *way* did not go on to outline how, in fact, heredity works.

Discovery activity 3.3   *Logical relations*

It's time to look at the whole of the *Genetics* text[35]. You should now be able to identify the logical relations between its sentences, showing how each sentence either anticipates the sentence that follows, or encapsulates some element of the sentence that preceded it.

3.3

> ### GENETICS
>
> The science of genetics explains why living things look and behave as they do. Advanced animals have two sexes, male and female. Each individual produces sex cells. If a male and female sex cell join, the female cell grows into a new individual. Each parent passes on certain characteristics to its offspring. This process is called *heredity*.
>
> Heredity works in an amazing way. Inside every cell are tiny *chromosomes*, largely made of a chemical called DNA. Different parts of each chromosome carry different coded messages. Each part is called a *gene*. The genes carry all the information needed to make a new plant or animal. They decide its sex and also what characteristics it inherits.
>
> Some inherited characteristics are stronger than others. They are dominant. Weaker ones are recessive. Genes for brown eyes, for example, dominate over the weaker genes for blue eyes.

Commentary ■ ■ ■

The following outline summarizes the logical relations between the sentences of the text.

(1) GENETICS	Statement of topic.
(2) The science of genetics explains why living things look and behave as they do.	The topic (*genetics*) is now a given, having been announced in the title and takes theme position. The definition that follows is the 'news' and takes the rheme slot. The embedded question (*Why do living things look and behave as they do?*) predicts an answer. The rest of the text in fact answers the question.
(3) Advanced animals have two sexes, male and female.	The topic (*advanced animals*) echoes part of the comment in (2) (*living things*) – this suggests that (3) is the beginning of an answer to (2).
(4) Each individual produces sex cells.	Again, the topic (*each individual*) is a re-focusing of the *living things, advanced animals* thread – same topic, new comment, with the word *sex* carried over. The dynamic verb

	(*produces*) suggests a process is being described (compared to (3), which describes a state), and since processes usually have stages, we can predict more sentences with more dynamic verbs.
(5) If a male and female sex cell join, the female cell grows into a new individual.	This sentence is almost entirely composed of ingredients from the previous two sentences: the topic combines elements from the comments of both sentences (3) and (4), ie *male and female, sex cell(s)*; the word *individual* is also carried over. Again, the dynamic verbs *joins* and *grows* confirm the 'process' hypothesis.
(6) Each parent passes on certain characteristics to its offspring.	Re-phrasing of parts of (5): *male and female = each parent; new individual = offspring*. New dynamic verb: will there be more stages to the process? And will these *certain characteristics* be itemized?
(7) This process is called *heredity*.	*This process* summarizes the text to date. *Heredity* is given special emphasis by the use of italics, suggesting it's a key word which will be further explained or elaborated on.
(8) Heredity works in an amazing way.	Previous comment becomes topic; *way* anticipates a description.
(9) Inside every cell are tiny *chromosomes*, largely made of a chemical called DNA.	*Cell* is carried over from (4); two comments: *chromosomes* and *DNA*. If this is the description of *a way something works*, it is incomplete, because so far there are no dynamic verbs. We expect more to follow.
(10) Different parts of each chromosome carry different coded messages.	*Chromosome* is carried over from (9). Dynamic verb (*carry*) suggests this is part of the *way* signalled in (8) and anticipates further sentences with dynamic verbs, since 'ways', like 'processes', have stages.
(11) Each part is called a *gene*.	The topic is the same as (10); new comment, given special emphasis (italics) which anticipates further commentary.

(12) The genes carry all the information needed to make a new plant or animal.	Previous comment becomes topic; *information* is similar in meaning to *coded messages* in (10).
(13) They decide its sex and also what characteristics it inherits.	Same topic as previous sentence. *Characteristics* is carried over from (6). Again, will the characteristics be itemized?
(14) Some inherited characteristics are stronger than others.	One of the previous comments becomes the topic.
(15) They are dominant.	Re-wording of previous sentence.
(16) Weaker ones are recessive.	*Weaker ones = others* in (14); the structure of the sentence imitates (15) – and is an example of parallelism (see page 22).
(17) Genes for brown eyes, for example, dominate over the weaker genes for blue eyes.	At last, and as expected, some specific characteristics are mentioned (see 6, 13 and 14); *dominant* becomes *dominate; weaker* is repeated; *genes* is repeated twice.

This analysis does not in any way exhaust the intricate network of intertwining themes and arguments in this one text: not for nothing does the word *text* derive from the Latin *texere,* to weave. In fact, some writers use the word *texture* to describe the combined effect of such structural features of a text as the topic-comment organization and of its internal cohesion, both grammatical and lexical. ■

It is important to stress, at this point, that texture is not simply a decorative or stylistic quality of texts, but that it fulfils a vital communicative purpose. When we are reading a text – or listening to spoken text – we are attending only to the immediate sentence or utterance. We cannot process the whole text all at once. (Of course, with a written text, you can glance back through it, but, generally, we don't.) Therefore, as readers and listeners, we need guidance as to what has gone before and what is yet to come. The immediate sentence has to represent the text *at that moment.* Or, as John Sinclair puts it, 'The text at any particular time carries with it everything that a competent reader needs in order to understand the current state of the text.'[36]

This view of a text unfolding *in time* has led Sinclair to propose a radical theory of text, which argues that the text is *only* the immediate sentence. This focal sentence either *encapsulates* the immediately preceding sentence, or it sets up an anticipation of the sentence that follows (what is called *prospection*). So far this argument is consistent with our analysis of the genetics text. In fact, its coherence is achieved almost entirely by acts of prospection, that is, by setting up an expectation that is immediately satisfied, as in:

> Heredity works in an amazing way. → Inside every cell are tiny chromosomes, largely made of a chemical called DNA. etc.

But Sinclair goes on to argue that, for all intents and purposes, the rest of the text apart from the immediate sentence exists only as a trace or an echo. It is not subject to mental consultation, hence there cannot really be such a thing as anaphoric (or back) reference. This is of course easier to argue with regard to spoken language, where it is simply not possible to consult the text in any physical way. But Sinclair extends the argument to written text as well. The interconnectivity of texts is only an artefact, he argues. It is available for us to study after the event, but it is not an accurate way of modelling what happens when we actually read. What *does* happen? As the focus of our attention proceeds from one sentence to the next, the state of our mental representation based on the text – the knowledge shared by writer and reader – is continuously updated through processes of encapsulation and prospection. Referents in the sentence, such as pronouns, do not 'point back' in the text. Rather, they point at what has become shared knowledge, much in the same way as definite articles or proper nouns do, as in the sentence from text 2.18: *And the apron will be perfect for Sant Pol barbies…* The referents are not in the text, but in the reader's and writer's heads, as it were.

Sinclair concludes that 'a text does not consist of a string of sentences which are intricately interconnected, but of a series of sentence-length texts, each of which is a total update of the one before'.[37] As compelling (and exciting) as Sinclair's argument is, it does not invalidate the study of cohesion in texts, but it does suggest that the processes of *encapsulation* and *prospection* demand more attention than they have been normally been given.

Reader expectations

Not all texts are as transparent as text 3.3, which, apart from anything else, was written for children and therefore is relatively straightforward and unadorned. Some texts do not yield their sense without more of a struggle. Nevertheless, as readers we approach a text assuming it will make sense until proven otherwise, even if it means putting our initial hypotheses on hold, or even abandoning them altogether. Take these two sentences, for example:

3.4

> (1) I learned to read around my sixth birthday. (2) I was making a dinosaur in school from crêpe bandage and toilet rolls when I started to feel as if an invisible pump was inflating my head from the inside.

Our understanding of the first sentence suggests that the second sentence will be connected to it either in some temporal or causal sense, eg it will relay the circumstances, or the cause, or the effect of the writer's learning to read. The past continuous in sentence 2 (*I was making a dinosaur…*) tends to support the temporal hypothesis, as it is a verb form often used to set the scene for some particular narrative event. It's only when we get to the 'invisible pump' that the hypothesis starts to wobble a bit. Perhaps the writer is implying that the experience of learning to read felt like his head was being pumped up. But how is the dinosaur related to reading? Is the dinosaur a red herring? Let's put our theory on hold and move on:

> (3) My face became a cluster of bumps, my feet dangled limp and too far away to control.

While this possibly relates to the sensations described in sentence 2, the theory that it has something to do with learning to read is becoming untenable. We are compelled to read on with no clear idea of what the connections are:

> (4) The teacher carried me home on her shoulders.

Well, now sentences 2, 3 and 4, are starting to cohere. Sentences 2 and 3 are related in an additive way (*What's more…*) and 3 is related in a causal way (*So…*). But we are still none the wiser as to how sentence 1 fits in. Much later in the same paragraph, after the writer has described in detail the onset of mumps, the connection at last becomes clear:

> (12) When I caught the mumps, I couldn't read; when I went back to school again, I could. (13) The first page of *The Hobbit* was a thicket of symbols, to be decoded one at a time and joined hesitantly together… (15) By the time I reached *The Hobbit's* last page, though, writing had softened and lost the outlines of the printed alphabet and become a transparent liquid, first viscous and sluggish, like a jelly of meaning, then ever thinner and more mobile, flowing faster and faster, until it reached me at the speed of thinking and I could not entirely distinguish the suggestions it was making from my own thoughts.[38]

It is now clear, in retrospect, that sentence 2 launched a long detour in which the circumstances leading up to the writer's learning to read are described in detail. Normally, this would have been signalled more obviously, eg *It happened when I was away from school with mumps…* Perhaps the writer wanted to suggest that there was more than simply a temporal connection between the experience of catching mumps and the experience of learning to read. The imagery of accelerating fluids in sentence 15 is not unlike the invisible pump image in sentence 2, as if learning to read *is* like catching mumps. The text is not only coherent but there is a coherent sub-text as well!

The writer has taken certain risks, testing the reader's faith in the coherence of his text, but it all comes clear in the end. (It's no coincidence, either, that the extract comes from a book about reading.) The writer is able to take these risks because he knows that readers are on the constant look-out for clues that will support their assumption that texts are, first and foremost, coherent – that they make sense. These clues are usually close at hand, in the associated text (or the *co-text*) – and often in the adjoining sentence. Or they may be in the *context* where the text is situated. (For more on co-text and context, see Chapter 5.)

When, occasionally, two sentences are juxtaposed whose relationship *cannot* be established, we have to conclude that their juxtaposition is accidental, as in this illuminated sign on a café in the USA in 2003:

3.5

> # OUR PRAYERS ARE WITH THE TROOPS
> ## TRY OUR FRESH TENDER HOME COOKED TURTLE

Discovery activity 3.4   *Rogue sentences*

Good readers can usually spot lack of coherence quickly – in fact, the capacity to do so is sometimes used as a test of reading ability. What, for example, is the sentence that doesn't fit in this text[39]?

3.6

> ### TORTOISE AND TURTLE
>
> (1) Unlike other reptiles, tortoises and turtles have hard shells to protect their bodies.
>
> Tortoises are land animals. (2) They live in warm countries and eat plant food. (3) A tortoise cannot run away from an enemy. (4) Instead, it tucks its head and legs into its shell. (5) Some tortoises can live to be much more than a hundred years old – older than any other animals.
>
> (6) Turtles live in the sea. (7) Some seaweeds can be eaten. (8) They have flatter shells than tortoises and use their legs as paddles for swimming. (9) On land they are very clumsy.
>
> See also REPTILE.

Commentary ■ ■ ■

The rogue sentence is, of course, number 7. A fairly easy exercise, you'll agree, but it can be made more difficult depending on the choice and length of the text and the choice of 'rogue' sentence. It can be made still more difficult if the text, along with its inserted sentence, is jumbled up (as in text 3.1a) – so that the exercise becomes a test of the ability to recognize cohesive ties as well as overall coherence. ■

The above exercise is a type of 'deletion' exercise. The opposite process involves insertion. Insertion exercises also require (and therefore test) the ability to recognize how coherence works and are now popular in some public ELT examinations.

Discovery activity 3.5   *Sentence insertion*

Here is a text from Henry Widdowson's *Teaching Language as Communication*[40] (in which the sentences have been numbered for convenience). The two sentences that follow (A and B) have been extracted from it (in no particular order). Can you re-insert them? As you do, consider the kinds of skills and knowledge that you need to enlist in order to do the task. How would you prepare students to do similar tasks?

A In some respects, however, it is unsatisfactory.
B But what exactly do we mean by this?

3.7

(1) The aims of a language teaching course are very often defined with reference to the four 'language skills': understanding speech, speaking, reading and writing. (2) These aims, therefore, relate to the kind of activity which the learners are to perform. (3) But how can we characterize this activity? (4) What is it that learners are expected to understand, speak, read and write? (5) The obvious answer is: the language they are learning. (6) We might mean a selection of lexical items recorded in a dictionary combined with syntactic structures recorded in a grammar. (7) In this view, the teaching of a language involves developing the ability to produce correct sentences. (8) Many teachers would subscribe to this view and it has been productive of a good deal of impressive language teaching material. (9) We may readily acknowledge that the ability to produce sentences is a crucial one in the learning of a language. (10) It is important to recognize, however, that it is not the only ability that learners need to acquire. (11) Someone knowing a language knows more than how to understand, speak, read and write sentences. (12) He also knows how sentences are used to communicative effect.

Commentary ■ ■ ■

To do this task requires more than simply recognizing cohesive ties (such as *however*, *but*, etc), although this is of course very important. It also involves the ability to understand and follow the thread of the argument, sentence by sentence, including recognizing what is 'new information' in each sentence. This in turn involves more than simply understanding the words and the grammar. Familiarity with the argument itself, and with this kind of text and writing style, is an obvious advantage.

To prepare learners for this kind of task requires, therefore, that attention be given to the formal ties between sentences, including the use of reference and conjuncts. It also means encouraging learners to read for meaning – stepping back, as it were, from the text in order to get its overall gist. For example, learners would be advised to read the whole text first, before attempting to re-insert the missing sentences. Knowing that the text is a complete paragraph would help matters. Since paragraphs (in academic writing) typically start out by presenting the writer's case, going on to elaborate it or give examples, before finally summarizing it, it's generally a good idea to pay special attention to the beginnings and endings of paragraphs. In the case of the above text, Widdowson's whole argument can be summarized in sentences 1, 11 and 12.

The missing sentences, by the way, fit in like this: **A** comes between sentences 8 and 9; **B** comes between sentences 5 and 6. ■

Classroom applications

End weight

The principle of 'end-weight' – of placing the newsworthy information at the end of the clause – is one that can form the focus of a number of classroom tasks. Asking learners to choose the best of a number of options for continuing a text can help draw attention to the way given and new information is typically distributed. For example:

Choose the sentence (a or b) that is the best way of continuing the text.

1 The ancient Egyptians buried their pharaohs in tombs called pyramids.
    a In Giza, near Cairo, are the most famous pyramids.
    b The most famous pyramids are in Giza, near Cairo.

2 Some pyramids are made of more than two million blocks of stone.
    a They were dragged into place by teams of workers.
    b Teams of workers dragged them into place.

3 The pyramids were built to house the body of the pharaoh.
    a Inside each pyramid is a secret chamber.
    b A secret chamber is inside each pyramid.

4 This is the tomb where the mummy of the pharaoh was laid.
    a Robbers have stolen most of these mummies.
    b Most of these mummies have been stolen by robbers.
  etc.

You'll probably agree that the best way of continuing the first sentence of the text is option **b**, where the end-weighted comment of the first sentence (*pyramids*) becomes the topic of the second. By the same principal, **2a** is the logical choice. In **3**, the new information is *a secret chamber*, which suggests it should go into the comment slot at the end of the sentence, as in option **a**. Similarly, *robbers* is new information, so **4b** is the preferred choice.

A similar kind of awareness-raising activity is to ask learners to spot the sentences that are 'back-to-front' in a text. The exercise on pyramids could serve as the basis for such a text. For example: What are the two awkward sentences in this text?

---

(1) The ancient Egyptians buried their pharaohs in tombs called pyramids.
(2) The most famous pyramids are in Giza, near Cairo. (3) Some pyramids are made of more than two million blocks of stone. (4) Teams of workers dragged them into place. (5) The pyramids were built to house the body of the pharaoh.
(6) Inside each pyramid is a secret chamber. (7) The tomb where the mummy of the pharaoh was laid is this. (8) Most of these mummies have been stolen by robbers.

(Answer: 4 and 7)

Passive constructions

Notice that a number of the alternatives in the exercise on pyramids involve a choice between active and passive constructions. This is a reminder that one of the chief functions of the passive is to allow for the possibility of placing the object of the verb in the theme slot – normally the domain of the grammatical subject – and at the same time placing new information in the rheme slot:

topic (theme)	comment (rheme)
Brutus	stabbed Caesar to death.
→ Caesar	was stabbed to death by Brutus.

If English only had active sentence constructions it would be difficult to divert the reader's focus on to what is newsworthy in a sentence. Moreover, it would be difficult to maintain topic consistency over extended stretches of text. Compare these two versions of the same text (passive verb forms are underlined):

3.8a

> Napoleon regained power in 1815. He ruled for a hundred days. But Wellington defeated him at the Battle of Waterloo. Napoleon surrendered to the British and they exiled him to St Helena, where he died in 1821.

3.8b

> Napoleon regained power in 1815. He ruled for a hundred days. But he was defeated by Wellington at the Battle of Waterloo. He surrendered to the British and he was exiled to St Helena, where he died in 1821.

This suggests another exercise type, where information is re-formulated according to a different point of view. For example, here are some short encyclopedia entries about famous people.[41] Can you re-write them so that they are about famous achievements instead?

Cervantes, Miguel de	He wrote *Don Quixote* in 1605.
Hill, Mildred and Patty	They wrote *Happy Birthday* in 1893.
Gates, Bill	He started Microsoft in 1975.
Fender, Leo	He invented the electric guitar in 1948.
Roddick, Anita	She started *The Body Shop* in 1976.

Don Quixote	*Don Quixote was written by Cervantes in 1605.*
Electric guitar	....
Happy Birthday	....
Microsoft	....
The Body Shop	....

The next stage might be some more productive activity, such as writing the description of a process from the point of view of the thing being processed (eg coal) or of the people who process it (eg coal miners). It is more likely that the former will require more use of passive constructions than the latter.

Cleft sentences

Certain constructions, such as *cleft sentences*, are used, like the passive, to alter the normal order of sentence elements, in order to place special emphasis on new information. For example, the second of these two sentences is a cleft sentence:
1 Robin paid.
2 It was Robin who paid.

Like the passive, cleft sentences are best understood and manipulated in context. Which of the above sentences, for example, best fits these mini-contexts?

A I was mistaken in thinking that Jan paid for dinner. _____ . Jan just left the tip.

B Jan, Robin and I had dinner together. _____ . Jan left the tip.

In this context it should be clear that the cleft construction adds extra emphasis in order to contradict, or correct, an earlier statement or inference (as in **A** above). The given information is 'Jan (or somebody else) paid.' The new information ('No, Robin did.') is superimposed on to this original statement.

We can represent the distribution of topic and comment like this:

topic (theme)	comment (rheme)
(1) Robin	paid.
(2) [It was]	Robin who paid.

In (2) *it was* is in brackets because it's not really a topic at all; it's simply a way of filling an empty slot, a bit like the *it* in *It was raining*.

The use of 'mini-contexts' to practise passive and cleft constructions would seem to be essential. An exercise that simply asked students to change statements like *Robin paid* into *It was Robin who paid*, with no reference to a context, would not be addressing the significance of the choice between the two constructions.

An exercise type that addresses a number of ways that sentences can be combined coherently is one in which learners are asked to *textualize*, ie turn into coherent text, a number of isolated propositions. For example:

Use this information to write a short text entitled 'Paper'. You can change the order of information in the sentences, but try to maintain the order of the sentences. You can combine sentences, if necessary.

The Chinese invented paper.
The Chinese originally produced paper from plant fibres and rags.
The Arabs introduced paper to Europe.
This happened in the Middle Ages.
Parchment had been the standard material for written and printed documents until then.
Paper eventually superseded parchment.
From the nineteenth century wood pulp was used to make paper.
Plant fibre and rags continued to be used to make some kinds of paper.
Waste paper is recycled to make most paper nowadays.
In France they introduced the first machines for making rolls of paper.
This happened in the eighteenth century.
Early paper was hand made.
Early paper consisted of single sheets.

One of several possible ways of textualizing these sentences might be the following:

(1) Paper was invented by the Chinese, who originally produced it from plant fibres and rags. (2) It was introduced to Europe by the Arabs in the Middle Ages. (3) Until then the standard material for written and printed documents had been parchment, but this was eventually superseded by paper. (4) From

the nineteenth century paper was made from wood pulp, although some kinds of paper continued to be made from plant fibre and rags. (5) Nowadays most paper is made by recycling waste paper.

(6) The first machines for making rolls of paper were introduced in France in the eighteenth century. (7) Early paper had been hand made and consisted of single sheets.

The textualizing process has involved the following kinds of operations:

- transforming active constructions into passive ones, in order to achieve end-weight (eg sentence 1)
- re-arranging the order of elements in the sentence, again in the interests of end-weight (eg sentence 3)
- combining sentences using relative pronouns (eg sentence 1) or linkers (eg sentence 4)
- using referring pronouns, such as *it,* to connect sentences and avoid repetition (eg sentence 2)
- changing verb forms in order to re-position events relative to other events (eg sentence 7).

Macro-level coherence: Topics

At the *macro-level,* texts achieve coherence because they are obviously *about* something, that is, there is an identifiable topic, or topics. This is a slightly different sense of the term *topic* than the one we have been using to talk about the themes of sentences. Of course, the topic of a text is often also the topic of at least some of the individual sentences in that text. Even without its title, text 3.6, for example, is clearly about *tortoises and turtles* since these comprise the topics of most of the sentences in the text. What other clues, apart from such obvious ones as headings and titles, indicate topical coherence?

Discovery activity 3.6   *Key words*

Key words are those words that occur with a frequency that is significant when compared to the normal frequency of these same words, as determined by corpus data. That is to say, if a word occurs, say, five times in a text that is a hundred words long, but only ten times in a general corpus of a million words, it is clearly disproportionately represented in the text. Chances are that the word's prominence in the text is not accidental, but is due to the fact that the word is intimately related to what that particular text is about.

Here are the key words of three texts. The first set of key words (which are ordered in descending order of significance) comes from a text you are already familiar with. Notice how just the key words alone convey a strong sense of what the text is about.

1 *heredity, genes, characteristics, weaker, cell, female, sex, male, carry, eyes, each, individual*

Can you work out the topic of each of the texts from which the two lists below were derived?

2 *striker, goalkeeper, ten, headed, penalty, corner, shot, ball, yards, cross, goal, home*

3 *paint, door, edges, frame, brush, colour, separately, painted, face, room, each, side*

Commentary ■ ■ ■

I shouldn't have to reproduce the texts to be able to prove that the second is the report of a football match (from a tabloid newspaper) and the third is from a DIY (*Do-it-yourself*) book and is about the painting of doors. The point of the exercise is simply to show that the *topic* of a text is, to a large extent, carried by its words. And that, moreover, these topic-carrying words tend to be nouns. ■

As we saw when we looked at cohesion, chains or threads of lexis ripple through texts and hold them together. This suggests some useful classroom activities, both in advance of and after reading a text, and also as preparation for writing or speaking. In advance of reading a text, for example, learners can be asked to brainstorm all the words they know that are related to the topic of the text, using dictionaries to top up, if necessary. In this way, they are well primed, cognitively speaking, to make sense of the text when they get down to actually reading it. Brainstorming the vocabulary related to a topic in advance of writing about the topic is also a useful pre-writing task – on the understanding, of course, that not all the words that have been brainstormed need to be included in the written text. The same goes for preparation for a speaking task.

Post-reading vocabulary work can involve the mapping of lexical chains in a text (or in the transcript of a listening text, too, of course). Scrutiny of these word sequences can help in the unpacking of difficult texts.

Discovery activity 3.7   *Lexical chains*

You may not be entirely sure what the following poem[42] is about, but you will probably agree that, because of the tight lexical chains running through it, it is about *something*. Can you identify at least two chains of words that run through it?

3.9

> *DEATH OF THE POET*
>
> *This year*
> *the roof of my hive*
> *broke open to the sky*
>
> *my bees buzz*
> *like anxious flies*
>
> *will they learn to feed on*
> *absence?*
>
> *my combs are filling*
> *with dark space.*
>
> *Forget selling myself*
> *to the first sweet tooth*
> *that sniffs along*
>
> *the night air is licking me*
> *clean out of honey.*
>
> *This year*
> *the roof of my hive*
> *gave up*
>
> *and let everything*
> *down.*
>
> *Does it matter*
> *that the moon is pouring*
> *through my holes?*

Commentary ■ ■ ■

There are at least two themes here that intertwine through the length of the poem. The first is the more obvious one, pertaining to bees and honey: *hive, bees* (and, by association, *flies*), *buzz, combs, sweet, honey.* The second has to do with the act of opening, emptying and thereby destroying something and consists of two sub-themes, represented on the one hand by these verb phrases: *break open, gave up, licking me clean out of, let everything down,* and on the other by these noun phrases: *absence, dark space, holes.* The combined effect of these interweaving themes is to suggest the destruction and exposure of a bee-hive, which – with or without the title – seems to be some sort of metaphor for the poet's own sense of implosion and creative emptiness. The point, though, is that, because of its lexical 'texture', the poem *seems* to make sense, even if we have to work hard to locate that sense. It's *about* something. ■

But word chains on their own are not enough to make a text coherent. Indeed, it would be quite possible to compose a text that is complete nonsense, but that is still lexically cohesive. Thus:
Ten cross goalkeepers shot a striker and then headed home from the ball…

The words of a text need to be organized in such a way that they form internal patterns within the text and also so that they relate to the world outside the text insofar as the reader understands it. We shall look at these two aspects of coherence in turn.

Internal patterning

The internal patterning of a text is realized locally in the way words – or their synonyms or derivatives – are carried over from one sentence to the next, as we saw in the discussion of information structure in sentences. Often the *comment* of one sentence becomes the *topic* of the next. In fact this 'carrying over' happens globally, too. That is to say, it occurs over quite long stretches of text. Here, for example, is the first sentence of a news report in a scientific journal[43]:

3.10

> (1) A draft version of the honey bee genome has been made available to the public – a move that should benefit bees and humans alike.

Not surprisingly, a number of words in this sentence flow over into the next two sentences (you might like to predict what they will be):

> (2) The <u>honey bee</u> (Apis mellifera) is multi-talented. (3) It produces <u>honey</u>, pollinates crops and is used by researchers to study <u>human</u> genetics, ageing, disease and social behaviour.

However, considerably further on in the text, parts of sentence 1 are still <u>popping</u> →*occur* up, to the point that sentence 11 paraphrases it almost exactly, using the same or *suddenly* similar vocabulary:

> (1) A draft version of the honey bee genome has been made available to the public – a move that should benefit bees and humans alike. [...]
> (11) The genome's publication is good news for beekeepers and victims of bee stings alike.

Note how the proposition *the honey bee genome has been made available to the public* has been 'nominalized' into the noun phrase *the genome's publication*. And notice how *should benefit* in sentence 1 becomes *is good news* in sentence 11 – another instance of nominalization (see page 27). The transition from *public* to *publication* is a form of indirect repetition based on derivation. The change from *benefit* to *good news* is one based on synonymy. By tracing these repetitions, both direct and indirect, through a text, we can get a clear sense of what the text is about, which in turn helps integrate the text into a coherent whole. Even in the very last sentence words from sentence 1 make a re-appearance:

> (1) A draft version of the honey bee genome has been made available to the public – a move that should benefit bees and humans alike. [....]
> (23) This is the first time that the amassed sequence data have been made publicly available.

Michael Hoey, in a fascinating study[44], has shown how these patterns of lexical repetition can extend further still, over the whole length of a book, in fact. He argues that it is the cohesion induced by these recurring patterns that accounts, to a large extent, for the sense we get of a text's coherence, a view that leads Hoey to question the whole cohesion–coherence dichotomy.

Discovery activity 3.8   *Lexical patterns across long texts*

You might like to test this theory on this very book. Flick ahead or back a few pages and take one or two sentences at random from the body of the text. How many words in those sentences are repeated on this page, either verbatim or in the form of derivations or synonyms?

Classroom applications: Key words

Traditionally, the checking of students' understanding of a text involves asking a series of comprehension questions, often about discrete details of the text. While this may be a valid testing activity (although I have my doubts), it does not provide much assistance in understanding the text if learners have no idea what the text is *about*. In the absence of any global understanding of the text, post-reading tasks may well be a waste of time.

One of the first things to establish, then, is the topic. This may require nothing more than to direct students' attention to the title (if it is obvious, like *Mozart*, for example), or to unpack the title if it is dense or otherwise not so obvious (eg *Honey bee genome sequenced*). In the absence of any title or headline, readers have only the text itself to guide them. Of course, the teacher could simply tell them, 'This is a text about bees.' But practice in identifying the topic is good training for learners.

As we have seen, the best indicators of the topic are the key words and the key sentences. The key words are those that are content words (ie not grammar words like articles, prepositions, etc) and ones that recur in the same sentences with some regularity, although possibly in different forms (eg *genome made public; genome's publication*). At least some of them will occupy the topic slot in the text's sentences fairly frequently.

The key sentences are those that begin the text, or come near the beginning, and which reflect the content of the headline, title and subtitle (if there is one). It often pays to focus initially on the first sentence of a text, eg by writing it on the board, dictating it, or having a student read it aloud, and to 'unpack' it, before going on to read the rest of the text. Other key sentences are those that repeat or paraphrase at least two, maybe three, elements of that first key sentence. And so on. Training learners to seek out these clues not only gives them an idea of what the topic is, but a mini-summary of the argument of the entire text.

Schemas and scripts

So far we have been looking at the internal relations and patterns operating across the words and the sentences that comprise a text. But however interrelated a text is, it doesn't make much sense if it doesn't somehow correspond to the reader's idea of the world *outside* the text. Take the word *bee*, for example. If we hear someone say *Be careful in the orchard. There are bees*, we can make perfect sense of this by reference to what we know about bees and the fact that, not only do bees like orchards because of their flowers, but bees sting. We have activated a 'bee schema'. A schema is simply the way knowledge is represented mentally. A bee schema includes the knowledge that bees frequent flowers and that bees sting. It is also likely to include the fact that bees make honey, they live in hives, they buzz and they are always on the move. Indeed, it's this last fact that enables us to make sense of language that is used metaphorically, such as *I'm as busy as a bee*. Of course, the depth and breadth of a schema will vary with each individual: a beekeeper's schema for *bee* will be much more elaborated than either yours or mine.

If, however, we heard someone say *Be careful in the orchard. There are goalkeepers*, we would be hard pressed to find anything in our orchard schema or our football schema that would help us make much sense of it. In the absence of an accessible schema, the text is senseless.

Related to the notion of schemas, are *scripts*. Scripts are the ways in which we come to expect things to happen. If a schema can be represented by a 'spider diagram', with various branches radiating from a central node, a script, being sequenced, is more like a list. For example, catching a bus in London used to follow this sequence:

- wait at stop
- board bus
- sit down
- pay conductor when he or she approaches.

Nowadays, the London bus script goes like this:

- wait at stop
- board bus
- pay driver
- sit down.

If you come from a culture where you are used to the former script, you may be caught off guard by the latter. (In fact, the London bus script is already being replaced by a new one, which involves buying the ticket from a machine at the bus stop and punching it when you board, something I learned to my cost recently.)

Discovery activity 3.9   *Scripts*

To take another example, take a minute or two to write a short description of your house or apartment for someone who has never visited it. Imagine, for example, it's part of a letter you are writing to a friend.

Commentary ■ ■ ■

Now, I am fairly confident that your description did not start with the colour of the walls, or the garden shed. Rather, you probably followed an apartment or house script and your description was possibly organized along similar lines to this e-mail I received from my niece:

3.11

> Dan and I have bought a house in Tanunda and move in next weekend.
>
> It's a circa 1950s house, with three bedrooms, a lounge, dining room, kitchen, one bathroom, cellar (for all that Barossa wine) and big backyard. We also have about four sheds ranging in size from an old outdoor toilet to a much bigger one and a carport. There's polished floorboards in the lounge, dining and kitchen. The kitchen and bathroom will eventually need renovating and there's room to expand out the back and make another living area – depending on how long we stick around.

In fact, there seems to be a 'macro-script' for describing anything static, of which the house script is one variety and of which text 3.11 is one instance. The macro-script organizes information according to the following parameters (among others):

- from general to particular (*it's a 1950s house with three bedrooms…*)
- from whole to part (*a lounge… there's polished floorboards in the lounge*)
- from 'including' to 'included' (*… cellar (for all that Barossa wine)*)
- from large to small (*three bedrooms, a lounge… one bathroom…*)
- from nearer to further, front to back, or outer to inner (*three bedrooms etc… and big backyard*)
- from possessor to possessed (*Dan and I have bought a house…*)
- from now to then (*Dan and I have bought a house… the kitchen and bathroom will eventually need renovating*).

These parameters are not carved in stone, of course, but to work in the opposite direction, eg from small to large, would create a marked effect. Sometimes, too, there is a tension between the parameters, so that, for example, the backyard, although bigger than the kitchen, is mentioned after the kitchen, because it is further away. ■

Macro-scripts

Other macro-scripts apply to processes, to biographies and to narratives. We saw, at the beginning of the chapter, how the 'biography script' determined the order of sentences in the text about Mozart (3.1). The biography script tends to follow a chronological order. But this is not the case with all past narratives. Take the news story script, for example. If you remember the story of the confused police dog in Chapter 1 (text 1.2), you may recall that the events are related in this order:

- A police dog (Shep) got the sack.
- A man was taken to hospital.
- Shep's handler had been called to a burglary.
- He was told the suspect was in the building.
- Officers carried out a search.
- Shep wandered off.
- He bit a man.
- A police spokesman commented on the incident.

The story appears to start with the *outcome* of the events, before filling in the narrative details of the incident itself and concluding with a comment. In fact, it would be more correct to say that the text starts with a condensed summary, including the main participants and the setting, of the story. This initial summary is, in turn, an expansion of the headline that precedes it:

Police dog sacked after biting innocent man

A police dog in Basel, Switzerland, has got the sack for biting an innocent | bystander at the scene of a burglary.

Bearing in mind that the purpose of news texts is to present *news*, ie that which is *newsworthy*, rather than simply to recount facts (as in an encylopedia, for example), it is not surprising that news stories focus on outcomes, especially when these are unusual or catastrophic. The dog's being sacked is more newsworthy than the fact that it bit someone. (An American newspaper editor famously said, 'When a dog bites a man that is not news, but when a man bites a dog that is news.')

News stories, then, set out to address the reader's (usually unvoiced) question when he or she opens the newspaper, or logs on to a news website, or turns on the TV: *What's new?* (or *What's happened?*) The purpose of the headline is to provide a succinct answer to the question. Typically, this will include some kind of activity or event, someone or something affected by the activity, an agent and possibly a reason. Either the agent or the affected party will take topic position in the headline, as in this sample of headlines from the website news service ananova.com:

topic	comment		
affected	*event*	*agent*	*reason*
Police dog	sacked	–	after biting innocent man
Pet kangaroo	hailed	–	for saving farmer
Caravan	damaged	by low flying cow	–

topic	comment	
agent	*event*	*affected*
Cat	saves	drowning lamb
Kitten	survives 70C tumble wash	–

If this attracts the reader's attention sufficiently, then the first sentence of the text addresses the reader's next questions: *Where? When? Who?* Having established the circumstances, the text goes on to answer the reader's next most likely question: *How did it happen?* At this point the narrative unfolds, each stage in it an answer to the reader's question: *What happened then?* Finally, the reader may be left still wondering as to the significance of the event, and the final comment, (usually by one of the participants or some kind of authority or expert), answers the question: *So what?* Or, more elaborately: *How has this affected things, or how will it affect things?*

In other words, the text is organized in order to answer the reader's evolving questions. All texts are organized to answer the questions that the reader puts to them and this is probably the single most important factor in terms of a reader's assessment of the text's coherence. The text will make sense if the reader, at any one point, is satisfied that his or her questions are being answered, and in the right order.

This helps explain why scripts are the way they are. The features of the house description script, as displayed in text 3.11, are not arbitrary, but respond to the reader's need to get the big picture first (*What does it look like?*), before having the details filled in (*What's it got inside?*). Likewise, the encyclopedia text (as in 3.1) answers the reader's need to know not *What's new?* but *Who was Mozart? What did he do? What did he do next?*

In this sense, texts are *interactive*. Or, as Michael Hoey puts it, 'Texts gain their meaning from a reader's interaction with them.'[45] As readers, we come to texts with unanswered questions (or what would be the point of reading them?). We search the text for answers: if the writer has been co-operative, the text will answer our questions, and in more or less the order we would expect. These expectations relate to cognitive factors (the way we think about things, or perceive or experience them, for example) and take the form of scripts. Over time, the way scripts are routinely realized through texts has given rise to certain predictable *text types* (the news story, the encyclopedia entry, etc), such that familiarity with the text type makes the interactive process even more fluid. (We will return to the topic of text types in Chapter 5.) The text will also raise further questions – and will provide answers, or at least explain why it *can't* provide them. The cumulative effect of this dynamic interaction between text and reader (or listener) is a measure of the text's coherence.

Discovery activity 3.10   *Keeping the reader in mind*

Before you read the following text, imagine you are faced with the challenge of painting a door. You have never painted a door before. You consult a DIY manual. What kind of questions would you want answered?

Now read the text[46]. What questions does the writer attempt to answer at each stage of the text? Did these correspond to your own questions? On balance, did the text answer most of your questions, and in the right order? Does it pass the 'coherence test'?

3.12

Doors have a variety of faces and conflicting grain patterns that need to be painted separately – yet the end result must look even in colour, with no ugly brush marks or heavily painted edges. There are recommended procedures for painting all types of door.

Remove the door handles and wedge the door open so that it cannot be closed accidentally, locking you in the room. Keep the handle in the room with you, just in case. Aim to paint the door and its frame separately so that there is less chance of touching wet paintwork when passing through a freshly painted doorway. Paint the door first and when it is dry finish the framework. If you want to use a different colour for each side of the door, paint the hinged edge the colour of the closing face (the one that comes to rest against the frame). Paint the outer edge of the door the same colour as the opening face. This means that there won't be any difference in colour when the door is viewed from either side. Each side of the frame should match the corresponding face of the door. Paint the frame in the room into which the door swings, including the edge of the stop bead against which the door closes, to match the opening face. Paint the rest of the frame the colour of the closing face.

Commentary ■ ■ ■

There are probably more answers than you had questions for in this text – but the writer has had to anticipate not only a variety of doors and colour schemes, but different degrees of background knowledge on the part of the readership. Nevertheless, these are some of the questions that you might have asked (and which the text answers):

What do I need to know before I start?
What is the effect I'm aiming at?
Is there any set procedure or order?
What precautions ought I take?
Where do I start?
What do I do next? (And next? etc)
What if I want to paint each side a different colour?
etc.

Of course, there are many other possible questions, including those raised by the text itself, eg *What if I lock myself in?*! But on the whole, the text is comprehensive. It is also very explicit and unambiguous: notice how often key words like *door* and *frame* are repeated, and consequently how few pronouns there are. Cohesion is achieved lexically, with few conjuncts. The definite article is used frequently, suggesting either a narrow field of reference, or a lot of shared knowledge, or both. The cohesion is more an effect, though, than a cause, of the text's sense-making capacity, ie its coherence. This coherence is achieved because the writer has the reader *in mind*. ■

Classroom applications: Macro-level coherence

There are many teaching implications of the kinds of macro-level features of coherence we have been looking at – such as topics, schemas and scripts. Some applications have already been mentioned, such as the usefulness of brainstorming topic-related vocabulary in advance of reading or listening and writing.

Other implications for classroom reading or listening activities include the following:

Schemas and scripts

Just as it is important to establish the topic of a text, so it is to establish the schema and/or script of a text – either in advance, by brainstorming around a theme, for example, or after reading (or listening to) the first one or two sentences, or after having read or heard the whole text. Some conventional text types have very clearly associated schemas and scripts. Consider, for example, how the following text openings set in train a number of associations, both in terms of the topics and their associated words and in terms of the organization of the subsequent text:

1 Once upon a time there was a king…
2 I am sixteen. I have been dating the same boy now for…
3 To select the required program, turn…
4 Unwanted facial hair can be embarrassing. Now…
5 This man walks into a bar and he says to the barman…
6 There was a young girl from Nebraska…

When dealing with texts in class, the teacher needs to estimate the extent of the learners' familiarity with both the content of the text and with the text type itself and to adapt the approach to the text accordingly. In Chapter 6, where text difficulty is discussed, we will look at more ways of doing this.

Comparing texts in the learners' mother tongue with the same kind of texts in the target language (eg English) can help alert students both to similarities and to differences in the way such texts are organized. Because human cognition is essentially the same, irrespective of language and culture, the organization of such basic scripts as narrative and description are likely to be more or less the same. This is good news for students: their expectations about a text are more likely to be met if they realize what kind of text it is and that it will be organized along similar lines to a text in their own language.

As with the text about painting doors, it is often a good idea to let the learners themselves decide the questions they would like answered in the text. Apart from anything else, it may be more motivating to answer your own questions than someone else's. To do this, though, it is essential that the learners have a clear idea of what the text is about, what kind of text it is and where it comes from.

Writing

Helping learners *write* coherently presents more of a challenge. Consider the following piece of written work, for example:

3.13

> *On balance, this is a very complex subject, still nowadays, in spite of the fact that this is not a new discussion. To find an easy answer and a more or less rapid solution for the problem is practically impossible, because it grows bigger and bigger every day. At this*

moment in our history too many people would have to work together and colaborate with one another and unfortunately it is something very uncommon in our days.

In my opinion, everything should be secondary in front of the fact of saving the lives of thousands of people, but there are some other things, apart from culture, that should be placed firstly in a secondary place. For example, I think it would be a good starting point if the rich countries reduced their expense of arms and used that money to send food to the more poor ones.

Only in the last sentence does the reader start to get a clue as to what the issue is that the writer is attempting to address, which is the contribution developed countries might make to global problems. One writer has called this kind of rambling, barely coherent style 'spaghetti writing'[47]:

> Spaghetti writing is the kind of loose-jointed composition writing which second-language students can produce in paragraph after paragraph. It is characterized by long incoherent sentences and a surfeit of subordinate clauses in search of a main one. All language stimulates expectations, but so often these expectations are not fulfilled in spaghetti writing and a *however* or a *so* leads the reader to a wrong conclusion. It is difficult to correct, because tinkering with a relative or a conjunction will not solve the problem and the usual correction shorthand (Sp, T, Art – spelling/tense/article) is inadequate: short of rewriting the passage, there is little the teacher can do.

Little the teacher can do *after* the event, perhaps, but there is quite a lot the teacher can do *before* the writing gets to this stage. I concluded the previous section by saying 'coherence is achieved because the writer has the reader *in mind*'. The challenge, in setting writing tasks that have any hope of achieving the production of coherent texts, is to devise ways of helping learners to *keep their readers in mind*. Here are some suggestions:

- When setting the writing assignment, make sure that the task rubric specifies a) the kind of text, b) the purpose of the text, and, most importantly, c) the reader. Ideally, the reader should be someone the writer knows who will actually read and respond to the text – for example, another student in the class or institution, or an on-line pen pal. If this is not possible, a 'putative' reader should be specified – that is, an imagined reader who would be typical of this kind of text's readership. And of course the reader could be yourself, the teacher, but not 'teacher-as-corrector'. Rather, 'teacher-as-reader'.

- Having established the readership, the writer should then brainstorm the kinds of questions the reader is likely to want to have answered. This is especially important in factual writing, but applies equally well to discursive writing of the type attempted in text 3.13.

- Suggest that the writer includes at least some of these reader questions in the body of the text, in the form of rhetorical questions. Note how Widdowson uses rhetorical questions to good effect in text 3.7: *What is it that learners are expected to understand, speak, read and write? The obvious answer is: the language they are learning. But what exactly do we mean by this?* etc…

- Challenge writers to sequence their sentences in such a way that no conjuncts (*so, therefore, finally,* etc) are necessary. Note that this is not always possible, especially with adversative relations, eg *but, however.* Where a conjunct *is* necessary, suggest they use one that includes the word *this*, as in *this means…, this is why…, because of this…, despite this…,* etc. This (!) will ensure that any conjuncts are firmly anchored.

- Remind writers that the topic and the way the topic is being considered, needs to be spelled out lexically and early on in the text. This may mean repeating, paraphrasing, or re-formulating elements of the rubric in the opening sentence. So, if the rubric asks the writer to *Suggest ways developed countries can contribute to global well-being,* an appropriate opening sentence might be: *How can developed countries contribute to global well-being?*

- Show learners how sentence topics are frequently carried over from the comments of previous sentences. Thus, a follow-on sentence to the opening one might begin: *Global well-being [depends on a number of factors… | can be defined as… | was once thought to mean…, etc].*

- Explain to writers that lexical repetition is not necessarily a bad thing. Show, using authentic texts, how effective writers use both direct and indirect repetition to convey their argument and to create cohesion. If the rubric includes words like *developed countries* and *global well-being,* these should re-appear in the body of the text, along with derived forms and synonyms, such as *development, developing, nations, international, welfare,* etc. This is where some pre-writing dictionary work might be useful – pre-activating not only key words, but derived forms and synonyms as well.

- Having written a first draft, learners should read this aloud to other students, in pairs, or at least silently read and then comment on each other's texts. Any point where their 'audience' asks for clarification should be considered a potential 'danger spot' and subject to re-writing. Ask students to summarize the gist of each other's texts, even if this has to be done in their first language. If they can't easily summarize their colleague's argument, then there may well be something wrong with the coherence of the text.

- As a last resort, be prepared, as teacher, to tell the writer, 'I'm afraid, this doesn't make sense.' This is best done on a one-to-one basis, if possible, where you can challenge the writer to tell you what it was he or she intended to say. Often this is enough for the bits to fall into place, for the logic to emerge, for coherence to kick in.

Conclusion

In this chapter we have looked at ways texts achieve coherence – ie how they make sense to the reader – through a combination of local (or micro-level) and global (or macro-level) effects. Writers use cohesion to help readers create coherence in a text, but it is the degree to which the reader is able to interact with the text that is the true test of coherence. Ultimately the reader has to decide whether the writer has kept the reader in mind.

The discussion has centred almost exclusively on written texts. Do the same principles apply to the production and interpretation of spoken texts? What makes spoken text coherent? What are the particular characteristics of spoken text that distinguish it from written? And what are the implications for teaching? These issues will be addressed in the next chapter.

Chapter 4 **Spoken texts**

In the last two chapters we have been arguing that a text is more than simply a random collection of sentences. We have shown that the parts of a text are interconnected (ie a text is cohesive) and that a text makes some kind of overall sense (ie it is coherent). But the discussion has been limited to written texts only. It's now time to re-assert the fact that texts are not only written, but are also spoken. (Remember that, initially, we defined a text as 'a continuous piece of spoken or written language' (p. 6).)

There are a number of reasons for emphasizing the spoken dimension. For a start, language originates in speech, both historically and in terms of an individual's own linguistic development. And most day-to-day language use is spoken. Moreover, from a teaching point of view, most (but not all) learners of a second language are keen to acquire at least a measure of oral fluency, so the study of spoken discourse ought to hold some interest for programme designers, coursebook writers, examiners and, not least, teachers themselves. And finally, there are a number of ways in which the boundary between spoken and written language is rather blurred, which suggests that to discuss one apart from the other may distort our understanding of how speakers and writers create and interpret text.

Discovery activity 4.1 *Differences between written and spoken texts*

In the following conversational extract[48], four Australian women, all related, are talking about the fact that one of them (Greta) will move into her parents' home while renovations are being done on her own. This leads into a discussion about the way computers become obsolete so quickly and mention is made of a scheme whereby old computers are re-cycled. The speakers are:
Joan (74), her daughters, Greta (47) and Claire (41), and her daughter-in-law, Alice (38), who is married to Joan's son, Philip.

(The sign ⌐ indicates an overlap, ie where one speaker starts speaking before another has finished.)

Skim the extract and note at least five features that characterize the text as being an instance of spoken language:

4.1

Computers

¹ **Greta** And um I'll take the I'll take the computer over because I've got my work stuff on computer so. Dad can play with the Internet or something.

² **Claire** I think I should give um Philip my computer and I'll keep the laptop I love it. [*laughs*]

³ **Greta** I had, I I took it into work to see whether they could load you know work stuff up on it. The guy sort of looked at me and said how old is this? And it's about four years old but of course you know in computer terms that's…

⁴ **Alice** Ancient.

⁵ **Greta** Ancient. So.

[6]	**Alice**	Oh I've got a laptop that's I don't know how older than Apple. You can't even write
[7]	**Joan**	⌊What's you know, the idea that you sort of, people
[8]	**Alice**	⌊but it's not even worth fixing. Just throw it out. You know.
[9]	**Greta**	⌊By the time they come out by the time they come out they've already improved them. You know. It's just extraordinary.
[10]	**Claire**	Well there is a big programme that ah people buying up computers you know we we but what d'you do with them you just chuck 'em out.
[11]	**Alice**	Mmm. No.
[12]	**Claire**	And there's a... a they're sort of doing... recycling them for use in you know underprivileged areas and third world countries and stuff.
[13]	**Joan**	Or give them to your relatives.
[14]	**Greta**	[*chuckles*]
[15]	**Claire**	Well. Yeah. I mean um. But it's just it's you know like all these analogue phones. In in in about four months' time you know they're gone.
[16]	**Alice**	⌊Oh don't talk to me about analogue phones.
[17]	**Greta**	Have you got an analogue phone?
[18]	**Alice**	No no

Commentary ■ ■ ■

You probably noted a number of obvious features of spoken language that are not usually present in written language, such as hesitations, false starts, repetitions and incomplete utterances. You may also have noted the frequent use of expressions like *you know, well, oh* and *mmm*, as well as several instances of vague language such as *sort of, … or something, … and stuff*. Perhaps you picked up on the informal register, as in *the guy* and *you just chuck 'em out*. And you may even have noticed how many sentences and clauses are connected by the relatively simple connectors *and, but* and *because*. What you won't have noticed, but what would of course have been present in the original conversation, is the use of stress and intonation to signal, among other things, what information is given and what information is new. ■

We can categorize these various features of spoken language according to whether they derive principally from a) its spontaneity, b) its interactivity, c) its interpersonality or d) its need to achieve coherence. We'll deal with each of these characteristics in turn.

Spontaneity

Most speech is produced 'on-line', that is to say in real time and with little or no time for much forward planning. This accounts for a number of characteristic features which we will call *performance* features. These include

- filled pauses: *I should give <u>um</u> Philip my computer*
- repetitions: *In <u>in in</u> about four months' time*
- false starts and backtracking: <u>*And there's a... a they're sort of doing…*</u> *recycling them*
- incomplete utterances: *What's you know, the idea that you sort of, people*

Another effect of the spontaneity of speech production is its 'one-clause-or-phrase-at-a-time' construction. Rather than being built up in sentence-length units, speech tends to be produced in smaller 'runs', each run representing a unit of meaning. These runs are tacked on to each other, rather than being embedded inside larger units (as is typically the case with formal writing) and are often linked by the highly frequent conjunctions *and, but* and *so.* So, Greta's turn 3 is constructed out of these elements:

The guy + sort of + looked at me + and said + how old is this? + And it's about four years old + but + of course + you know + in computer terms + that's... ancient

This cumulative construction principle tolerates the addition of sentence 'slots' that in written language would be considered ungrammatical. For example, when Greta says *I'll take the computer over because I've got my work stuff on computer so.,* the final *so* occupies the sentence 'tail': a place reserved for some kind of comment on, or qualification of, what has been said. (The same speaker uses the same tail in turn 5: *Ancient. So.*) Common tail-slot-fillers include question tags (*isn't he?, didn't they?),* adverbials that convey speaker attitude (*actually, really, quite frankly),* vagueness expressions (*and that sort of thing*) and topic clarifiers, as in *It needs a bit of a prod that fire.*

A similar slot is available at the *head* of utterances, which is typically used to 'announce' the topic of the utterance that follows, so that Alice might have said: *Analogue phones. Don't talk to me about analogue phones.*

To make on-line production even easier, many of its individual runs consist of 'chunks'. Chunks are multi-word units that behave as if they were single words and typically consist of short formulaic routines that are stored and retrieved in their entirety. In the above extract *sort of, of course* and *you know* are typical chunks, but so also is *in computer terms,* where *computer* fills a variable slot in the frame *in X terms.* Likewise, *about X years old* is another example of a frame with a variable slot.

Of course, this segmentation into bite-sized chunks not only makes production easier, but it makes processing on the part of the listener easier too. This is a fact that is sometimes forgotten when materials writers write texts for listening practice that are constructed out of sentence-length units, rather than clause- or phrase-length ones. In a well-intentioned attempt to 'tidy up' spoken language, they may, in fact, be making it harder to process.

Interactivity

Talk of the type represented by the conversation about computers is clearly interactive: the speakers interact by taking turns to speak, keeping silent when others are speaking, interrupting at times and signalling their agreement or amusement by grunts, laughs and chuckles. An obvious instance of this interactivity is the asking and answering of *questions,* as in:

[17] **Greta**   Have you got an analogue phone?
[18] **Alice**   No no

Speakers also acknowledge their audience by asking and answering their own (rhetorical) questions:

[10] **Claire**   ...but what d'you do with them you just chuck 'em out.

Another interactive device is the *back-channelling* that listeners do in order to register that they are following the speaker's drift, as in:

¹⁰ **Claire**   …but what d'you do with them you just chuck 'em out.
¹¹ **Alice**   Mmm. No.

Of course, with so many speakers jockeying to have a turn, it's not all plain sailing, and this is reflected in the number of interruptions and overlapping turns which the transcription attempts to capture:

⁶ **Alice**   You can't even write
⁷ **Joan**   ⌊What's you know, the idea that you sort of, people
⁸ **Alice**   ⌊but it's not even worth fixing. Just throw it out.
             You know.
⁹ **Greta**   ⌊By the time they
             come out by the time

In order to manage the cut-and-thrust of interactive talk as smoothly as possible, speakers use a number of linguistic devices, called *discourse markers,* to signal their intentions and to show how what they are going to say, or have just said, is connected to what went before or what is coming up. Discourse markers are not unlike the gestures and devices that drivers make use of in order to indicate their intentions in heavy traffic. Take, for example, turn 15:

¹⁵ **Claire**   Well. Yeah. I mean um. But it's just it's you know like all these
             analogue phones.

The speaker/driver starts the turn/manoeuvre by using the markers/indicators *well* and *yeah* to provide a fairly non-committal response to what has just been said (Joan's light-hearted suggestion of giving old computers to one's relatives rather than to some charity). This is followed by the marker *I mean* that signals that some kind of clarification is going to follow; then *but* signals that this clarification perhaps contrasts with what has gone before (Joan's flippant remark) and *you know* appeals to the shared knowledge of the other speakers as a new topic is introduced (analogue phones).

These discourse markers signpost the shifts and turns in the on-going interactive progress of the talk. They also have a connecting function identical to that of the cohesive devices that we looked at in written texts. They connect the elements within speaker utterances and across them. Notice, too, that they frequently take the form of multi-word units, or chunks: *I mean…, you know…*

What is not so obvious from the written transcription of this conversation is the way that changes in pitch and emphasis, ie *intonation,* also serve to signpost the direction and interconnections of the talk. So when Claire says *like all these analogue phones* the words *analogue phones* are emphasized by means of a marked step up in pitch, conferring on them the status of new information and a new topic of conversation.

Interpersonality

Conversation is not simply the exchange of information, but has a strong interpersonal function. That is, it serves to establish and maintain group solidarity. Casual conversation is often punctuated by laughter, or at least chuckles. (Interestingly, people who are speaking tend to laugh more than people who are listening.) Even when speakers disagree, they do it in such a way as not to threaten the *face* of other speakers. Hence, speakers use *hedges*, such as *yeah but,* in order to blunt the force of a disagreement. Or they use *vague language* in order not to sound too assertive and opinionated:

12 Claire   ... they're <u>sort of</u> doing... recycling them for use in you know underprivileged areas and third world countries <u>and stuff</u>.

And they are constantly referring to shared knowledge and appealing for agreement through the use of markers like *you know,* question tags (such as *isn't it? don't you?*) and rising intonation.

They also demonstrate empathy by completing and repeating each other's utterances, as in this example:

3 Greta   ... but of course you know in computer terms that's...
4 Alice   <u>Ancient.</u>
5 Greta   <u>Ancient.</u>

These attempts to harmonize the joint construction of talk are further demonstrated in the frequent use of exaggeration and strongly evaluative language. The choice of *ancient* rather than simply *old* is a case in point. The use of evaluative language acts as a means of flagging the speaker's attitude to what is being said, in order to minimize the chance of misunderstanding and also to bring the talk into line with the views of the other speakers:

9 Greta   ... by the time they come out they've already improved them. You know. It's <u>just extraordinary</u>.

And, a little later in the conversation, Claire and Alice, who have been discussing the uses that mobile phones are put to, comment:

Alice   Oh they're <u>amazing</u>.
Claire   <u>Unbelievable</u>.

This on-going evaluation of talk can also take the form of swearing and the use of expletives, a distinctive feature of some conversational registers. A (relatively mild) instance occurs a little later in the conversation:

Greta   It is is just quite extraordinary what is on that on that <u>bloody</u> Internet. Absolutely extraordinary.

When conversationalists fail to demonstrate 'high involvement' in any of these ways, they risk being considered cold or even hostile. The character Joe in the British TV comedy *The Royle Family* is almost catatonically uncooperative[49]:

Dad   [*struggling for conversation*] Antiques Roadshow's on in a minute.
Joe   Oh aye?
Dad   Barbara's mother's down, why don't you nip through and say hello?
Joe   No.
[*pause*]
Dad   So life treating you all right, is it?
Joe   Can't complain. [*pause*] Nice bit of cake.
Dave   Did you hear the thunder last night?
Joe   No.
Dave   Slept right through it then?
Joe   Must have done.

When Joe finally leaves, Dad comments:

Bloody hell, he's hard work, ain't he?

Coherence

Conversation that is stripped of those features that result from its spontaneity and those that signal its interactive and interpersonal character, reads fairly flat on the page – not unlike written language. Here, for example, is the beginning of text 4.1 stripped down:

Greta I'll take the computer over because I've got my work stuff on computer. Dad can play with the Internet.

Claire I should give Philip my computer and I'll keep the laptop. I love it.

Greta I took it into work to see whether they could load work stuff up on it. The guy looked at me and said how old is this? It's about four years old but in computer terms that's ancient.

Alice I've got a laptop that's older than Apple. You can't write but it's not worth fixing. Throw it out.

But there is no doubt that, even when stripped of the characteristic features of spoken language, the text makes *sense*. That is, it is *coherent*. (In fact, without the distraction of all the *ums* and *ahs*, it is possibly *more* coherent, which is one reason, perhaps, why fictional dialogue, as in novels or drama, usually dispenses with these features. It is also one reason, perhaps, why textbook dialogues are like they are: transcribed conversations, such as 4.1, are notoriously difficult to make sense of – an issue we will return to shortly.) But unlike written text, whose coherence is principally the responsibility of one person, the writer, coherence in the computer conversation is a collaborative enterprise. The speakers co-operate to ensure that what they say is relevant to what has been said before and to the overall purpose of the talk. Failure to co-operate in this joint work is likely to result in conversational breakdown, and the resultant lack of relevance is often a characteristic of the speech of mental patients, as in this instance[50]:

Doctor What is your name?

Patient Well, let's say you might have thought you had something from before, but you haven't got it anymore.

Doctor I'm going to call you Dean.

A less pathological example of conversational incoherence is this transcript of an on-line chat exchange, in which the initiator ('ten') doesn't realize that he is chatting not with a human being, but with a computer program (AOLiza[51]) that has been designed to simulate conversational interaction:

4.2

ten how you been?

AOLiza have you asked anyone else?

ten no, should I?

AOLiza why 'no'?

ten i don't know, like to get it from the source. what's up?

AOLiza does that trouble you?

ten does what trouble me?

AOLiza are such questions much on your mind?

ten sorry, missed the last. could u resend?

AOLiza i've told you that apologies are not required.

ten ok. so how are you?

AOLiza why do you ask?

ten	just wondering. how's the job? the family? stuff like that.
AOLiza	have you asked anyone else?
ten	about what?

The 'conversation' continues in this rather bizarre fashion for another 35 moves, before 'ten' says:

ten	i don't know. i feel like i'm having a conversation with myself.
AOLiza	don't you really know?
ten	what are you talking about?
AOLiza	what comes to mind when you ask that?
ten	i'm just trying to figure out what this is all about
AOLiza	do you enjoy being just trying to figure out what this is all about?
ten	what's that supposed to mean?
AOLiza	why do you ask?
ten	good bye
AOLiza	i'm not sure i understand you fully.
ten	that makes two of us

Avere Tolerance

Discovery activity 4.2   *Coherence in talk*

What is it about the preceding 'conversation' that threatens its coherence and raises doubts in 'ten's' mind? At the same time, how is it that AOLiza does in fact succeed in keeping 'ten' chatting on-line for a total of 70 turns?

Commentary ■ ■ ■

There are a number of ways that AOLiza's responses might set alarm bells ringing. For a start, he/she (/it?) doesn't follow the 'script', that is, the conventional way of conducting certain routine exchanges. In the initial greeting, for example, AOLiza departs from the usual script by following the question *how you been?* with another question, *have you asked anyone else?* Moreover, several of AOLiza's questions seem to have no obvious connection to what preceded them, as in:

ten	… what's up?
AOLiza	does that trouble you?

On the other hand, some of AOLiza's questions do seem to connect with the preceding comment and this is no doubt one reason why 'ten' was persuaded to keep chatting. For example:

ten	sorry, missed the last. could u resend?
AOLiza	i've told you that apologies are not required.

Because AOLiza has been programmed to respond to the word *sorry* by making an explicit reference to *apologies*, some degree of relevance can be inferred. Likewise, when 'ten' comments:

ten	i'm just trying to figure out what this is all about

AOLiza incorporates his utterance into its own response (albeit somewhat awkwardly):

AOLiza	do you enjoy being just trying to figure out what this is all about?

This technique conveys at least the illusion of relevance and is sufficient incentive for 'ten' to keep on trying. ■

Relevance

In his lectures on logic and conversation, the philosopher Grice proposed a number of conversational *maxims* (or rules) to which speakers adhere and without which conversation would simply break down. One of these maxims concerns the relation of the speaker's utterance to the 'accepted purpose or direction of the talk-exchange'. Grice sums up this conversational maxim as: *Be relevant.* This means that, unless given explicit indications to the contrary, speakers assume that each other's utterances both relate to a mutually agreed topic and follow on from one another. Even where the relevance is not explicit, we will attempt to infer it.

One very obvious way that speakers signal the relevance of what they are saying is by repeating all or part of what previous speakers have said.

AOLiza's technique – of incorporating bits of the other speaker's utterance into its responses – is well attested in studies of the development of child language, as in

| **Adult** | You do that one |
| **Child** | Now I do that one |

Indeed, amongst themselves, children seem to be able to sustain long conversations that consist entirely of repeating or slightly modifying one another's utterances. In this transcript of two three-year-old twin boys interacting[52], the 'conversation' is sustained almost purely through the repetition of three words:

B1	you silly you silly
B2	no Toby's silly
B1	you silly
B2	no you silly no not, you silly
B1	you silly
B2	no not no silly
B1	no silly
B2	no no you silly you silly
	(etc, for another 36 turns)

Similar, though less prolonged, 'incorporation sequences' are common in adult conversation. Later on in the computer conversation cited earlier, for example, the following sequence occurs:

Claire	No no I want to buy I've got an analogue I've got an analogue.
Greta	⌊No no she's wants she's got an analogue. She's got an analogue.
Alice	Oh you've got an analogue as well?

Alice and Greta 'echo' Claire's phrase *got an analogue* in such a way that the exchange is tightly bound together and maximum cohesion is ensured.

Repetition serves at least two functions: it binds utterances together, thereby enhancing the sense that speakers are being relevant. It also creates a sense that all participants are in harmony – that they are 'singing to the same hymn sheet' – and thereby supports conversation's interpersonal function. One researcher of conversational repetition concluded, 'Repetition is a resource by which conversationalists together create a discourse, a relationship and a world.'[53]

Lexical repetition is a good indicator that the speakers are all 'speaking to topic'. This notion of *topic* is a key one in terms of conferring coherence on talk. It is the lack of a consistent topic that characterizes the AOLiza chat, such that, at one point, 'ten' comments, 'i'm just trying to figure out what this is all about'. In the computer conversation (text 4.1), there is no doubt as to what the conversation is about. Not only are the words *computer* and *laptop* repeated, but also the phrase *work stuff* and different permutations of *old* and *ancient*, all in just six turns:

Greta   And um I'll take the I'll take the <u>computer</u> over because I've got my <u>work stuff</u> on <u>computer</u> so. Dad can play with the Internet or something.

Claire   I think I should give um Philip my <u>computer</u> and I'll keep the <u>laptop</u> I love it. [*laughs*]

Greta   I had, I I took it into work to see whether they could load you know <u>work stuff</u> up on it. The guy sort of looked at me and said how old is this? And it's about four years <u>old</u> but of course you know in <u>computer</u> terms that's...

Alice   <u>Ancient</u>.

Greta   <u>Ancient</u>. So.

Alice   Oh I've got a <u>laptop</u> that's I don't know how <u>older</u> than Apple.

Here it is clear – just from the words that are repeated – that the speakers are 'speaking to topic'. Of course, topics can change, and there is a good example of that in turn 15 of the same conversation when Claire says:

Claire   it's you know like all these analogue phones

which prompts Alice to respond:

Alice   Oh don't talk to me about analogue phones

which, in fact, signals the beginning of a long sequence where they talk about nothing else! This is a good example of how topic shift is co-operatively managed (and another instance, incidentally, of how repetition across turns reinforces the sense of shared purpose).

Alongside direct repetition, there are various forms of indirect repetition that also serve to maintain topic consistency and to bind talk together. One of these is the use of *lexical chains*, such as other words relating to the theme of computers: *Internet, Apple, load up;* and the use of *referring* expressions, as in these instances of the pronouns *it, they* and *them:*

Greta   I took <u>it</u> into work to see whether <u>they</u> could load you know work stuff up on <u>it</u>.
... by the time <u>they</u> come out they've already improved <u>them</u>

As in written text, conjuncts, such as *so, and, but, or,* make connections within and across utterances:

Claire   <u>And</u> there's a... a they're sort of doing... recycling them for use in you know underprivileged areas and third world countries and stuff.

Joan   <u>Or</u> give them to your relatives.

And we have already seen how *discourse markers,* such as *oh* and *well,* signal the speaker's intentions as to the direction that the conversation is taking. All these features, then, contribute to the overall coherence of the talk.

Macrostructure

But there is another, more top-down, way that talk is imbued with sense and that is the way it conforms to certain fairly predictable organizational sequences, or *macrostructures*, which extend over several turns. We saw how AOLiza failed to adhere to the standard greetings script:

| **ten** | how you been? |
| **AOLiza** | have you asked anyone else? |

Predictable two-way exchanges, such as greetings, or saying thank-you, are called *adjacency pairs*:

| **A1** | Hi! |
| **A2** | Hi there. |

| **B1** | Thanks for that. |
| **B2** | You're welcome. |

Three-part exchanges are characteristic of a lot of classroom talk, where they are called IRF (initiate – respond – follow up) exchanges, as in this example:

Teacher (*initiates*)	What is the capital of Peru?
Student (*responds*)	Lima.
Teacher (*follows* up)	Good.

In the following joke, the student fails to recognize the script:

Teacher	What's the protective outer layer of a tree called, Tom?
Tom	I don't know.
Teacher	Bark, Tom. Bark!
Tom	Woof, woof!

Even longer predictable sequences characterize *transactional* talk – that is, talk whose purpose it is to achieve the exchange of goods or information.

Discovery activity 4.3　*Service encounters*

Here is a transactional dialogue from a coursebook[54]. How could you describe its macrostructure? To what extent do you think it is a typical example?

4.3

Assistant	Yes?
Riaz	Could I have a packet of aspirins, please?
Assistant	Here you are. Anything else?
Riaz	Have you got any toothbrushes?
Assistant	Yes, these are five pounds, and those are seven pounds fifty.
Riaz	One of those, please. How much is that?
Assistant	Five pounds eighty for the aspirins and seven pounds fifty for the toothbrush. That's thirteen pounds thirty, please.
Riaz	Here you are. Thanks a lot.

Commentary ■ ■ ■

The dialogue embodies a number of features of what are called *service encounters*, such as:

Assistant	Yes?	*sale initiation*
Riaz	Could I have a packet of aspirins, please?	*sale request*
Assistant	Here you are. Anything else?	*sale compliance*
Riaz **Assistant**	Have you got any toothbrushes? Yes, these are five pounds and those are seven pounds fifty.	*sale enquiry*
Riaz	One of those, please.	*sale request*
Riaz **Assistant**	How much is that? Five pounds eighty for the aspirins and seven pounds fifty for the toothbrush. That's thirteen pounds thirty, please.	*sale*
Riaz	Here you are.	*purchase*
	Thanks a lot.	*purchase closure*

What is slightly unusual about the dialogue is that there is no second *sale compliance*, ie after *One of those, please*. Research suggests that the sequence *sale request* and *sale compliance* form obligatory elements in service encounters and the seller would say something like *Here you are* or *There you go* plus *Anything else?* or *Will that be all?* Also missing (but not obligatory) is an opening and a closing. These typically consist of greetings, like *Good morning* and formulaic parting shots like *Have a nice day*. Depending on how well the seller and buyer know one another, openings and closings may be quite extended and chatty, as in this example, recorded at a supermarket check-out in New Zealand[55]:

[O = Operator; C = Customer]

O   Good morning.
C   Morning.
O   How are you?
C   I'm fine thanks.
O   You look well. You look nice.
C   ... had – had ten days in hospital.
O   Oh, did you? You feeling better?
C   I've had a new hip put in.
O   Oh, well good for you. As – is – you going well with it?
C   Yep.
O   Super.
C   Down to – ah – one crutch.
O   Good for you.
C   On my right side. Tell me, the Sheba pet food. You've got beef cuts, beef and kidney, but no turkey in... ■

Opening and closing

As with service encounters, conversation between friends also has its openings and closings. A famous example of the latter is the prolonged closing attributed to the heir to British throne, in a secretly recorded mobile phone conversation with his girlfriend, part of which went like this[56]:

He	Don't want to say goodbye.
She	Neither do I, but we must get some sleep. Bye.
He	Bye, darling.
She	Love you.
He	Bye.
She	Hopefully talk to you in the morning.
He	Please.
She	Bye. I do love you.
He	Night.
She	Night.
He	Night.
She	Love you forever.
He	Night.
She	G'bye. Bye my darling.
He	Night.

and so on for another 24 turns!

Story sequences

It might seem, though, that apart from openings and closings, casual conversation has no structure at all. However, researchers have identified several organizational features of casual conversation that suggest that it does in fact have predictable macrostructures. One of these features is the regular occurrence of *story* sequences, story being defined very generally as to include:

- a temporal location
- specification of participants
- a sequence of events
- evaluation

So, in the conversation about computers quoted earlier, Greta's short account of her interaction with the technician at work constitutes a rudimentary story:

Greta	I had, I I took it into work to see whether they could load you know work stuff up on it. The guy sort of looked at me and said how old is this? And it's about four years old but of course you know in computer terms that's…
Alice	Ancient.
Greta	Ancient. So.

The temporal location is simply in the past, no further specification being given. The participants include herself and the technician. The sequence of events is captured in the main finite verbs: *took it in, looked at me, said…*

The evaluation expresses the speaker's attitude to the story and underscores the point of the story. The use of the word *ancient* deliberately exaggerates the age of the computer and accounts for the technician's look and question. The point of the story would have been lost if the speaker had simply said:

It could, of course, be argued that coursebook dialogues are a genre apart (we'll be looking more closely at *genre* in the next chapter) and that their function is less to replicate the features of spoken language than to contextualize targeted language items in typical but intelligible contexts. Besides, many of the more idiomatic or regionally localized features of spoken language may be of little use or interest to learners whose objective is English as an *international* language.

What's more, if learners are being exposed to a regular diet of spoken language in their classrooms, through, for example, their interactions with their teacher, then there may be less onus on the coursebook to provide realistic models. Unfortunately, as it happens, this is not always the case.

Discovery activity 4.6   *Teacher–learner interaction*

Here, for example, is an extract of actual teacher–learner interaction. In what ways is it similar to – and different from – naturally-occurring conversation of the type exemplified in the Computers extract?

4.6

Phil Collins

T	OK, look at the last text on the sheet that Cathy gave you OK?... What's it about? ... the last text.
S1	The last text...
T	Who's it about?
S2	It's about Phil Collins' life.
T	Yeah. It's about Phil Collins... erm ... what does Phil Collins do?
S2	... singer
S1	... plays drums I think
T	He's a singer and he...?
S3	Plays drums
T	He's a singer and he plays the drums so he's a...?
S4	Drummer, he's a drummer.
T	OK. Does he sing well? Does he sing well? Is he a good singer?
Ss	Yes [*laughter*]...

Commentary ■ ■ ■

It should be obvious, from this small extract, that the 'conversation' is very one-sided, with the teacher asking all the questions and the students answering them, using the three-part IRF framework that we looked at on page 72.

T	Who's it about?	(*initiate*)
S2	It's about Phil Collins' life.	(*respond*)
T	Yeah.	(*follow up*)

Several of the questions are in fact less questions than oral gap-fills:

T	He's a singer and he...?

Moreover, the teacher's questions are all *display questions*, ie questions that require the learners to display knowledge that is already known by the teacher. Such questions, apart from being rare in naturally-occurring conversations, usually require only one- or two-word answers and therefore provide the respondent with little conversational 'rope' to play with. Compare them with *real questions*, such as *Who's your favourite singer?* or *Do you play an instrument?* ■

In short, the spontaneous, (two-way) interactional and interpersonal features of conversation are almost totally absent from this kind of discourse. This does not disqualify it as a form of discourse in its own right: this kind of 'teacher talk' has a long tradition and it serves a very useful pedagogical purpose. But it can no way be considered a valid model for – or practice of – casual conversation. Hence, learners who are exposed only to this kind of interaction might emerge less than fully prepared for the realities of fast-moving, interactive, chat. And it is often 'conversation' that learners nominate when asked what it is they most hope to improve on.

How, then, are learners to acquire conversational skills?

Discovery activity 4.7   *Conversational skills*

Look at these two activities. Both are targeted at the development of conversational competence. How do they compare?

Activity 1

Conversation

Form groups of three to five.
Write the following topics on cards:

– last weekend
– a recent film
– a good restaurant
– some sports news
– an animal story

Make more cards by adding two or three more topics of your choice.

Shuffle the cards and place them face down in front of you.

One student takes a card, reads it aloud and the group discusses the topic.

When the group feels that there is nothing more to say about the topic, the next card is picked up, and so on.

Activity 2

Conversation

1 Listen to this recording of a real conversation and answer these questions:

How many speakers are there?
Which speaker speaks the most?
Which speaker speaks the least?
How many turns does this speaker have?
Which speaker interrupts another speaker?

2 One speaker tells a story. Put the stages of the story in order:
significance of the story
time and place
solution
problem event
characters

I've tried this out on a number of people and they have come up with some original, even ingenious, suggestions, such as that it is the sign leading to the relevant section of a railway museum. If you turn to page 185, you'll see that it is indeed a sign, but a road sign, and it is situated in an area of geothermal activity (Rotorua, New Zealand, to be specific) in order to warn motorists of the possibility of reduced visibility due to steam. Without this contextual information, the text is open to a variety of interpretations.

In fact, it took an anthropologist to realize that, without context knowledge, the meaning of a text is difficult, if not impossible, to unpack. It was Malinowski, working in the early years of the last century in the South Pacific, who first observed that 'An utterance becomes intelligible only when it is placed within its context of situation.'

Of course, very occasionally not even these contextual clues can help. Here is an English text I found on a hot water thermos flask in a hotel room in China (and which I have already mentioned, in Chapter 2):

5.3

> *I like a pumpkin.*
> *I like a celery.*
> *Go toward the 21st century.*

With the best will in the world, I cannot get this text to make sense. I can only conclude, therefore, that this is not text at all, but simply decoration, in the same way that random words are sometimes incorporated into fabric design.

On the whole, however, the relation between a text and its context are more transparent. This is partly due to the knowledge we have, as members of a shared culture, as to what texts are likely in what contexts and what the distinguishing characteristics of these texts might be.

Discovery activity 5.1   *Contexts of use*

Identify the likely context for each of these texts (the first of which you have met already). What clues helped you do the task?

5.4

> **For the perfect cup**, use one tea bag per person and add freshly drawn boiling water. Leave standing for 3–5 minutes before stirring gently. Can be served with or without milk and sugar.

5.5

> **TEA**
> Tea is made by pouring boiling water on to tea leaves. The leaves come from tea bushes, which are grown mainly in India, Sri Lanka and China. Tea first came to Europe from China in the 1600s. At first it was brewed and stored in barrels, like beer.

5.6

S1	Chris, do you want some cream on yours or?
S2	Just a little bit.
S1	It's terrible for your arteries. [inaudible].
S5	Have a cup of tea and wash it down.
S6	So Adam, coffee?
S5	I'll have a coffee as well thanks.

5.7

> We followed John into the tiled café. It was set back from the road and was not so far from where our van was now parked.
>
> 'It's a French hotel,' John whispered. 'I think it might be a bit expensive.'
>
> 'We'll just have some tea,' Mum reassured him and we sat down in the shade of the terrace.
>
> The tea they brought was made from mint leaves and was very, very sweet. Mum looked into the pot. 'It's like syrup in there,' she said.

Commentary ■ ■ ■

Even without reading the texts closely, the lay-out alone should have helped you identify the text types (assuming you were familiar with such text types). And it should be obvious that text 5.6 is the transcription of a spoken text, while the others are all written. A closer look at the language of the written texts helps classify them as, respectively, *instructions* (note the imperative verbs, for example), *factual information* (the passive constructions help identify this) and *narrative* (the past tenses and quoted speech are a giveaway). The spoken text (5.6)[57] seems to be taking place in the context of a meal: note the offers and acceptances.

It doesn't need sophisticated text analysis skills to conclude that both texts 5.6 and 5.7 are probably extracts from longer texts. The pronoun *yours* and the linking expression *as well* in 5.6. seem to refer back to prior information, while, in text 5.7, the writer seems to assume that the reader already knows who *John* and *Mum* are and that *the tiled café* and *our van* have already been mentioned.

A still closer study of the texts enables us to refine our predictions. For example, we can deduce that the instructions in 5.4 were written not simply to give instructions but also to promote a positive feeling towards the product itself. Note the choice of words with positive connotations such as *perfect, freshly drawn, gently*. This in turn suggests that the text is part of the packaging of the product, rather than, say, an extract from a reference book. (The text does in fact come from the wrapping of a teabag.)

Text 5.5 may have been written with younger readers in mind, since it is relatively simple in terms of the language used and the concepts it conveys. (In fact, it comes from a children's encyclopedia[58].)

The people in text 5.6 would seem to be on familiar terms, judging by the use of first names and the use of informal expressions such as *just a little bit, wash it down*. Also, the comment about *arteries,* which might be considered impertinent in a more formal context (eg tea with the Queen), suggests a jokey familiarity.

And 5.7 might either be a memoir (it's written in the first person (*we, our*) and the writer refers to one of the characters as *Mum*) or fiction, or a combination of the two. (In fact, it comes from a novel[59].) ■

Context, text type and text

To sum up, the language choices in these texts – such as the use of the imperative, or of the passive, or of narrative tenses, or of informal vocabulary, or of words with positive connotations – seem to reflect the kind of text each one is. And, in turn, the kind of text each one is seems to be a reflection of particular context factors, such as the text's purpose and topic, its audience and its mode (ie whether spoken or written). That is, there is a direct relation between the lower-level choices of grammar and vocabulary – what, for convenience, I will call *text* (uncountable) – and the text type itself. In turn, there is a relation between text, text type and the context in which the text operates. We can illustrate this relation like this:

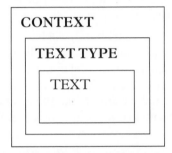

One immediate implication of this relationship is that, given text, it is possible to make confident predictions about both the text type and the context (as we saw with the example 5.6 above, for instance). Conversely, given sufficient information about the context, we can make accurate predictions about the kinds of texts you would be likely to find there and the textual features of these texts as well.

Discovery activity 5.2   *Predicting text type in context*

What texts would you expect to find in the following contexts? In what ways might these texts be similar or different?

- the noticeboard in the teachers' room of a language school
- inside a bus
- a magazine targeted at teenage girls.

Commentary ■ ■ ■

If your teachers' room is anything like mine, it will contain an assortment of short texts, some of which will be purely administrative and factual (such as schedules, announcements of room changes and of meeting times and topics, lists of stand-by duties, minutes of meetings, etc). There will be others which will have a more regulatory function (appeals to teachers to clean up after eating, to fill in class registers, and so on). Here is one from my own school:

5.8

> # DO'S and DON'TS
> ### Reception
>
> – Registers belong in reception except during class-time.
> – Don't make any changes in registers – send students to reception.
> – Don't put students up or down without seeing Jenny, then send student to reception.
> – Phone reception and Jenny before 1pm if you're sick (evening teachers).
> – Phone reception as soon as possible if you're sick (morning teachers).
> etc.

And there will also be such ephemera as texts advertising local services, or offering domestic items for sale, or asking for donations of books for a specific charity. There may also be some light-hearted material of only marginal relevance, such as a cartoon clipped from a satirical magazine. And a postcard or two from teachers who are currently on vacation.

The bus, on the other hand, will have a more restricted range of texts and none of them will be as informal as, say, holiday postcards. But, like the teachers' room, there will be a mix of factual material (eg information about routes and fares), advertisements and rules-and-regulations-type texts, although these are likely to be more formally worded than the teachers' room notices. As an example of the degree of formality, the following comes from an intercity bus:

5.9

> In the interests of **safety and comfort** if you wish to use this seat you **must** wear the seatbelt provided. In addition, passengers are asked to remain seated until the coach comes to a complete stop at your requested bus stop.

The teen magazine will include a variety of text types, from the factual–informational (*Jane's fashion news, Meet the boys, I quit school to save the forest*), to the more interpersonal advice-type texts (*Ask anything, Quiz: What's the secret of your success?, The style council*) plus *a lot* of advertising. The style, of course, is likely to be less formal even than the teachers' room board. Here, for example, is some teenage advice[60]:

5.10

> # Rule 1:
> ### Give him sweet treats.
>
> **S**abrina Everyone likes presents, I know I do! Keep love sweet by surprising your boy with prezzies. It doesn't matter what you give – it'll make him feel appreciated and loved. And if your luck's in, you'll get a big thank you snog too!

■

We have seen, then, that given a text (as in examples 5.4 to 5.7), it's possible to work out its context, and given a context, it's possible to predict the kind of text you would find there (as in examples 5.8 to 5.10).

Text functions

Given a context… But what is it about a context that determines the way a text is realized? What are the features of the context that impact on the way that language is used in that context?

Various theories of language and context have been proposed, each identifying the contextual factors that most significantly affect the language choices involved in text production and interpretation. Most theorists agree that a key factor determining the structure and language in a text is its *function*. In fact, Michael Halliday (the father of functional grammar) defined text as 'language that is functional. By functional, we simply mean language that is doing some job in some context, as opposed to isolated words or sentences that I might put on the blackboard.' [61]

We saw, for example, that the texts typically found in a teachers' room or in a bus divide more or less into two main categories: those that are *factual–informational* and those that are more like *rules and regulations*. Various systems have been devised to itemize and classify key language functions. Here, for example, is one such list of 'macro-functions', that is, the larger functions under which more specific functions are subsumed:

1 **referring** – that is, using language to convey or solicit information
2 **expressing feelings** – for example, saying what you like or dislike
3 **regulating** – using language to influence people and get things done, such as requesting, ordering, giving or refusing permission, promising, warning, etc
4 **interacting** – using language to establish and maintain social relations (also called the social or interpersonal function)
5 **playing** – using language imaginatively and playfully.

Discovery activity 5.3   *Text functions*

Categorize the following texts according to their macro-functions:

5.11
> The ladies and gentlemen who smoke are kindly requested to use the ashtrays and to leave them in the corridors. We would also be pleased if they refrain from smoking in the classrooms. Thank you very much for your cooperation.

5.12
> **Thank you for NOT SMOKING.**

5.13
> **TOBACCO**
>
> Tobacco is made from the dried leaves of the tobacco plant. It originally grew wild in America. The Spaniards brought tobacco to Europe in the 1500s and today tobacco is grown in Asia, Africa and Europe as well as America.
>
> Tobacco leaf can be made into pipe, cigar or cigarette tobacco, or snuff. Smoking is a harmful habit. It is especially bad for the lungs and heart.

5.14
> **I loved** McFly's first single and can't wait for their album to come out. Me and my mates made up a dance to it and it's well funny. I even caught my dad singing along to it on the radio. *Sarah, Glasgow.*

5.15

```
so    go
go    so
sl    ow
go    oh
low   ow
oh
```

5.16

Scott,
Thanks for sendingme the disk.
Sandy mckay

Commentary ■ ■ ■

Text 5.11 is clearly regulatory. Basically, it's a very elaborate way of saying *You can smoke in the corridors but please don't smoke in the classrooms.* **Text 5.12**, commonly found in taxi cabs, is of course also regulatory, but adopts a slightly more subtle approach than 5.11. In fact it disguises the regulatory function using a form that is more often associated with the interpersonal function of *thanking.* That is, the literal (or semantic) meaning and the pragmatic meaning don't necessarily match. As noted above, pragmatics is the study of how we 'read between the lines' of texts like this. The reason that text 5.11 is so elaborate and 5.12 so indirect is that, of all the language functions, the regulatory one is the most sensitive. Telling people what to do or not to do carries certain risks – what are called threats to *face*. In order to reduce this potential threat, we are often compelled to resort to linguistically quite complex evasion strategies.

By contrast, text **5.13** (which comes from the same source as text 5.5, incidentally,) is basically referential, in that it conveys factual information. Of course, it could be argued that there is an implicit message in the final two sentences that has a more regulatory intention, such as *to warn*. It's significant, for example, that the message SMOKING CAUSES HEART DISEASE (on a cigarette packet) is called a *health warning* rather than, say, a *medical report*. This is another instance of how context affects our interpretation of a text's purpose.

Text 5.14 (from a magazine for teens) expresses the writer's feelings about a pop group, so has an expressive function. Text 5.15 is a poem[12], part of a longer sequence, and simply plays with words that have the 'oh' sound – the form of the words taking precedence, temporarily, over their meaning. Hence its function is mainly playful.

Text 5.16, because it is simply the polite acknowledgement of something that someone has done, is essentially interpersonal. In fact, apart from the implication that the disk has arrived, there is very little informational content at all in this text. However, it fulfils an important social function, as do other 'content-less' expressions like *Hi! How are you?*, *Have a nice day!*, etc. Such 'polite noises' are said to have a *phatic* function. (This does not mean, though, that all expressions of *thanks* are purely phatic: see text 5.12 as a case in point.)

Pragmatics also explains how we read text 5.1 (the instructions on the hand-dryer) as regulatory (telling us how to do something) rather than purely referential, as it might initially appear on the basis of the first sentence. When there is a mismatch between the surface form of a text and its context we are compelled to look for alternative 'readings'. As we have seen, these alternative readings often have a regulatory function – what on the surface looks like a statement of fact is actually trying to get us to do something. Take the health warning on the cigarette packet, for example.

One implication of the fact that texts don't always mean what they say they mean is a legal one. A great deal of litigation is expended on interpreting the intentions of writers or speakers. You only have to think of President Clinton's legalistic squirming when asked if his claim that 'there is no improper relationship' with Monica Lewinsky was true:

> 'It depends upon what the meaning of the word 'is' is… If the… If he… If 'is' means 'is and never has been', that is not an… that's one thing. If it means 'there is none', that was a completely true statement.'

Nearer to home, a colleague of mine once sent a joke postcard to his Director of Studies claiming he was having such a wonderful time on holiday that he'd decided not to come back for the next school term. Not being a student of pragmatics, perhaps, the Director of Studies took it literally and he came back to find he had been replaced! This shows how it is not just individual words or phrases, but whole texts, that can be misconstrued. ■

Context and register

We have seen how the purpose of a text affects its production, although not in ways that are always completely transparent. What other contextual factors determine the choices of language we make when we create a text? And can we relate these factors directly to specific formal features of the text?

Of all the possible components of the context that might impact on the language choices in text production, just three seem to be particularly significant:

- the *what* of the situation – what kind of social activity is going on, and about what sort of topic (what is called the *field*)
- the *who* of the situation – the participants, their relationship and so on (what is called the *tenor*)
- the *how* of the situation – the means by which the text is being created, eg e-mail, fact-to-face talk, broadcast talk, written monologue and so on (what is called the *mode*).

These three contextual dimensions – field, tenor and mode – determine what is called the *register* of the resulting text. That is to say, different configurations of these dimensions demand different kinds of choices at the level of grammar and vocabulary, and these choices create textual effects that we recognize as being appropriate to the context of the text's use. Thus, the register of a teenage magazine allows for such words as *prezzie* and *snog* that would be inappropriate in a children's encyclopedia or in academic correspondence, for example. By the same token, you would not expect expressions like *ladies and gentlemen…, are kindly requested to…, we would also be pleased if…,* on a teabag wrapper.

Let's look at an example of register at work. I once sent an article to a prestigious academic journal and was pleased to get the following e-mailed response from the journal's editor:

5.17

> Dear Professor Thornbury,
> It appears that we will be including your Forum commentary in the spring issue.
> I would greatly appreciate it if you could send a disk copy of your response for
> production purposes to my office at San Francisco State University. Please label
> the disk with the word processing program you are using.
> Thank you in advance,
> Sandra McKay

The *field* in which the text is situated is very generally academic publishing and accounts for the presence of words such as *spring issue, disk copy, production purposes, word processing program.*

The *tenor* is very formal, even frozen, influenced by the fact that neither of the participants have met, nor know much about each other's status. By addressing me as Professor Thornbury, the writer avoids causing any offence, in case I am indeed a professor (which I am not). The use of highly indirect and modalized language (ie language using modal verbs such as *would, could*) is another way of creating a safe distance.

The *mode* is e-mail communication, usually a rather informal medium, but the writer uses the conventions of a formal letter, again, just to be on the safe side.

In my reply, while the field and mode remain the same, I seem to deliberately have adjusted the tenor, opting for a less formal wording, but still maintaining some of the conventions of a formal letter, eg in the address form and the closing:

5.18

> Dear Sandra McKay,
> I sent the disk off today. I hope it opens OK – let me know if there is any problem.
> Thanking you for your interest,
> Scott Thornbury

The response is quite startling in the degree to which the writer has picked up on the adjustment to the tenor:

5.19

> Scott,
> Thanks for sendingme the disk.
> Sandy mckay

The text is much more in keeping with the informality of e-mail communication (including uncorrected errors of punctuation). But, of course, it would not have been appropriate to have initiated the exchange in this style. Nor could the adjustment to tenor have occurred had the writer not been sensitive to the signs I sent out in text 5.18. This is a good example of how register is both jointly

number and complexity of the noun phrases, including the frequency of proper nouns and dates. In fact, one of the dangers of a genre-analytic approach is that there is no end to what is analysable and teaching genre can sometimes become all analysis and no synthesis. The analysis should not be pursued at the expense of allowing learners opportunities to apply this analysis in the production of their own texts.

What is important is that all these factors can be related to the kind of context in which the genre will be used. The audience (children) requires a level of transparency that is reflected in the brevity and syntactic simplicity of the texts, although this is counterbalanced by the lexical density – the result of having to pack quite a lot of information into a short space. The didactic function accounts for the assertive and unproblematic way that the information is presented and also accounts for the one or two instances of explicit evaluation. And the absence of human agents (apart from the historical Spaniards and Chinese) may even suggest an ideological stance, since no mention is made of the people (possibly lowly paid and exploited) who are currently involved in the cultivation and production of these products. Such hidden 'sub-texts' are particularly susceptible to the kind of analysis advocated by proponents of a genre-based view of text.

What, then, is the difference between a *text type* and a *genre?* Many writers use these terms interchangeably, or avoid the term *genre* altogether, preferring to reserve it for the description of literary texts. For others, the term *genre* is intimately associated with Halliday's *systemic functional linguistics,* which attempts to describe language in terms of its social purposes. Thus, genre analysis doesn't simply describe how texts are structured, but tries to account for these structures in terms of the social and cultural forces that shaped them. It is not simply descriptive (as in text linguistics) or even interpretative (as in literary criticism), but *explanatory.* A text, such as a headstone, a text message, or an encyclopedia entry, takes the form it does, not through accident, but because its construction reflects its social purpose, specifically its particular configuration of the variables of field, tenor and mode.

Classroom applications

The interdependent relationship between texts and their contexts has significant implications for language teaching and these can perhaps best be summed up by paraphrasing Malinowski:

> A text becomes intelligible only when it is placed within its context of situation.

This maxim applies equally to the *understanding* and to the *production* of texts. Let's look at understanding first.

A lot of teaching texts, such as those that learners read or listen to in the classroom or in examinations, are de-contextualized. That is, there are few or no clues as to where the text originated. This is particularly the case with recorded audio material, where learners hear only the disembodied voices of complete strangers. Typically, learners are asked to read or listen to such texts and then to answer comprehension questions about them. These questions often focus on specific details in the text, overlooking the fact that, until the learners have an idea of where the text originally came from – its context of situation – such details might be unintelligible. This is because, as has been argued in this chapter, the context of situation, including the text's original purpose and audience, determines the way the text is constructed. Without context knowledge, learners may feel a bit like the writer V. S. Naipaul from Trinidad, who, on his first trip to the United States, attempted to make sense of *The New York Times:*

> 'I was interested in newspapers and knew this paper to be one of the foremost in the world. But to read a newspaper for the first time is like coming into a film that has been on for an hour. [...] It made me feel a stranger, that paper. But on the front page, at the bottom, there was a story to which I could respond, because it dealt with an experience I was sharing. The story was about the weather. Apparently it was unseasonably cool and gray for the end of July, so unseasonable that it was worth a story.'[63]

Nowadays, coursebooks are much better than they used to be at situating the texts they use. The fact that many classroom texts are authentic – or appear authentic – helps learners to make accurate guesses as to the type of text they are – whether, for example, they are news articles or advertisements or informal letters. The problem is more acute when texts have been 'wrenched' from their context, re-typed, possibly simplified and re-presented to learners without any visual clues as to their origin: foundling texts, in fact. (We will return to the issue of authenticity in the next chapter.)

One of two 'context-flagging' strategies is therefore recommended when using texts in the classroom:

- situate the text firmly in its context before learners read or listen to it
- ask learners to guess the context after an initial exposure.

The first strategy might involve nothing more than saying, 'You are going to read a text that comes from the problem page of a teenagers' magazine.' Or 'You are going to listen to a conversation that takes place at the information desk of an airport.' This may be all learners need in order to activate their *schemas,* ie their mental representations of how things happen, specifically where language is involved (see page 55).

The second strategy might involve them reading the first few lines, or skimming the text quickly, in order to answer the question: *Who wrote the text, what about, to whom and why?* If the text is a recorded one, the learners can be asked to listen to the first few utterances and answer the question: *Who is talking to whom, about what and why?* Having established the context, a follow-up question might be: *And what do you think is going to happen?* The idea is to activate the learners' predictive skills. By testing their predictions against the evidence of the text as it unfolds, they become more active and involved readers and listeners.

Discovery activity 5.6   *Activating schemata*

Try it yourself with this text – part of an authentic conversation between two women[64]. Cover the text with a piece of paper. Reveal one chunk of text at a time, and each time ask yourself: *What are they talking about? Why? Who is going to say what next?* Then check to see how accurate your predictions were:

S1	I didn't get one with roots this year
S1	I'm ever so pleased with it but I did my usual <LAUGHS>
S2	what?

S1	I went out Thursday
	I went down to Carpenter's Nurseries
	cos you know I got my trees from there
S2	yeah

S1	and he'd got lots of rooted ones
	and I thought 'No,
	I'm not gonna bother with roots this year',
	cos it's always a pain to me,
	I never – never takes in the garden.
	I thought 'Sod it,
	I'm not gonna have any worries'
S2	yeah
S1	so

	I bought a beautiful tree,
	fiver,
	beautiful tree
S2	mhm

| S1 | when I got home it was too big to go in the house |
| | *<SPLUTTER OF LAUGHTER>* |

S1	and that's the third year running I've done that,
	I thought, 'He'll kill me,'
	I thought, 'No he won't,
	I'll see to it myself.'
	Here's me six weeks out of hospital

| | I'm sawing away at this tree. |

	But five pounds for a nine foot tree
S2	Incredible
S1	and it is the most beautiful shape

Commentary ■ ■ ■

If you still haven't worked out what they are talking about, you probably feel like many learners do, trying to make sense of texts in the absence of sufficient contextual information. In this case, there is cultural context to take into account as well, since the women are talking about *Christmas trees*. Learners unfamiliar with the pre-Christmas custom of buying a tree, with or without roots, would have considerable difficulty with the text, even if they had been told what the word *one* (in the first line) referred to. Nevertheless, the technique of alternating the gradual disclosure of a text with discussion as to what is going on is a useful one. It is easier to manage, of course, with recorded texts, but a written text can also be revealed gradually using either an overhead or a data projector. ■

Text production

As with receptive skills work, many classroom writing tasks are de-contextualized, of the type:

> Write 250 words about your favourite pop group.

or

> You have just won $10,000. What will you do with the money? (10 sentences)

or

> Discuss the pros and cons of examinations. (One page)

or

> A day in the country. (You have 30 minutes.)

In the absence of any context – including a purpose, an audience and details about the mode, such as whether it is a letter, a magazine article and so on – it is not surprising that learners often produce texts of startling banality. In the absence of a real-life purpose, the task is likely to be interpreted as involving nothing more than the display of accurate grammar.

Discovery activity 5.7   *Contextualizing writing tasks*

Choose one or two of the writing tasks above and think of ways that you could contextualize them, in order to make explicit their function, field, tenor and mode.

Commentary ■ ■ ■

Some possible ways of adapting these tasks might include:

> Your favourite band are playing in your town soon. Write an email (250 words) to a friend, who doesn't know or doesn't like the band, and try to persuade the friend to come with you to hear them.

Or

> You've been asked to write some cover notes for your favourite group's latest album. Write two or three paragraphs, explaining why you like them so much.

For the second task:

> You've just won $10,000. You are going to be interviewed by a local newspaper. What questions do you think they will ask you? Prepare your answers.

For the third:

> Your school is considering dropping examinations from the curriculum, but is asking for everyone's opinion. Write to your school board, outlining the arguments for and against keeping the exams and stating your own opinion.

And finally:

> A travel magazine is offering free flights for the best account of a day spent out of town, which they will publish in their section called 'A day in the country'.

You may feel that these tasks are a little bit contrived and that they are therefore no better a safeguard against banality than the originals. Of course, the best tasks are those that are motivated by the learners' own need to communicate their individual interests, wishes, concerns and so on. Establishing a regular channel for doing this may obviate the need to contrive artificial writing tasks of the above type. One way of contextualizing writing in this way is to ask learners to write letters to you regularly and to reply to them in kind. While this may seem time-consuming, it is probably no more so than the reading and marking of traditional written homework, especially if both teacher and learners have access to e-mail. And, of course, the content is bound to be more interesting than that generated by more traditional writing tasks. ■

Using a genre-based approach

Finally, what does a *genre-based approach* have to offer for text production, both spoken and written? Typically such an approach begins not with a creative task but with the analysis of representative examples of a text genre, in much the same way that we analysed the entries in the children's encyclopedia. This analysis will focus on:

- the macrostructures of the text – how, for example, it is organized into obligatory and optional elements and how these are ordered
- the *texture* of the text, that is, the way that the text is made cohesive through, for example, the use of linking devices
- the lower-level features of grammar and vocabulary that encode the register of the text, that is, its field, tenor and mode.

A genre-based approach is particularly well-suited for text types that are both fairly formulaic and whose mastery confers social advantages on the user. For example, the ability to write a convincing CV, along with an accompanying letter, would be an asset for an immigrant looking for a job. Both the CV and the letter are fairly formulaic and their generic features can be highlighted through the study of representative examples. This utilitarian motivation partly accounts for the popularity of a genre-based approach in Australia, with its large immigrant population.

In theory, however, a genre-based approach is aimed at more than simply the ability to reproduce formulaic text types. By relating texts to their contexts, including their social purposes and by raising awareness as to the meaning-making potential of register features, genre teachers hope to *empower* their learners – to give them access to the means of text production that are valued in the target culture. This worthy objective may be jeopardized if the analysis becomes too academic. As noted above, there is a real danger of genre analysis becoming overly pre-occupied with the minutiae of textual features, when what learners probably need most is to 'have a go'. The 'have a go' approach, now known as *process writing,* is decried by proponents of genre-based approaches, however. They associate it with uncontrolled self-expression and the perpetuation of mediocrity.

In the next chapter we will look at ways whereby these two positions might be accommodated.

Meanwhile, a 'light' form of genre-based teaching might include the following elements:

- Learners read a text chosen to represent features of a particular genre and their understanding of the text is checked, using standard approaches, eg checking of understanding of the overall gist first, followed by more detailed questions.
- At this point it is important to establish the *function* of the text, its intended audience and its role in the target culture.
- They then look at more examples of the text type. For this reason, it helps if the examples are not too long: short texts are best for genre analysis. If this is not possible – for example, in the case of academic assignments – the focus can be on selected parts of the text, eg the abstract, the introduction, or the bibliography.
- Learners compare the texts and identify generic features, first of the overall structure, including the obligatory and optional elements and then in the use of language within these structures. It is best if learners do the analysis themselves, working in pairs or groups, with teacher guidance, as the features they identify themselves are likely to be more memorable than features that are simply pointed out to them.
- An alternative approach might be to contrast the text with a text that shares some generic features but is significantly different in one or more respects. For example, a formal letter on a specific topic can be contrasted with an informal one on the same topic. In other words, the field and mode remain constant, while the tenor changes. In this analysis stage it is important that the features that are identified as generic are significantly so and that the analysis doesn't get bogged down in detail.
- Learners then attempt to reproduce the genre in a text of their own. Or they can 'play' with the genre, formalizing a text that is informal (a change in tenor), for example, or turning a spoken text into a written one (a change in mode). Or they use their knowledge of the genre to write a parody: this usually involves a change in field. Writing a children's encyclopedia text on the topic of, say, garden gnomes or chewing gum would be an invitation to parody the genre.

Conclusion

In this chapter we have looked at the relation between texts and their contexts of use. Key context variables include the *field, tenor* and *mode* of the situational context, that is, the *what, who* and *how* of the language event. The way that these variables combine and interact determines the *register* of the text. Certain recurring register combinations become institutionalized over time and are known as *genres*. Genre theory argues that language is best learned through the analysis and mastery of specific genres, since such an approach best reflects the way language is shaped by – and shapes – its social contexts of use. Moreover, mastery of the genres that are valued by a specific community offers the learner access to that community. Critics of genre-based approaches query both its ideological stance and the emphasis on analysis that is often associated with the study of genres and they remind us that learners need not only to analyse language, but to put it to use. Nevertheless, any approach that highlights the relation between a text and its context, so long as it doesn't get bogged down in terminology, should serve to raise learners' awareness about the way texts are produced and interpreted.

One context of use that hasn't been mentioned is the classroom context. Is there a genre that is specific to classrooms? What are its functions and features? That is the subject of the next chapter.

Chapter 6 **Classroom texts**

In the opening of his play *The Bald Prima Donna*[65], the playwright Eugene Ionesco satirizes the kind of language and values that – in his day, at least – were associated with foreign language classes:

MRS SMITH.　Goodness! Nine o'clock! This evening for supper we had soup, fish, cold ham and mashed potatoes and a good English salad and we had English beer to drink. The children drank English water. We had a very good meal this evening. And that's because we are English, because we live in a suburb of London and because our name is Smith. [...] Mashed potatoes are very nice with cold ham. The mayonnaise was quite fresh. The mayonnaise from the grocer round the corner is much better quality than the mayonnaise from the grocer opposite, it's even better than the mayonnaise from the grocer at the bottom of the hill...

Ionesco realized that the bland, unexciting world of coursebook characters and the somewhat surreal detail with which their daily routines are described was a genre in its own right – distinctive enough to be recognized by his audience and surreal enough to fit neatly into the tradition of absurdist theatre. It was familiar to his audience because of texts such as this one[66], from the same period:

6.1

It is ten past seven now. Are Roger and David still in the bedroom? No, they are not in the bedroom now, they are in the bathroom.

David is having a bath. He has a bath every morning. Roger is standing at the wash-basin. He is washing his hands and face. Roger has a bath in the evening, before he goes to bed.

What are Roger and David going to do next? They are going back to the bedroom. They are going to dress.

As banal as this text may seem to us now, there were in fact good reasons for such texts being like this. For a start, language teaching texts needed to be intelligible, even for beginners, and so a degree of simplification was considered necessary, both in terms of syntax and vocabulary. In this sense, the writers of these texts were 'keeping their audience in mind', or, in Hallidayan terms, respecting the *tenor* of the discourse. Moreover, these texts were not designed in order to inform their readers about the world nor to influence them to change it: they had a purely *pedagogic* (that is to say, teaching) function. Part of this teaching function was to display the target language in contexts that would make it both comprehensible and also learnable. And part of what makes a language learnable is that its patterns are frequently and prominently displayed, thereby increasing the chances that they will be attended to (or *noticed*) – either consciously or subliminally. Hence the repetition and alternation of these grammar patterns:

- present continuous: *David is having a bath... Roger is standing at the wash-basin,* etc and
- present simple: *He has a bath every morning... Roger has a bath in the evening...*

In fact, *not* to be either simplified or repetitive would be a sure sign of their failure as appropriate texts for teaching purposes, one would have thought.

Nevertheless, a reaction against texts of this type set in at the same time as a more *communicative* approach to language teaching was being advocated. It was felt that such texts provided poor models of real (or *authentic)* language use and, moreover, were obsessively concerned with the *forms* of the language, particularly its grammar patterns, at the expense of more communicative features of text, such as vocabulary and discourse features. Especially since the advent of *corpus linguistics*, ie the systematic study of (often vast) data bases of naturally occurring texts, artificially doctored classroom texts have been subject to extensive criticism, even derision. The fact, for example, that few if any scripted dialogues in coursebooks include such highly frequent items as the discourse markers *you know, I mean, but, erm* and so on, is just one instance of their lack of representativeness. Worse, many coursebook texts actually distort the evidence, presenting language items in ways that they would rarely or never be used in naturally occurring language use. In this dialogue in a beginners' course[67], for example, the modal verb *must* is presented for the first time, but in a way that seems rather forced:

6.2

MRS JONES:	Come in, Bessie.
	Shut the door, please.
	The bedroom's very untidy.
BESSIE:	What must I do, Mrs Jones?
MRS JONES:	Open the window and air the room.
etc.	

What must I do? with its connotations of self-imposed moral obligation, seems an odd choice in this context. (A corpus search shows that the phrase *what must I do…* often collocates with … *to be saved?* Maybe Bessie has other things on her mind.)

Simplification in coursebook texts could lead to distortion, not just at the sentence level, but at the level of the entire discourse. The following dialogue[68] not only misrepresents the way telephone openings and closings are ordered and elaborated, but seems to have no communicative purpose, in that the speaker phones simply to tell the listener something he already knows:

6.3

CHRISTINE:	Hello. Is that Uncle Bob?
UNCLE BOB:	Yes?
CHRISTINE:	This is Christine. I'm in my hotel in New York.
UNCLE BOB:	Hello, Christine! How are you?
CHRISTINE:	I'm fine. I'm very excited. How are you?
UNCLE BOB:	We're all fine.
CHRISTINE:	My plane arrives in Montreal at seven fifteen this evening.
UNCLE BOB:	Yes, that's right.
CHRISTINE:	See you very soon. Bye.
UNCLE BOB:	Goodbye Christine.

One argument for simplification in coursebook texts was that this made them easier to understand. It's true that at the level of vocabulary and grammar the conversation between Uncle Bob and Christine is easy to process. But as coherent discourse, it is less transparent. Uncle Bob's response to Christine's informing him about her arrival time (*Yes, that's right*) doesn't make sense unless Christine's utterance is some kind of coded message (are they secret agents?) or he is hard of hearing. Moreover, he doesn't appear to share her feelings of excitement. Maybe Uncle Bob is a computer program, like AOLiza?

In fact, the lack of correspondence with any kind of reality may have made some coursebook texts *harder*, not easier, to understand. And, as we saw in Chapter 4, when spoken language is stripped of all its repetitions, filled pauses, false starts and discourse markers, it can become very dense and hence difficult to process in real time.

Finally, coursebook texts were boring. They provided little intrinsic motivation for learners to *want* to read or listen to them. Only a perverse imagination could have responded with anything but a yawn to Roger's and David's bathroom antics, or to Christine's electric conversation with her uncle.

The communicative approach ushered in a re-evaluation of such texts and one response was to look to *authentic* texts for guidance. Accordingly, *authenticity* became the standard by which classroom texts were judged, and authentic texts, ie texts not written specifically for teaching purposes, started to make an appearance in coursebooks. Here, for example, is a text from a beginners' course published in 1982[69]:

6.4

parties	**MAKING FRIENDS IN LONDON**
discos	
pub evenings	is a challenge even for the most sociable of us. You can't just go up to strangers and say: 'Hi, I'd like to meet you.' If you enjoy meeting people LONDON LINKUP could be just what you've been looking for. We are a friendly cross-section of mostly unattached young people aged 20–40, equally divided between the sexes. Our aim is to become involved in things that really interest us and to make worthwhile use of our spare time. There's always lots happening all over London amongst our 1,500 members who organise over 150 events each month.
wine bars	
films	
concerts	
folk	
jazz	
ballet	To find out all about us, just drop into one of our informal introductory talks. These take place at both 6.30pm and 8.00pm on the following days (excluding public holidays).
cooking	
bridge	Mondays and Thursdays. At the International Sportswriters' Club, Great Russell Street. (Opposite the YMCA near Tottenham Court Road tube.)
chess	
football	
waterskiing	If you would like a chat beforehand, please ring us 01-606 1750. We look forward to welcoming you.
horseriding	
astrology	**LONDON LINKUP**

In order to deal with texts like this, teachers were faced with at least two challenges: how to ensure that their learners understood such texts, and how to decide which language features of these texts should be selected for teaching purposes. Inevitably, a number of compromises, especially at lower levels, resulted. One was to select only the simplest authentic texts, such as restaurant menus and bus timetables, for use at lower levels. But even purists recognized that this minimalist strategy risked depriving learners of a sufficiently varied diet of texts and language input. Another was to produce so-called *semi-authentic* texts, that is, texts that replicated features of authentic texts, but which had been simplified linguistically. This strategy is still widely adopted, especially with texts designed for listening practice.

Discovery activity 6.1   *Authentic texts*

Which of these texts – all from coursebooks – is a) authentic (ie not originally designed for classroom use), b) an authentic text adapted for classroom use, or c) completely contrived? What features of each helped you decide? How successfully simulated is the 'semi-authentic' text?

6.5

Dog bites policeman

WHEN POLICEMAN Alan Handley received an emergency call from a fellow officer, who was trying to arrest three thieves in a local park, he responded immediately. When Handley arrived on the scene, the officer and his police dog were losing the fight, so Handley bravely jumped in. However, the dog did not recognize him and bit him on the arm, allowing the thieves to escape. 'I was wearing my uniform, but maybe he didn't recognize my number,' joked Handley.[70]

6.6

Sarah's surprise

Shapely Scottish singing sensation Sarah Sownes broke off her engagement with American transport millionaire Laurie Van Truck yesterday. Sarah has been seeing Laurie since her marriage to film star Steve Newman broke up two years ago. She said, 'I've decided to break with Laurie completely. I don't love him. He was helping me to break into the film industry, but nothing's happened.'[71]

6.7

Police hold 18 football fans in dawn raids

POLICE investigating football violence arrested eighteen people yesterday in dawn raids on homes in London and the Home Counties.

Detectives said they hoped they had 'broken the back of a hard-core element' of violent football fans. Weapons including knives, coshes and a crossbow were seized by the ninety officers involved in the raids.[72]

Commentary ■ ■ ■

It should be fairly obvious that text 6.6 is the contrived text. Even without the cutely invented names, the unusually high frequency of instances of the verb *break* gives the game away and suggests that there is a language agenda here, ie phrasal verbs. Nevertheless, the text does replicate some of the stylistic features of tabloid text, including pre-modified proper nouns (*American transport millionaire Laurie Van Truck*), alliteration (*shapely Scottish singing sensation*) and the use of direct speech. Even the relative simplicity of its language is probably just as much a characteristic of tabloid newspapers as of coursebook texts. What is less typical is the absence of any idiomatic language, apart from the phrasal verbs themselves.

Text 6.7, however, makes no concessions to learners, either in terms of syntax or the choice of vocabulary. The average sentence length of seventeen words contrasts with twelve in the text about Sarah Sownes, suggesting greater syntactic complexity. There is no evidence of any form of simplification: rare words, such as *coshes* and *crossbow*, have not been omitted. Nor have the relatively uncommon words *dawn* and *seized* been replaced by more common synonyms, such as *early morning* and *taken*. And the idiomatic expression *broken the back of* is left intact.

Text 6.5, on the other hand, does show signs of simplification, while remaining true to the generic features of this kind of text. It may be interesting to compare the coursebook version with the original on which it was based[73]:

6.8

Dog bites man

Hereford, England – Policeman Colin Kerfoot responded instantly to an emergency call from a fellow officer who was tackling three burglars in a local park. When he arrived at the scene, the other officer and his police dog were losing the battle, so Kerfoot bravely jumped in. However, the dog failed to recognize its ally and bit PC Kerfoot on the arm, allowing the suspects to get away. 'God knows what he would have done if he'd been on their side,' joked the officer.

Notice for a start that low frequency words, such as *tackling, burglars, battle* and *ally*, have been replaced by more common synonyms, as has the idiomatic phrasal verb *get away*. In the interests of clarity, a pronoun has been replaced by its noun phrase referent (*When he arrived* → *When Handley arrived*) and *joked the officer* re-written as *joked Handley*. Also, the last sentence has been completely re-cast so as to eliminate the relatively difficult third conditional structure and replace it with something that is grammatically more transparent. (The change of proper names, by the way, has nothing to do with simplification and more to do with copyright.) On the whole, the text succeeds in sounding like an authentic text, while being a little more accessible to learners than the original. ■

Another way of addressing the authenticity issue when it first emerged was to argue that a complete understanding of such texts was not necessary – nor even desirable. After all, who completely *understands* the instructions in a computer manual, and who needs to understand them? Accordingly, tasks were designed to discourage learners from 'reading every word', despite many learners' strongly felt desire to *want* to read every word.

Discovery activity 6.2   *Grading the task not the text*

In order to cope with the difficulty of ungraded authentic texts, a methodology was devised based on the slogan: *Grade the task, not the text*. That is, the learner's load in processing the text could in theory be eased by tinkering with the reading (or listening) tasks, rather than by simplifying the text itself.

The following tasks are designed to be used with text 6.4 above. Rank them in terms of the relative depth of text processing required. That is to say, which tasks require processing of the text at only a superficial level and which require deep processing?

Task A
Which of the following are typical Linkup members?
a a married 30-year-old man
b a single 25-year-old woman
c a single 50-year-old man
d a divorced 35-year-old man

Task B
What is there to do in London if you like...
music?   outdoor sports?
meeting people?   indoor games?
the arts?

Task C
Who is London Linkup aimed at?
– bored people
– lonely people
– shy people
– sociable people
– unattached people

Task D
You are interested in becoming a member of London Linkup. What do you do next?

Commentary ■ ■ ■

Tasks A and D both require a fairly detailed understanding of a small part of the text, but not necessarily the whole text. Task B (which in fact is the task that is offered in the coursebook) requires no processing of the body of the text at all, but only of the list of activities on the left. In fact, with a little common sense learners should be able to answer the questions without even referring to the text. It's difficult, therefore, to understand why the text was included at all. This raises the question as to whether the strategy of *grading the task, not the text* may not sometimes be taken too far, resulting in tasks that are trivial and texts that are redundant.

Task C, on the other hand, could require a quite detailed reading of the text, since it is not immediately obvious whether the purpose of London Linkup is to 'become involved in things' and 'to make worthwhile use of … spare time', or 'making friends'. Moreover, members are described as 'friendly' and 'unattached': the words *shy* and *lonely* are never used. Yet the 'sub-text' suggests that it is precisely these kind of people who are being targeted. However, processing the text at this level of subtlety would be beyond the means of most beginner students. Teachers using the text at this level might be content, then, to use the title (*Making friends in London*) to elicit ideas as to the kind of organization London Linkup is, and then set tasks A and D. ■

Texts designed for the classroom

Despite the ingenious attempts on the part of teachers and writers to accommodate authentic materials, some scholars, such as Henry Widdowson and Guy Cook, have begun to question the whole notion of authenticity itself. For a start, isn't the classroom a specific context with its own standards of authenticity? The whole point of studying a language in a classroom setting (it is argued) is so that the learning process can be purposefully engineered and streamlined, eliminating the hit-and-miss nature of 'just-picking-it-up-in-the-street' type of learning. One way of doing this engineering and streamlining is by deliberately contriving texts in order to maximize their educational potential. The resultant texts are appropriate to the context for which they were designed: the classroom. They are authentic classroom texts, just as prayers and sermons are authentic place-of-worship texts, or sports commentaries are authentic sports arena texts. The coursebook text *genre*, in fact, has a long history, and few learners would have been surprised by the Roger-and-David type texts that they encountered in the classroom. (It would be a different matter if they encountered them *outside* the classroom, of course.) Learners are quite happy, on the whole, to suspend their disbelief about such texts. In fact, some learners, like the writer Vladimir Nabokov, came to cherish them:

> I learned to read English before I could read Russian. My first English friends were four simple souls in my grammar – Ben, Dan, Sam and Ned. There used to be a great deal of fuss about their identities and whereabouts – 'Who is Ben?' 'He is Dan', 'Sam is in bed' and so on. Although it all remained rather stiff and patchy (the compiler was handicapped by having to employ – for the initial lessons, at least – words of not more than three letters), my imagination somehow managed to obtain the necessary data. Wanfaced, big-limbed, silent nitwits, proud in their possession of certain tools ('Ben has an axe'), they now drift with a slow-motioned slouch across the remotest backdrop of memory…[74]

Nabokov's story is a good example of the way learners make 'non-genuine' texts authentic for their own learning purposes: that is, they *authenticate* them. According to this view, authenticity is not a property of texts, but more a property of the learner's response to the text: authenticity is in the eye of the beholder.

Authentic tasks

A preoccupation with text authenticity has also been questioned on the grounds that the authenticity of the text may be of less importance than the authenticity of the tasks that learners engage in when using the texts. After all, it doesn't require an authentic menu in order to perform a restaurant role-play. If the task is to collaborate in choosing a meal, a simplified menu would do just as well. An inauthentic task, on the other hand, would be to read the menu aloud from start to finish, or to write a summary of it, or to turn it into a gap-fill exercise. Such tasks, it is argued, de-authenticate the text, turning it into a mere linguistic object.

Despite these arguments, however, the issue of the interest-raising – and hence motivational – potential of real texts doesn't go away. The 'suspension-of-disbelief' principle may work up to a certain point. But how much satisfaction is to be gained from working with texts that were merely designed to display language? And how much spin-off, in terms of authentic classroom *talk*, can be milked out of a text like the Roger-and-David one above? Or, to cite a more recent example, the text about Suzy Stressed (on page 18)? Of course, such texts don't *have* to be banal. Even a little tweaking – by giving the 'story' some narrative twist, for example – might serve to turn the Roger-and-David text into something quite interesting. Could their very colourlessness be in fact a subterfuge? Could they be aliens in disguise? Undercover agents? Lovers?

But what happens when learners encounter a text like this[75]?

6.9

THE POP STAR AND THE FOOTBALLER

DONNA FLYNN & TERRY WISEMAN

TALK TO *HI! MAGAZINE* ABOUT THEIR LOVE FOR EACH OTHER

This is the most famous couple in the country. She is the pop star who has had six number one records – more than any other single artist. He has scored fifty goals for Manchester United, and has played for England over thirty times. Together they earn about £20 million a year. They invited *Hi! Magazine* into their luxurious home.

Donna: A lot of the time since we've been together, one of us has been away. We really have to try hard to be together. We have both flown all over the world just to spend a few hours together.

Terry: Obviously people say, 'Oh, you've got all this money, what are you going to spend it on?' But the best thing is that money buys us the freedom to be together.

Donna: It hasn't changed us. We are still the same people. Newspapers have told terrible stories about us, but it's all lies.

Terry: Our perfect Saturday night is sitting in front of the telly with a take-away. Our favourite programmes are Blind Date and Friends. You won't find photos of us coming out of pubs and clubs drunk, having spent the night with a whole load of famous people.

Here is a text that is obviously based on people who will be familiar to most learners (the footballer David Beckham and his wife Victoria), but who have unaccountably morphed into coursebook characters. Unlike fictitious Roger and David, Donna and Terry hover somewhere between fact and fiction, such that the set question *Who is the couple in the interview?* can be answered in any number of ways. This peculiar alienation effect makes the text difficult to exploit for anything other than its superficial language features. As a springboard into a discussion about the rights and responsibilities of the rich and famous, for example, it will be all but useless, unless everyone agrees to remove the surface 'film' and to talk about the real people underneath. A genuine text, on the other hand, is much more likely to elicit a genuine response.

As evidence of which, here is the description of a lesson that a colleague, Peter Coles, who teaches in Turkey, posted on a teachers' website:

> My weekend students have an exam next week in which they have to write an 'informal letter'. This is how it [the lesson] went.
>
> Stage 1.   Get students to look at the sample letter in the coursebook and then we analyse the language and style together. (3 mins)
>
> Stage 2.   Group discussing informal letters, noting how even informal letters conform to certain conditions eg always ask how one is at the beginning etc. (1 min)
>
> Stage 3.   I thought 'What the bloody hell am I doing?' (2 secs)
>
> Stage 4.   Opened my diary and found an e-mail from my brother-in-law, ran to the photocopy room, ran back (out of breath) then we looked at a real informal letter together. Again noting the style, content etc in pairs and as a group. (wasn't looking at the time)
>
> Stage 5.   Students wrote letters to me for their homework.
>
> The result: Yesterday I received 18 of the most wonderful, genuine, honest pieces of writing that I have seen. Expressing thoughts about the course, their families, their love lives et al.
>
> Real people writing about real things.

Discovery activity 6.3   *Purposes of classroom texts*

Peter's lesson reminds us that texts are used for different purposes in the classroom: in his case, the text served as a model for a writing task. It was only incidentally used to develop reading skills, or to focus on grammar, for example. But what about some of the other coursebook texts that we have been looking at? What do you think was the purpose (or what were the purposes) that motivated their inclusion in the coursebook? And how successful are they, in the light of their purposes?

Look specifically at texts 6.3 (Christine and Uncle Bob), 6.4 (London Linkup) and 6.6 (Sarah's surprise).

Commentary ■ ■ ■

The phone conversation between Christine and Uncle Bob was probably designed to contextualize the language of phoning, particularly the potentially problematic use of *this* and *that,* as in *This is Christine, Is that Uncle Bob?* Hence, we can say that the purpose is primarily *linguistic* and specifically *pragmatic,* in that it focuses on the way language is used in specific contexts. As we have already noted, it might have been more successful had the conversation more closely reflected real-life discourse structures, but it does have the virtue of being short and easy to process. There may also have been a secondary motive for the text, which is to develop the book's 'storyline': Christine's adventures continue in the next few units.

The London Linkup advert, on the other hand, was not included for any specifically linguistic purpose, but more as material for *skills development* and, specifically, the development of strategies for processing text beyond the learner's current linguistic competence. It has been argued that learning how to cope with authentic texts involves using such strategies as:

prediction: eg predicting the content of a text on the basis of its title

skimming: eg identifying the gist of the text

scanning: eg finding specific information in the text and ignoring everything else

recognition: eg identifying familiar words in the text

selection: eg selecting as key only those words that carry the main informational load of the text.

 The development of these skills involves choosing authentic materials – the content being less important than the fact that they *are* authentic – and setting tasks that mobilize these skills and, importantly, which discourage a tendency on the part of the learner to 'read every word'.

As we have seen, the task that was originally set for this text was perhaps less than adequate as a means of activating these strategies. But, more recently, this whole 'strategy-based' approach has been called into question. For a start, it has been argued that encouraging learners to process text at this very superficial level – eg by skimming and scanning – may be counterproductive, since successful reading involves a much greater degree of engagement with the text than such an approach allows. Successful readers may, indeed, 'read every word', at least some of the time. By discouraging learners from processing texts at anything other than a very superficial level, teachers may be giving learners the wrong message.

Finally, the text called *Sarah's surprise* is, as we have noted, clearly written to display a specific language feature (phrasal verbs with *break),* and therefore its purpose is primarily linguistic. The fact that the writers have chosen to co-opt an existing genre (the gossipy news item) suggests that a secondary motive may have been to provide not just a context for the targeted item but some incidental skills development as well. Exposing learners to examples of different text types (even if not authentic) might arguably improve their ability to handle these text types in real life. Certainly, success in processing an example of a text type may at least motivate some learners to read beyond the text book. ■

To sum up, we have identified at least two main reasons for including texts in coursebooks: a *linguistic* purpose, such as providing contextualized instances of grammar structures, vocabulary items, pragmatic functions, or as a model for text production (as in the case of Peter's informal letter), and a *skills development* purpose, ie as material for the development of reading and listening skills.

We should add a third purpose, which we will call *text-as-stimulus* – that is, the text is used to introduce content into the classroom that learners can then respond to, in the form of discussion or role play, for example, or as a prompt for some writing task or even project work. Finally, some texts are included in coursebooks purely for their informational content, as for example, when cultural information is being conveyed. An example of this might be a text in a business English course about the conventions involved in accepting an invitation to dinner at a business colleague's home.

Of course, one text may serve a variety of purposes, just as one purpose may be served by a variety of texts. On the whole, however, linguistic purposes have usually involved using invented texts, while, for the purposes of skills development, genuine or 'adapted-genuine' texts are now favoured. For texts-as-stimulus it's likely that genuine texts will work best, on the principal of, as Peter Coles put it, *real people writing (or talking) about real things*.

If genuine texts are going to be used effectively, however, teachers need to be able to address the issue of *difficulty*. Specifically, what makes a text difficult and what measures can teachers take to reduce difficulty, or to help their learners cope with it?

Discovery activity 6.4   *Level of difficulty*

Read these four texts and rank them in order of difficulty. What criteria did you use?

6.10

> **COLUMN 8**
>
> ☐ A COUPLE from Dandenong arrived at the Manly Pines Motel the other day. 'Did you come here through the tunnel?' asked Brian Marshall, the manager. 'Well we did and we didn't,' he was told. They had been driving through the city, had got into the tunnel and come out the other side. But they hadn't realized they'd passed under the Harbour – and knowing that to get to Manly they had to cross the Bridge, they did. Whoops, back in the city…

6.11

> Dear Mr Thornbury
>
> In response to your letter dated 15th May, I regret to inform you that I am unable to carry out your instructions to send your Debit Card to the destination requested. The reason being that the signature we hold on file differs from that on your letter. Therefore, could you please sign and return the enclosed Signature Slip and provide a copy of your current Passport.
> I look forward to hearing from you shortly.
>
> Yours sincerely,
>
> C...... M......
> Senior Customer Services Clerk

6.12

> **Tea bags** can cure sick building syndrome, say Japanese researchers. People who move into a new house can suffer nausea and sore throats due to the chemicals from fresh paint and glue. One of the chief culprits is formaldehyde. Now the Tokyo Metropolitan Consumer Center has found that tea bags scattered around the house soak up the formaldehyde, aided by tannin in the tea. They found that the concentration of formaldehyde in the air fell by between 60 and 90 per cent. Dry black or green tea is said to work best.[76]

6.13

> Last month my big sister bought a flash new car. It was perfect timing, as I was going to a disco and thought it would look really good if she picked me up in her new cool-mobile. She couldn't though and neither could anyone else, apart from my nan [...] The disco was fab – especially as I'd managed to chat up Josh – the guy I'd fancied for ages. As the night came to an end, they played My Heart Will Go On and I snuggled up to Josh for a slow dance. Then, just as we were about to go for our first romantic snog, the music stopped and the DJ said, 'Could Lucy Sage please come to the front of the hall, your nan's waiting to take you home!' I just wanted the ground to open up and swallow me, as Josh looked at me and burst into laughter! Talk about uncool!
>
> Lucy, Freddie Prinz Jr fan, Essex[77]

Commentary ■ ■ ■

All four texts present varying degrees of difficulty and the relative degree of difficulty will depend to a large extent on the individual learner, so there is no one 'right' answer to this task. The kinds of difficulty specific to each text include the following:

Text 6.10: The vocabulary is unspecialized and non-idiomatic (apart from *whoops*) and should present no major problems so long as the key word *tunnel* is known. The grammar and syntax shouldn't present too many difficulties either, despite the preponderance of past perfect verb forms. More problematic might be the use of grammatical substitution, that is the use of *did* and *didn't* in place of full clauses. What, for example, does the last *did* stand for? The text type is a narrative, which provides a familiar *schema* on which to construct the events, but because it is unfinished, the point of it is rather elusive. Also, it is not clear what kind of text this is: it is too vague (*a couple..., the other day...*) to be a news report, but the use of real names (*Brian Marshall*) rules it out as a joke. But the greatest source of difficulty will be the fact that most readers will have no idea of the geography that is being described: in other words, they lack the necessary background knowledge to make sense of the events or to understand the point of the story. It is in fact a columnist's anecdote from the Sydney Morning Herald[78].

Text 6.11: The vocabulary is more specialized in this text, the field being banking and bureaucracy, and the register is formal, which in turn means that the language is syntactically complex (there are six verbs in the first sentence alone!). However, the text type (a formal letter) is immediately recognizable, as well as its purpose:

the discourse structure (apology → reason → consequence) is not only a familiar one, but is clearly signalled, both lexically (*regret, the reason, please*) and through the use of linking words (*therefore*). The text is both coherent and cohesive. Because the letter is a response to an earlier letter, readers are missing some of the background to the text, but this is fairly easily recoverable from the first sentence.

Text 6.12: The scientific register may be difficult for non-specialist readers and this is evidenced in the technical vocabulary, such as *formaldehyde* and *tannin*, as well as the relatively high number of low-frequency words: only 80% of the words in the text fall within the top 2000 most common words in English (proper nouns excluded). Those that fall outside this range include: *aided, chemicals, concentration, consumer, researchers, culprits, soak, glue, nausea* and *syndrome*. That means that a learner with a recognition vocabulary of 2000 words would have difficulty processing the text, even using context clues to guess the meaning of the unfamiliar words. Compare this to the two previous texts which have a high frequency quotient of 94% and 92% respectively, which means that the same learner would recognize more than nine out of every ten words. Moreover the tea bag text is relatively dense: the proportion of grammar words (like *can, of, into, the*) to content words (like *sick, paint, scattered*) is very low – just over a third of the words being grammar words. This is largely due to the high proportion of multi-word noun phrases in the text, such as *sick building syndrome, Japanese researchers, fresh paint and glue*, etc. In the text about the tunnel, however, there is double the proportion of grammar words, which suggests that the information is much less densely packed. The debit card text falls somewhere between the two, being roughly half grammar words and half content words.

On the plus side, text 6.12 is totally self-contained and doesn't rely on the reader having detailed background knowledge nor being familiar with another dependent text. The argument is presented logically and follows a recognizable discourse structure, that of the scientific research paper, summarized down to just five sentences.

Text 6.13: The text type may not be familiar to many readers, being a reader's letter to a teenage girls' magazine describing an embarrassing moment, a regular feature of such magazines. Lack of familiarity with the text type may be compounded with lack of familiarity with the style and the concerns of teenage magazines in general. But because it is clearly a coherent narrative, told chronologically, it presents no real cognitive challenge to readers in terms of their being able to construct a matched mental schema of the events. It has the universally familiar narrative structure of *circumstantial information* followed by a series of *past events*, which include a *complication* and its resulting *outcome*, interspersed with frequent *evaluation*. Moreover, the situation – the unwelcome appearance of an older relative and the speaker's consequent humiliation – is a fairly well-known, and hence easily recognizable, one. Of course, the whole story depends on knowing that *nan* is a colloquial term for *grandmother*. More than that, it is the idiomatic and 'in-group' vocabulary that would make this difficult for readers accustomed to more standard varieties of English: 'slang' terms, such as *flash, fab, chat up, fancied, snuggled up, snog* and *uncool* would present problems, but the context would probably resolve many of these.

In short, a 'comprehensibility ranking' of the four texts would leave little to choose between texts 6.11 and 6.13, with texts 6.10 and 6.12 more difficult but for different reasons.

To summarize, then: the factors that influence text difficulty include:

'Top-down' factors

- topic familiarity, including background knowledge
- context familiarity
- cognitive complexity, eg density of information
- visual support, eg pictures, maps, diagrams, etc
- length
- layout and signposting
- organization of text
- internal cohesion, eg linking of sentences

'Bottom up' factors

- sentence length and complexity
- grammatical familiarity
- lexical familiarity and idiomaticity
- lexical density ∎

Classroom applications

However you define authenticity, there is little doubt that texts that come from genuine sources have a great many advantages in the language classroom. Not only do they offer the learner reliable data about the language, but they have a greater chance of capturing the learner's interest – and therefore attention – than fake or imitation texts. But, being ungraded, they are often less accessible than purpose-built texts. The challenge facing the teacher, then, is how to alleviate text difficulty. Various options are available and the choice of these will depend largely on the factors that make the text difficult in the first place, as well as on the classroom purposes for using the text.

We can divide possible approaches into those that involve adapting the text in some way (*text-adaptation strategies*) and those that involve designing appropriate tasks (*task-design strategies*).

Text-adaptation strategies

shortening

Cutting out unnecessary sections, and thereby reducing the length of the text, is one way of easing the processing load, but it is done at one's peril. If the editing threatens the overall coherence, eg by omitting a key stage in a narrative or argument, it will make the text harder, not easier.

segmenting

Dealing with the text in short sections, one at a time, can ease the processing load. A long article from a scientific journal, for example, might best be dealt with in sections: the abstract, the background, the research question, the method, etc. However, splitting the text between different readers (or listeners) who then interact to reconstruct the gist of the text (the so-called *jigsaw* technique) compounds reading or listening difficulty exponentially. For example, reading the

their knowledge. And *not* pre-teaching vocabulary will encourage learners to work out meaning from context. The amount of challenge you want to incorporate into a reading or listening task will depend on your assessment both of the text's difficulty and the learners' capacity to overcome any difficulties on their own. Either way, the factors that influence text difficulty (listed on page 116) provide a useful reference when considering how to calibrate text-based activities.

TAVI vs TALO

As we have seen, the main reason that texts like 6.1 (the Roger and David text) or 6.9 (the fake David Beckham text) are the way they are is because their primary purpose is not to inform or entertain us but rather to display features of the language that have been pre-selected for teaching purposes. The not-so-hidden agenda for the Roger and David text is to contrast present continuous and present simple. The fake-Beckham text is used to contrast present tense forms (*They have lived in their new home since April, They like watching TV on Saturday night*) and past tense forms (*They met after a football match*). When the aim is solely language display, then texts don't need to be true or interesting.

But there is the other – skills-development – reason for reading or listening to texts in the classroom. Learners need to become more efficient readers and listeners in their second language. Part of being an efficient reader/listener is having the capacity to extract information from a text, especially the information that you need or are interested in. It follows that learners need to hone their reading and listening skills by using texts that are truly informative and where the information is of a type that learners may be motivated to seek out. Hence, not only should learners be exposed to texts designed to display pre-selected language features, that is, *texts-as-linguistic-objects*, or TALOs, but they should also learn to cope with *texts-as-vehicles-of-information*, or TAVIs.

For the first purpose, ie TALO, it used to be thought that contrived texts of the Roger-and-David type would do. We now know that these kinds of texts tend not to be sufficiently representative of language 'as it is really used'. For the second purpose, ie TAVI, authentic texts were felt to offer the best training for real-life text processing. However, authentic texts, as we have seen, are often too difficult for learners to deal with, and rather than developing fluent reading or listening, they may actually inhibit it.

The solution? Combine the two purposes in the one text. The text can be simplified – in the interests of intelligibility – but also informative. Moreover, it can be re-jigged so as to include pre-selected language items. Or, better, it can be chosen because it *already* includes pre-selected language items. And the tasks that accompany the text can focus both on its content (ie TAVI-type tasks) and on its linguistic forms (TALO-type tasks).

Discovery activity 6.6   *How useful is the text?*

Here is a text from a contemporary coursebook[80]. It has been adapted from an authentic newspaper text. Assess its usefulness as both a *text-as-vehicle-for-information* (TAVI) and a *text-as-linguistic-object* (TALO). Design tasks that would support each of these purposes.

6.14

TINA I first met Will when I was looking for someone to share the house I was renting. I put an advertisement in the local student newspaper and he was one of the people who answered it. When we met, we hit it off straightaway and I told him he could move in.

Living with Will was fun. We soon found out that we had a lot in common and quickly became close friends. We always had really good discussions about everything that was important to us at the time: politics, the environment, literature and other less important things like cooking. We also liked the same music and that's important when you're sharing a house. We fell out a couple of times about the housework. Will thinks I'm untidy but I think life's too short to worry about things like that.

When we graduated three years ago, we went our separate ways and since then our lives have been very different. I went back to my home town and got a job as a production assistant for art exhibitions. I like my job because I'm helping young people to get involved in the arts. I'm living with my parents because I'm not earning very much. Will thinks I'm crazy because money is very important to him now, but I get a lot of personal satisfaction from my job. He's earning a lot of money, but he doesn't have time to spend with his family and his friends. I don't see him very often now. When he comes down for the weekend we have a laugh, but our lifestyles are so different now that we don't have very much to talk about.

WILL Tina and I got on very well together at university. When we first met, we clicked straightaway and we ended up sharing a house for nearly three years. We had the same attitude to the important things in life and the only thing we argued about was the housework. I'm a Virgo so I'm very tidy whereas Tina's the opposite. I don't think she ever found out where we kept the vacuum cleaner!

When I left university, I moved to London and got a job in a finance company. I have to work long hours and I don't really enjoy what I'm doing but I earn a very good salary. I'm very ambitious and I want to get to the top of my profession. I enjoy spending money on CDs, clothes, a nice car and going out to good restaurants. Tina's working really hard as well, but she's not earning much. I don't understand why she's doing it. I think she's having a holiday - it seems very idealistic to me. Anyway, it means that our lifestyles are very different now so we've drifted apart. We haven't fallen out or anything. We still talk on the phone and when I go down to visit her, we have a laugh. I know she'll always be there for me.

Commentary ■ ■ ■

As information, the text has general, human interest, but not a great deal more. Unless you know Tina and Will personally, there is not a lot here that you will be motivated to study intensively. Most readers, however, will find something to relate to, since the text documents a fairly universal aspect of the human condition, that is, the gradual detachment from one's former friends. Therefore, it has lots of potential as a springboard for generating learner text in the form of anecdotes, reminiscences, even letters. And the photos add faces to a text that would otherwise be a bit disembodied.

The photos are exploited in the coursebook pre-reading task, which aims to stimulate learners' curiosity in the text, by asking them to make predictions:

> Look at the photographs of Tina and Will. Do you think the following statements are true or false?
>
> a) Tina and Will had similar interests when they were at university.
> b) They chose similar careers when they finished their studies.
> c) They have similar lifestyles now.

Some students might respond, a little cynically perhaps, *How am I supposed to know?* but they will at least have a little more motivation for reading the text now than had it been simply 'served cold'.

The corrected version of the statements above could then usefully serve as a rubric for a closer reading of the text with a view to 'peeling' off further layers of meaning from it, but still treating it as a 'vehicle-of-information', ie TAVI. For example:

> What interests did Tina and Will share at university?
> How did their career paths differ?
> How are their lifestyles different now?

The text may not be gripping reading, but as a linguistic object it is extremely rich and exploitable. At the lexical level, the text is rich in language relating to the processes of getting to know someone and becoming friends: *we hit it off, we clicked, we … became close friends, we fell out, we've drifted apart,* etc. This is, in fact, the focus that the coursebook develops:

> Tina and Will use several expressions to talk about their friendship. Complete as many of these expressions as you can from memory. Compare them with a partner. Then look at the article again to check.
>
> a) Two expressions that mean 'we liked one another immediately'
>   *We clicked… We hit …*
>
>   etc.

There's also a fair bit of vocabulary relating to housing and domestic chores and to careers and lifestyle. And, because the essence of the text is a contrast between *then* and *now,* there is lots of opportunity for a contrastive tense focus, not only between past and present simple, but between past and present continuous (*the house I was renting, I'm helping young people*). Learners could be sent on a simple 'grammar hunt': find five statements about the past and five statements about the present. (This could be turned into a race, for more competitive-minded students.) Likewise, the hunt could be narrowed to continuous forms.

Apart from the continuous forms, there are also a variety of other uses of the *-ing* form: *Living with Will was fun… things like cooking… we ended up sharing… I enjoy spending money….* Again, learners could be set the task of finding all the *-ing* words and classifying them.

Even more interesting, perhaps, is the wide variety of uses of the verb *have:* as a lexical verb (*he doesn't have time, we don't have very much to talk about*)*;* as a de-lexical verb, ie part of a verb-plus-noun expression where the verbal meaning is expressed by the noun, such as *we have a laugh, we always had really good discussions;* as a modal verb (*I have to work long hours*) and as an auxiliary verb (*we haven't fallen out*). A task to draw attention to these different uses of *have* might be to ask learners to use the text to make their own *concordance.* That is, they search the text for examples of *had/have*, etc and organize them vertically, along with their immediate contexts:

> we **had** a lot in common
> we always **had** really good discussions
> our lives **have** been very different
> he doesn't **have** time to spend with his family
> we **have** a laugh
> we don't **have** very much to talk about
> I **have** to work long hours
> she's **having** a holiday

Learners can then attempt to classify the different uses of *have*. This kind of focus on the short, often overlooked, high-frequency words in a text is a particularly effective way of re-visiting 'old' grammar under the guise of vocabulary, and the discovery approach, using 'home-made' concordances, respects learners' ability to seek out patterns themselves. And, of course, any text can be used for this purpose, since any text will have a representative selection of high-frequency function words in it. ∎

Finding appropriate texts

I said above that, rather than re-writing a text to include targeted language items, it might be better if the texts were chosen because they *already* included such items. The integrity (even sanctity) of the text is not threatened, its authentic flavour is retained and, on top of that, the targeted item is displayed to best effect. This is because the fact that *text X* embeds *grammar item Y* is seldom a chance thing. As we saw in the discussion on genre, in order to realize their context-specific purposes, different kinds of texts encode distinctive clusterings and patterns of linguistic forms. The fact, for example, that the passive is used in an encyclopedia text, or that subject pronouns are ellipted (ie left out) of tea packet instructions, is not arbitrary. The choice of linguistic form is influenced by the genre. This means that, given a specific genre, it's normally possible to predict the specific language forms that will constitute it. And, vice versa: given a specific language form, it is often an easy matter to predict in which text types that form will be prominent. The predictability of this interrelationship between text and forms is a boon to course designers, in that it offers clues as to where to find exploitable texts and relieves them of the need to invent their own.

Discovery activity 6.7   *Choosing authentic texts*

In what kinds of texts would you expect to find the following language forms?

- comparative and superlative adjectives (such as *faster, best, most expensive*)
- prepositions of place (such as *in, behind, next to*)
- present tense with past reference
- intransitive verbs (ie verbs that don't take objects)

Commentary ■ ■ ■

Comparative and superlative adjectives, especially ones with positive connotations, are likely to occur in advertising texts. A quick scan of the ads in *Glamour* magazine[81], for example, threw up the following:

GQ THE MOST STYLISH MEN'S MAGAZINE IN THE WORLD	**It's a fact.** With Clarins, life's more beautiful.
It shaves you so close, your skin stays smoother, longer.	Now there's an easy way to enjoy a healthier lifestyle – with Twinings' Herbal and Fruit Infusions every day. Using only the finest ingredients and most experienced blenders, Twinings create tantalizing infusions of mouth-watering fruit flavours and healthy herbs…

Prepositions of place are bound to be fairly concentrated in instructions and directions (eg how to change the toner in a photocopier, how to reach a specific destination), as well as in descriptions of buildings, such as those found in guide books or in real estate advertisements. Here, for example, is an extract from a guide book[82], with the place prepositions underlined:

Talismán & Ciudad Hidalgo

The road <u>from</u> Tapachula heads 9km northeast <u>past</u> Izapa to the international border <u>at</u> Talismán bridge, <u>opposite</u> El Carmen, Guatemala. A branch south <u>off</u> the Talismán road leads <u>to</u> another cross-border bridge <u>at</u> Ciudad Tecún Umán. There are hotels and places to change money <u>at</u> both borders.

Present tense with past reference occurs in narrative genres of the *synopsis* type, eg descriptions of the plots of plays, operas and films; and in *jokes*, both spoken and written: *A sandwich goes into a bar, and the barman says, 'I'm sorry, we don't serve food here.'*

Finally, intransitive verbs often occur with significant frequency in texts that describe events or processes that aren't deliberately caused, or whose causes are best not mentioned, as in factual or scientific writing:

> The Earth <u>came</u> from a cloud in space. Scientists think the Earth <u>formed</u> from a huge cloud of gas and dust around 45000 million years ago. A star near the cloud <u>exploded</u>...[83]

> A war fought in many different parts of the world is known as a world war. The first, known as World War One, <u>broke out</u> in 1914 and <u>did not come to an end</u> until 1918. World War Two <u>broke out</u> in 1939 and <u>lasted</u> until 1945....[84]

Choosing texts that display grammar items in prototypical ways helps learners become familiar both with the text type (the genre) and with the specific grammar items themselves. ■

Text-based syllabuses

The interdependence of text and grammar suggests a more central role for texts in the design of language courses. Normally the process of course design begins with a list of pre-selected grammar items, such as *the past continuous, the second conditional, adverbs of frequency,* etc. Texts are then found – or created – that have these items embedded in them. Next, tasks are designed to exploit the texts as *texts* (TAVI-type tasks) and to tease out their language features (TALO-type tasks). The process can be summarized like this:

design grammar syllabus → write or find texts → design tasks

An alternative, more radical, approach to course design is to start not with the grammar items, but with the *texts.* Texts are selected and then analysed for their characteristic language features. These features are then taught not as entities in themselves, but as components of the high-order structures of language, ie texts. The process of course design can be represented like this:

find texts → extract grammar syllabus → design tasks

Such an approach prioritizes texts over grammar and targets only the grammar that is necessary to produce and interpret particular texts. But what is the rationale for text-driven course design? One argument is that, as one scholar put it, 'Language always happens as text, not as isolated words and sentences.'[85] That is to say, people use language not to trade grammatical structures back and forth, but to produce coherent text – both spoken and written. A knowledge of discrete items of grammar is no guarantee that learners can produce whole texts. Whereas a familiarity with whole texts does entail some kind of grammar competence – not as an end, but as a means.

Moreover, the meaning and use of many grammar and vocabulary items are simply not inferable at the level of the sentence. (The use of the words *whereas* and *does* in the last sentence of the preceding paragraph is a case in point.) By basing a course on texts rather than sentences, it is argued that teaching and learning are more firmly grounded and have a better chance of success.

A text-based course is particularly suited to learners whose textual needs can be clearly identified, for example, a group of learners preparing to study a specific subject at an English-speaking university. Or a group that has to interpret instruction manuals for the machinery that their company has invested in. Where specific purposes can be identified, a text-based syllabus would seem to be the direct route, as opposed to the scenic, grammar-based, one.

Even with general English it's not impossible to imagine a text-driven course where texts are selected and graded on the basis of such criteria as:

- frequency: how common is this text type?
- usefulness: how likely is it that the learner will need to produce or interpret this text type?
- difficulty: how difficult are texts of this type, on the whole?

So long as the range of text types chosen is sufficiently broad, including both spoken and written ones, and the example texts are sufficiently representative, then learners should be getting all the grammar they are likely to need. They will also be getting exposure to all the text types they are likely to meet. With a purely grammar-driven syllabus, however, such a wide-ranging exposure to different kinds of texts occurs accidentally, if at all.

As I said, such an approach represents a radical departure from conventional course design and it may simply not be feasible in contexts where a traditional grammar syllabus is imposed from above. Even so, teachers may still be able to select their own texts, or some of them. In which case, they should at least try to select texts that not only meet the syllabus requirements – by embedding instances of the target grammar, for example – but that also expose learners to a range of different text types and of topics, so that the chances of incidental learning are maximized. Moreover, if the texts are at least notionally relevant to the learners' own needs, experiences and interests, there is a better chance, perhaps, that they will engage with these texts in ways that encourage a deeper level of language processing.

Discovery activity 6.8   *Text types*

The following list of text types comes from the *Common European Framework of Reference for Languages (CEF)*, a document that provides exhaustive descriptions of what is involved in language mastery. Examine the coursebook you are using or one that you are familiar with. Which of these text types are represented?

Spoken, eg:
public announcements and instructions
public speeches, lectures, presentations, sermons
rituals (ceremonies, formal religious services)
entertainment (drama, shows, readings, songs)
sports commentaries (football, cricket, boxing, horse-racing, etc)
news broadcasts
public debates and discussion
interpersonal dialogues and conversations
telephone conversations
job interviews

Written, eg:
books, fiction and non-fiction, including literary journals
magazines
newspapers
instruction manuals (DIY, cookbooks, etc)
textbooks
comic strips
brochures, prospectuses

leaflets
advertising material
public signs and notices
supermarket, shop, market stall signs
packaging and labelling on goods
tickets, etc
forms and questionnaires
dictionaries (monolingual and bilingual), thesauri
business and professional letters, faxes
personal letters
essays and exercises
memoranda, reports and papers
notes and messages, etc
databases (news, literature, general information, etc).

Commentary ■ ■ ■

On the whole, coursebooks include a fairly narrow range of text types. Most listening texts are of the 'interpersonal dialogues and conversations' type, fleshed out with telephone conversations and service encounters (oddly, not included in the *CEF* list). Longer, monologue-type texts, such as lectures and presentations, are rare. As for written texts, many contemporary coursebooks now favour magazine-article-type texts, probably on the grounds that these are intrinsically more interesting than, say, brochures and prospectuses. However, the rather restricted register of coursebook texts, and their ephemeral nature, has come under criticism. One writer, for example, decries the current fashion for 'coursebook-as-magazine' and suggests 'returning to books and good writing as a source of language texts that are deeply rewarding to read'[86].

Although books written for more specialized markets, such as business English, usually have a more representative range of text types, the range offered by general English courses is relatively limited. ■

Classroom applications

Whether or not you adopt a text-driven syllabus, the ability to exploit texts both as *texts* (ie as vehicles of information) and as *linguistic objects* will stand you in good stead. For a start, you will be developing learners' text-attack skills, such as how to work out word meaning from context, or how to infer the writer's point of view. And you will also be raising awareness about the linguistic features of the text: its grammar, vocabulary, cohesive devices, and so on. Also, the ability to exploit a text thoroughly can save lesson preparation time, in that one text can form the basis for a whole lesson, providing both a grammar and a vocabulary focus, as well as practice in a variety of skills. And, as we saw in Chapter 1, the text doesn't have to be long in order to yield a *lot* of grammar. In fact, the advantage of short texts is that they require less processing, allowing more time for language focus and subsequent practice.

Discovery activity 6.9   *Exploiting authentic texts*

Here, for example, is a short authentic text[87]. How could you exploit this text, at an elementary level, to productively fill an hour's lesson?

6.15

How to recycle a goat

Give a widowed mother a goat.

The widow gives a goat back.

The goat produces milk.

The widow keeps a goat.

Her children don't go hungry.

The goat produces more goats.

The goat produces manure.

The widow sells more crops.

Commentary ■ ■ ■

There are many possible ways that this text could be used in class, both from a linguistic and a language skills perspective. With regard to the former, the least interesting aspect of the text (for me) is the use of the present simple. I'm assuming that learners at this level will have had plenty of exposure to it and will not need (another) full-blown presentation. Nor is its use here typical, in that it describes single events, narrative style, rather than routine habits. So, in the ideas that follow, I have chosen not to pay it much attention. More interesting are the verb patterns, especially the two-object verb *give*, and the use of articles. So I have selected these for the language focus.

Here, then, is my lesson (bearing in mind that this is just one of many possible lessons):

1 **Warm-up**
   Give the class instructions which they have to act out. For example,
   José, give Pilar a pen.
   Marina, can you pass Sergio the dictionary, please?
   Sergio, hand Juan the dictionary.
   Pilar, give José back his pen.

   Teach them to say *Here you are* or *There you go*, as they hand the objects over and *Thank you* as they receive them.

   The verbs *give, pass, hand, give back* are written on the board. Students then take turns to give one another similar instructions.

2 **Schema activation**
   Ask the class: what would be the single most useful thing you could give to a widowed mother in an African village? (Take time to explain the meaning of *widowed.*) Let the class discuss this in small groups and then present their ideas, including their reasons. Alternatively, provide a list of items and ask them either to choose an item, or to rank them in terms of usefulness, eg

a bicycle
a tractor
a radio
a goat
a fruit tree
a laptop
a mobile phone
a husband

3 Text: first contact

Learners read the text (6.15) silently, using dictionaries. Their initial task is to decide what kind of text it is. Is it a story? Is it a poem? Is it a news article? They compare their ideas with classmates.

4 Response to text

Establish the text type. (It comes from a charity brochure, appealing for donations.) Ask the class what they think of the idea and provide the following expressions so that they can tell their classmates what they think:
It's a good/nice idea.
I like it.
Yes, but…
What happens if…?
I don't understand this bit…
Can you/anyone explain…?
What does this mean?

5 Text: closer reading

Ask the following questions, one at a time; learners scan the text for answers and write the answers down, then compare.
What does the mother get?
What three things does the goat produce?
What does the mother do with the milk?
What is the manure good for?
What happens to the baby goats?

6 Text: reconstruction

Learners turn the text over and from memory, fill in the gaps:

Give a widowed mother a goat.
The goat produces _____ .
Her _____ don't go hungry.
The goat _____ manure.
The _____ sells more crops.
The goat produces more _____ .
The widow _____ a goat.
The widow gives a goat _____ .

7 Language focus: articles

Again, without looking, learners complete the gaps with either *the* or *a*.

Give _____ widowed mother _____ goat.
_____ goat produces milk.
Her children don't go hungry.
_____ goat produces manure.
_____ widow sells more crops.

———— goat produces more goats.
———— widow keeps ———— goat.
———— widow gives ———— goat back.

Ask learners what they think the rule is. They can then test their understanding
of the rule using this text (which could be dictated):

Last night I felt like seeing ———— film. I bought ———— ticket. I put ————
ticket in my pocket. Then I met ———— friend outside ———— cinema. He
didn't have ———— ticket so I bought another one. Unfortunately, ———— film
was not very good.

8 Language focus: verb patterns
Write the following grid on the board:

1	2	3	4	5
Give	a	widowed hungry	mother child	a goat some food

Using dictionaries, learners work together to think of more words that could go
into columns 3, 4 and 5.

They read out their sentences and comment on them, using prompts such as:
Why? – Because…
That's an interesting idea.
What does … mean?

9 Writing
Learners work in pairs to produce a brochure (like *How to Recycle a Goat*). They
write a text of at least six sentences. The following sentences are written on the
board, as possible ideas, but learners are also invited to think of their own.

Give a lonely person a mobile phone.
Give an unemployed youth a bicycle.
Give a smart child a dictionary.
Give a poor family a garden.
Give a disabled person a laptop.
Give a homeless person $10.

They then read each others' texts and decide which one makes the best
campaign.

10 Listening and speaking
Tell a short anecdote about something that you were given that proved really
useful, or totally useless. Ask learners to think of similar stories of their own and
provide prompts on the board:

Once, someone gave me a …
It was the best/strangest/worst present.
It is (not) very …
I love/don't like/hate it.
I keep it in/under/on…
I use/wear/put/ it …

Learners tell their stories in small groups and volunteers tell their story (or their
classmate's story) to the class.

For homework, they can write up their, or a classmate's, story.

Conclusion

Texts have always been an integral part of language learning, but the purposes for which they are used, and hence their nature, have changed over the years. Generally, they serve one of two main purposes:

- as contexts for pre-selected language items
- as material for skills development.

The two purposes can, of course, be combined in the same text, in which case tasks need to be devised that target one purpose or the other. And for both purposes authentic texts have many advantages: they provide attested, as opposed to invented, contexts for language study and they provide more realistic preparation for subsequent out-of-classroom text encounters. They are not without their problems, however, not the least being their potential difficulty. But with a little ingenuity these difficulties can often be overcome. The texts themselves can be adapted without sacrificing all of their more exploitable features; and the tasks that are designed to mediate these texts can be selected and sequenced so as to get the most out of them. When texts are thoroughly exploited both for their informational content and their linguistic features, there is a case for proposing a text-based syllabus, that is, a syllabus where texts are the central organizing feature and not just an add-on. Even when this is not possible, texts should be chosen that not only demonstrate the 'structure of the day' but that can be used for a range of purposes, not the least being to 'turn up the heat' in the classroom and thereby (to paraphrase a famous marketing campaign slogan that was used to sell beer) 'to reach the parts that other texts do not'.

One kind of text that demands a level of engagement deeper than that demanded by more traditional classroom texts is the literary text, and that is the focus of the next chapter.

Chapter 7 **Literary texts and loaded texts**

Literary texts

In the last chapter a contrast was made between, on the one hand, texts whose main function is to display language items, and, on the other, informative texts, those that are 'vehicles-of-information'. Most of this book has been concerned, so far, with one or the other. But of course there is a whole class of texts that are intended neither to display nor to inform, but whose function is primarily expressive. These are literary texts. What exactly distinguishes literary texts from non-literary ones?

Discovery activity 7.1   *Literary texts*

Here are some texts. Which would you classify as literature – and why?

7.1

> **The dream is green**
> You wear our memories like a cloak:
> bedecked with flowers in spring
> and the summer dew
> bestrewn with gold in the fall
> and the winter frost.
> You spread yourself beneath our dreams
> like a carpet:
> our kid's games and our poolside barbecues
> and weekend picnics and the days of rest.
> You celebrate us.
> We nurture you.
> Green. You are the dream.

7.2

> **Leave-taking**
> *He took her hand. She took his money.*
> *He took a lover.*
> *She took exception. He took leave of his senses. She took advice. He took*
>   *fright.*
> *She took him to the cleaner's. He took to drink.*
> *She took a holiday.*
> *He took his life.*
> *She took up ballroom dancing.*

7.3

The Rainbow
Even the rainbow has a body
made of the drizzling rain
and is an architecture of glistening atoms
built up, built up
yet you can't lay your hand on it,
nay, nor even your mind.

7.4

The elderly passenger sitting on the north-window side of that inexorably moving railway coach, next to an empty seat and facing two empty ones, was none other than Professor Timofey Pnin. Ideally bald, sun-tanned and clean-shaven, he began rather impressively with that great brown dome of his, tortoise-shell glasses (masking an infantile absence of eyebrows), apish upper lip, thick neck and strong-man torso in a tightish tweed coat, but ended, somewhat disappointingly, in a pair of spindly legs (now flannelled and crossed) and frail-looking, almost feminine feet...

7.5

CHERYL COMES BACK IN.

Barbara   Ahhh Cheryl, congratulations!
Denise   I'm dead, dead, dead pleased for you.
Cheryl   Thanks, everyone.
Michelle   What's all this about?
Barbara   Ah well, Cheryl went to see a clairvoyant yesterday and she said she'd find true love in two days, two weeks, two months or two years.
Michelle   Who told you this, Cheryl?
Cheryl   Gemini Astrid, up the precinct.
Michelle   Gemini Astrid?
Cheryl   Yeah.
Michelle   For three quid?
Cheryl   Yeah.
Michelle   She talks complete bollocks, she does, love, I'd take no notice.
Barbara   Oh Cheryl. You'd found love and now you've lost it.
Mary   Better to have loved and lost then never to have loved at all.
Barbara   Yeah.
Cheryl   Yeah.
BIG PAUSE.

Commentary ■ ■ ■

Although they differ widely, these texts are clearly not simply transactional: they do not serve merely to trade information, goods or services. Rather, and to varying degrees, they use language expressively, imaginatively and sometimes playfully. One or two are obviously very carefully crafted: they display a high degree of conscious artifice and a deliberate use of sometimes rare or abstruse language. There are several instances of language 'drawing attention to itself', through the use, for instance, of repetition, or the way the text is laid out on the page. And there are cases where the language seems to be saying one thing but meaning another – where the meaning is not *literal*, but has to be inferred. In that sense, they are all *literary* in style, although some are perhaps more literary than others. Let's look at them individually.

Text 7.1 is about a colour, green, but the colour is given agency: it wears our memories like a cloak, and it spreads itself like a carpet. Clearly, the text is not literally true, but is in some way *metaphorical*: the effect of green is *like* an animated cloak or carpet. Metaphorical use of language is, of course, associated with poetry. But is Text 7.1 a poem? It is laid out like one, and there is a kind of rhythmic repetition of elements (called *parallelism*), such as:

> *bedecked with flowers in spring*
> *and the summer dew*
> *bestrewn with gold in the fall*
> *and the winter frost.*

But is it poetry? You may have your suspicions. The inclusive use of *our* and *we*, for a start, seems odd. The writer seems to be speaking not just to, but on behalf of, the reader. Moreover, the definite article *the* in *the dream* implies that the writer and reader share knowledge of what that dream is. In short, the writer is not detached and introspective, as might be expected in lyric verse, but is complicit with the reader in the expression of a – let's admit – rather trite sentiment. Don't we feel that, just perhaps, this complicity only thinly disguises the fact that we are being sold something?

In fact, the text comes from a magazine advertisement for lawn fertilizer, and the design of the advertisement leaves no doubt that it is the *American* dream that is being invoked. Having a nice green lawn is a part of that dream, is the message.

The use of the conventions of literary language in advertising is, of course, not uncommon. Think of the playful use of rhyme in slogans like *Beanz Meanz Heinz*. But the fact that advertising co-opts features of literary style does not make it literature. As one researcher noted, 'Ads are a parasite discourse which has attached itself to literary discourse (among other types) as a host.'[88] Nevertheless, ads can be productively used when highlighting features of literary style, especially by comparing them to and contrasting them with, the 'real thing'. For example, here is a 'real' poem about grass[89]. Like the 'green' text, it also humanizes an inanimate object and uses parallelism and direct repetition to create its effects. But its voice is not the adman's, trying to cosy up to us. Nor does the sub-text extol the American dream. Quite the contrary:

7.6

> **Grass**
> *Pile the bodies high at Austerlitz and Waterloo.*
> *Shovel them under and let me work –*
> > *I am the grass; I cover all.*
>
> *And pile them high at Gettysburg*
> *And pile them high at Ypres and Verdun.*
> *Shovel them under and let me work.*
>
> *Two years, ten years and passengers ask the conductor:*
> > *What place is this?*
> > *Where are we now?*
>
> > *I am the grass.*
> > *Let me work.*   *Carl Sandburg*

Text 7.2 bears a strong similarity to language teaching texts, in that one linguistic feature (the verb *take*) is prominent to an almost absurd degree. Compare it, for example, with text 6.1 in Chapter 6. Yet it's not uncommon for literary texts, too, to exaggerate a single linguistic feature, whether a sound or a word or a phrase, in order to create an insistent, rhythmic effect. Take, for example, the beginning of a poem by Allen Ginsberg[90]:

7.7

> *America I've given you all and now I'm nothing –*
> *America when will we end the war?*
> *America when will you be angelic?*
> *America when will you take off your clothes and be human?*
> *America when will you give me back my mother?*
> *America when will you give me back my love? …*

In other ways as well, text 7.2 has literary attributes. It tells a story and the story is self-contained. One way that non-literary texts are often distinguished from literary ones is that, while the former make connections with our social world and practices – they are situated and contingent – literature creates a disassociated and self-contained world of its own. Text 7.2 makes no reference to known people, nor actual events nor even places. There is nothing to suggest that it is a true story. It is probably pure invention and the persistent use of *took* underscores its inventiveness. In that sense it aspires to the literary. On the other hand, its inventiveness is a little self-conscious: a bit too clever by half. Whereas Ginsberg's use of repetition creates an effect that is like a prayer or an incantation, the repetition of *take* in text 7.2 is like nothing other than an exercise or a word-game. Could it have been an entry in a competition?

Indeed it could. It was a prize-winning entry in a British newspaper's regular 'mini-saga' feature. [91] A mini-saga is a story of exactly 50 words: no more no less. So popular was the competition that, as the writer Victoria Glendinning comments, 'The mini-saga is here to stay and is all set to join the limerick and the haiku as one of those short, apparently easy, but actually pretty tricky, literary forms that catches everyone's imagination.' Granting the mini-saga literary status may be premature: even the novel had to wait a long time before it was admitted into the select group of genres that constitute Literature. But as literature with a small *l*, the mini-saga has certainly a greater claim than advertising copy. Nor does the 50-word 'rule' disqualify the mini-saga: many other literary genres, such as the sonnet, have similarly highly constraining rules.

More interestingly, for our purposes, is the mini-saga's utility in the language classroom. Its brevity allows it to be exploited in various ways in the course of a lesson. The example I have chosen (text 7.2) could be used first as the basis of a reading task: learners can use dictionaries to 'unpack' all the different meanings of *take* and write a more transparent version *not* using the verb *take*, e.g. *He became an alcoholic* instead of *He took to drink*. They could then 'interview' the woman, as a form of role play, to get her version of events. And they could then write their own mini-sagas, based around another high-frequency verb, such as *go*, or *make*, or *do*.

Text 7.3 is a late poem by D. H. Lawrence (1885–1930) and qualifies therefore as 'capital L' literature. As a poem it shares some of the poetic features of text 7.1, including the layout, some instances of repetition (*built up, built up*) and some internal half-rhymes (*drizzling, glistening*). But instead of appealing to an inclusive *we*, it uses the informal but impersonal *you* to make a general statement that represents the poet's introspective thoughts. It is not trying to sell us anything, nor even change us particularly, apart from making us think. And the statement that it makes, like its subject, the rainbow, is itself elusive, so that you 'can't lay your hand on it'. The poem is about the rainbow, but about something else too. The first word, *even*, suggests a prior idea, of which the rainbow is being advanced as further proof. Try taking away that *even*: the poem still makes perfect sense, but we are no longer compelled to look beyond the poem, to search for an idea with which the rainbow correlates. The poem loses some of its mystery. And that is a very literary 'trick': that a poem about mystery should itself be mysterious. It is also a quality of (good) literature that texts don't surrender their (multiple) meanings without a struggle. Compare this to the trite didactic tone of the advertising text (7.1). The Lawrence poem simply suggests, and leaves it up to the reader to fill in the gaps. That may be another feature of good literature: its economy. It is the unsaid that is as important as what is said. Only by hinting at something can there be resonance.

However, in this case there *are* clues beyond the text. As one literary critic has noted, 'Lawrence's poems are less framed and finished products than fragments of a larger discourse. Images circulate from one poem to another, one poem flows into another or acts as raw material for it, and the whole process is criss-crossed by resonances, redundancies, repetitions.'[92] The poem that precedes 'The Rainbow' in my edition of Lawrence's poems is called 'The Body of God' and begins 'God is the great urge that has not yet found a body...' In the light of this, the *even* that begins 'The Rainbow' starts to reach out and take root, making a connection to the 'larger discourse' about the insubstantiality of God. We shouldn't forget, either, that Lawrence wrote a novel called *The Rainbow*, at the end of which the heroine, contemplating the bleak industrial landscape of the north of England, sees a rainbow begin to form in the sky:

> She saw in the rainbow the earth's new architecture, the old, brittle corruption of houses and factories swept away, the world built up in a living fabric of Truth, fitting to the over-arching heaven.

Note that, in both the novel and the poem, Lawrence describes the rainbow as *architecture* and uses the verb *built up*. Only in the novel, though, is the connection between *architecture* and the rainbow's *arch* made explicit.

This characteristic of literary texts – to connect to a larger discourse – is called *intertextuality*. Sometimes the connection is explicit, as when a writer quotes directly from another text. The poem that follows 'The Rainbow' begins:

> *The man of Tyre went down to the sea*
> *pondering, for he was a Greek, that God is one and all alone and ever more shall be so.*

Many readers of these lines will recognize the phrase *[One] is one and all alone and ever more shall be so* as forming part of the refrain of a traditional English song (which has the, possibly unintended, effect of trivializing the Greek's theological reflections).

Often, intertextual references are veiled, taking the form of puns, for example. This is a characteristic of many newspaper headlines in English, such as *The Blame In Spain*, a headline that appeared in *The Guardian* about troubled relations between Britain and Spain and which makes reference to the song *The rain in Spain*. An article about Stradivarius, the violin maker, was titled *Lord of the Strings*, coinciding with the success of the film version of Tolkein's *Lord of the Rings*. Or texts reflect the *structure* of other texts: *genres* are a product of intertextuality, as, over time, writers replicate the structural features of particular texts until they become institutionalized. Reading a limerick, for example, we are reminded of all the other limericks we have read. Indeed, one critic, Bakhtin, has suggested that *all* language use is intertextual and that *all* texts contain echoes of the texts that preceded them.

As a feature of literary texts, intertexuality will prove elusive to many second language learners, who may lack knowledge of the shared background, both cultural and linguistic, with which the text interconnects. But intertextuality is also a feature of literature that lends itself to classroom exploitation: simply put two related texts together and ask learners to make the connections. Whatever connections are made, the process of seeking them out will encourage a closer than normal reading of the texts.

Text 7.4 is the opening of a novel, *Pnin*[93], by the naturalized US writer, Vladimir Nabokov. The elaborateness of the description, including the choice of many uncommon words (*inexorably, infantile, apish, spindly*), identifies this as distinctively literary. The text conveys a great deal more than would be necessary, in normal circumstances, to identify the person being described. In fact, an interesting exercise for learners would be to re-cast the text in the form of a non-literary text type, such as a 'missing persons notice':

> **MISSING**
> Timofey Pnin (Professor)
> Elderly; bald, clean-shaven, tanned complexion, wears glasses; thick-set.
> Last seen wearing tweed coat and flannel trousers.

What makes the literary version distinctive is the *point of view*. Pnin is being observed in minute detail by an anonymous narrator who is not even physically present at the scene: note the empty seats and the use of the distancing determiner *that* in *that inexorably moving railway coach*, as if we were seeing it all from a long way off. This disembodied narrator's voice is both detached and ironic. His lack of involvement is underscored by the use of the modifiers *rather* and *somewhat*. The passenger is *none other than* Professor Pnin, perhaps a little dig at the character's sense of self-importance. He is described as *beginning* and *ending*, which has faintly comical overtones: people, after all, don't normally begin and end. But these verbs are consistent with a description that is all about externals: we have no idea as to what is going on inside Pnin's head.

But we know a lot about what is going on in the *writer's* head. The description is thick with evaluations (*ideally, impressively, disappointingly*) – all the *writer's* evaluations, note, not the subject's. Pnin is being both observed and judged and is, of course, blissfully unaware of the fact. Note also how the description mirrors the person described, beginning sonorously with the *great brown dome* and ending lamely with a fizz of fricatives: *flannelled, frail-looking, feminine*. The use of language that, through its actual shape or sound, *means* what it describes is called *iconicity* and is yet another feature of literary texts. In an earlier novel, *Lolita*, Nabokov celebrates the iconic nature of the protagonist's name:

> Lolita, light of my life, fire of my loins. My sin, my soul. Lo-lee-ta: the tip of the tongue taking a trip of three steps down the palate to tap, at three, on the teeth. Lo. Lee. Ta.
>
> She was Lo, plain Lo, in the morning, standing four feet ten in one sock. She was Lola in slacks. She was Dolly at school. She was Dolores on the dotted line. But in my arms she was always Lolita.

In the extract from *Pnin*, the wry detachment of the observer, coupled with the caricatured nature of the observation, seems to be setting the protagonist up for some kind of unexpected downfall. This expectation is reinforced by our familiarity with narrative texts in general, in which circumstantial information (characters and setting) typically presage a complicating event. (At this point, if you were using this text in class, you could ask learners what they think is about to happen. This is always a good strategy, as it both directs attention to the narrator's technique and encourages more active, engaged, reading.)

Sure enough, a paragraph later, we read:

> Now a secret must be imparted. Professor Pnin was on the wrong train…

Pnin is not only oblivious to 'us' observing him, but is oblivious to his fate. Again, we hear the arch, ironic voice of the god-like narrator: not *I must tell you a secret*, but the agentless passive and the rather portentous choice of verb: *a secret must be imparted*. The choice of the modal verb *must* is also significant. Compare this, for example, with *a secret will be imparted*. *Must* implies some kind of moral obligation. The writer is deferring to the reader's 'right to know' what is going on, even if Pnin himself has no right to know. The writer and the reader are sharing the joke at Pnin's expense. This capacity of writers – both to adopt a point of view and to situate the reader in relation to this point of view – is an extremely potent one and we will return to it in the section on ideology below. Meanwhile, as a point of comparison, it's worth contrasting the description of Pnin with another description, also of a person on a train, and also in the first chapter of a novel (*Mr Norris Changes Trains* by Christoper Isherwood). Note how the narrator's point of view differs from the one adopted by Nabokov's narrator:

7.8

> My first impression was that the stranger's eyes were of an unusually light blue. […] He had a large blunt fleshy nose and a chin which seemed to have slipped sideways. It was like a broken concertina. When he spoke, it jerked crooked in the most curious fashion and a deep cleft dimple like a wound surprisingly appeared in the side of it. Above his ripe red cheeks, his forehead was sculpturally white, like marble. A queerly cut fringe of dark grey hair lay across it, compact, thick and heavy. After a moment's examination, I realized, with extreme interest, that he was wearing a wig.

The most obvious difference with *Pnin* is that here the point of view is that of a first-person narrator who is physically present in the situation he is describing. Nouns like *impression* and *examination* and verbs like *seemed* and *realized* all attest to the physical and cognitive processes of looking, absent in the Nabokov extract. Moreover, the observer is not just observing from a distance, but doing so from close up and with *extreme interest*. This is reflected in the adverbs and adjectives he chooses: *unusually, most curious, surprisingly, queerly*. We get the sense of the narrator as an involved, engaged participant in the encounter, his gaze flitting from feature to feature, gathering a series of somewhat disconnected impressions in real time: *my first impression... when he spoke... after a moment's examination....* This cumulative, rather 'cubist' approach to description is reflected both in the similes he chooses: *like a broken concertina, like a wound, like marble*, and the highly contrastive colours: *blue, red, white, dark grey*. (Curiously, in another of his 'Berlin novels' Isherwood described his narrative technique in these terms: 'I am a camera with its shutter open, quite passive, recording, not thinking...' In fact, he is anything but passive, and his thought processes are much more easily read than Nabokov's all-knowing but inscrutable narrator.)

In short, apart from the fact that both Pnin and Mr Norris border on the grotesque, and that both descriptions end in bathos, they could not be more different. These two extracts demonstrate how writers of literary texts, like directors of films, can manipulate point of view to create a diverse range of effects. One of the most crucial of these effects is whether we, as readers, are positioned to view the events through the eyes of one of the participants, or through those of a detached narrator. This in turn can have an important influence on how we interpret what we are reading or listening to.

Text 7.5 is an extract from a television comedy series, *The Royle Family*[94], which charts the fairly uneventful lives of a working class family in the north of England. Because it is popular entertainment, purists might discount it as literature altogether, or classify it as a *sub-literary* form. But it does have many, if not all, of the defining features of 'high' drama, including plot, characterization and dialogue. And it creates a self-enclosed world, one that closely *parallels* the real world, but where the characters are slightly more exaggerated and where the events are 'tidied up' in order to bring out their humour or pathos. Thus, the incident where Cheryl's expectations of finding true love are dashed, has a beginning, a middle and an end, whereas in real life it probably would not be so neatly packaged. And the characters are 'types': we recognize (and perhaps identify with) Cheryl's credulity and Michelle's cynicism, and we can laugh at (because we recognize) Mary's misguided attempt to console Cheryl (her daughter) with the platitude: *Better to have loved and lost then never to have loved at all.* (The irony is, of course, that Cheryl *hasn't* loved.) Despite this 'tidying up' of characters and events, the language which the characters use has many of the qualities of naturally occurring language – qualities we looked at in Chapter 4. Part of the skill of the dialogue writing is in the way it mirrors vernacular language use, as in:

> She talks complete bollocks, she does, love, I'd take no notice.

It is *like* real speech, but we know it's *not* real speech. Features of casual conversation – such as its elliptic and often inconsequential nature – have been accentuated, as they are in the plays of Harold Pinter, for example. But whereas in Pinter's plays the effect is often sinister, in *The Royle Family* it is gently mocking. In short, this is a text that doesn't directly *refer* to the real world, but *re-presents* it. The distinction between (non-literary) *referential* texts and (literary) *representational* ones, is one that is frequently made in the study of literary discourse. ■

To sum up, then, characteristics of literary texts include the following:

- Language is used expressively, ie to express feelings, emotions.
- Language is used playfully, ie forms are chosen and repeated purely for their effect.
- Language is used iconically, ie forms are chosen because their form is (part of) their meaning.
- Language is used imaginatively, to conjure up alternative worlds, or, put another way, texts re-present reality, rather than simply referring to it.
- Language is used metaphorically, ie to say one thing in terms of another, and because of this literary texts are meaningful on different levels.
- The point of view of the writer may be detached or involved, and this in turn affects the way the reader interprets the text, eg as irony, as matter-of-fact, etc.
- The text's meaning is partly intertextual, ie the text may only be fully understood by reference to other, related, texts.
- Texts conform to, and are constrained by, certain generic features; very broadly they can be classed as poetry, prose, or drama.
- Texts are often highly valued by the culture, at least in the case of 'literature with a capital L'.

Of course, any of these characteristics may be shared by other, non-literary, kinds of texts. We have seen how advertising discourse makes expressive and playful use of language. And there are certain other types of texts – such as inspiring political speeches of which Martin Luther King's 'I have a dream' speech is an example – that are highly valued without necessarily being classed as literature. Moreover, literary texts are no different from non-literary texts in many fundamental respects. There is the expectation that they will make sense, and to this end they exhibit internal cohesion. Take the Lawrence poem, text 7.3, for example:

> Even the rainbow has a body
> made of the drizzling rain
> and is an architecture of glistening atoms
> built up, built up
> yet you can't lay your hand on it,
> nay, nor even your mind.

Here cohesion is achieved by exactly the same means that non-literary texts achieve cohesion: through the use of lexical chains (*rainbow… drizzling rain; body… atoms; architecture… built up; hand… mind*); the use of conjuncts and other discourse markers (*and, yet, nay*); pronoun reference (*lay your hand on it*), verb tense consistency (*has, is, can't*); parallelism (*you can't lay your hand on it [and you can't lay] your mind [on it]*); and ellipsis (*and [it] is an architecture…; nor even [can you lay] your mind [on it]*). All this in the short space of 35 words!

The poem – like all texts – has an *architecture* that is *built up*. The difference between the poem and other, more mundane, texts is that it is harder to 'lay your mind on it'. But, apart from whatever local difficulties they present, there is no reason why literary texts cannot also be used, alongside non-literary texts, as effective vehicles for highlighting such textual features as cohesion, discourse organization and grammar and vocabulary use.

So, do literary texts have any advantages over non-literary ones, from a teaching point of view? And do they require a different approach?

There are at least five reasons for using literary texts in the classroom:

1 **Variety** – they provide exposure to other kinds of texts and language functions, especially those not covered by the more utilitarian text types associated with work, studies, obtaining services, etc, and they provide an antidote to the kind of ephemeral, magazine-type, texts that are now the norm in most coursebooks (and which were criticized in the last chapter).

2 **Language awareness** – since literary texts are also authentic texts, they offer instances of real language use and therefore qualify, like any other authentic texts, as useful sources for raising language awareness (although it would be a shame if they were used *only* for this purpose).

3 **Challenge and skill** – being generally more difficult than non-literary texts, they raise the level of challenge and they help train learners in the more interpretative kinds of text processing skills, such as inferencing (reading between the lines), identifying the writer's point of view, etc.

4 **Pleasure** – since literary texts are originally designed to entertain and give pleasure, this purpose should not be lost or ignored in the classroom; moreover, helping learners to appreciate literary texts in the classroom may motivate them to further reading outside the classroom.

5 **Cultural knowledge** – literary texts typically encode a lot of cultural knowledge about the society that both produced and values the texts and therefore they offer a source of such knowledge for those learners who may be interested in integrating into the culture, or at least understanding other texts produced by that culture.

Discovery activity 7.2   *How is the approach to using literary texts different?*

Let's look at the Carl Sandburg poem again. Imagine you plan to use this in the classroom. How might your use of it be similar to – or different from – the approach used for the Christian Aid brochure in Chapter 6 (see page 128)?

> **Grass**
> *Pile the bodies high at Austerlitz and Waterloo.*
> *Shovel them under and let me work –*
> *   I am the grass; I cover all.*
>
> *And pile them high at Gettysburg*
> *And pile them high at Ypres and Verdun.*
> *Shovel them under and let me work.*
>
> *Two years, ten years and passengers ask the conductor:*
> *   What place is this?*
> *   Where are we now?*
> *   I am the grass.*
> *   Let me work.*

Commentary ■ ■ ■

Essentially there needn't be any major differences between the approach to using non-literary texts and the approach to using literary ones. However, you might have to work harder at the *pre-text* stage, providing any helpful background knowledge (including cultural and biographical information) and you might have to intervene more at the *comprehending* stage, ie the stage where learners are attempting to construct a coherent mental *schema* of the text. What is important (as with non-literary texts) is that at some point you should solicit the learners' *response* to the text, including their feelings about it: did they find it moving, funny, difficult, thought-provoking, etc? And why or why not? At some point, and especially if the text is a poem, learners should be given the opportunity of hearing the text read aloud. Often, because of such factors as *iconicity,* for example, the text doesn't properly come alive until it is heard. ■

Classroom applications

A possible sequence of activities based around Sandburg's 'Grass' (and one that closely mirrors the lesson plan in Chapter 6) might be:

1   **Warm-up**

Play a guessing game. Describe a view and ask the class: *Where am I?* For example, *There are three huge buildings. They are made of stone. They each finish in a point. They are surrounded by sand. Where am I?* (Answer: The Pyramids at Giza.) Learners take turns to do the same in small groups.

2   **Schema activation**

Write the single word *grass* on the board and ask learners to work together and brainstorm sentences beginning *Grass....* They should divide these between facts and opinions: say, five of each. Provide any vocabulary needed, or allow learners to consult dictionaries. Ask individuals to read out selected sentences.

3   **Text: first contact**

Learners read the poem in order to answer the question: *Where is the grass?* (Answer: on battlefields.) They should have a chance to discuss this in pairs. Answering this question will require learners to recognize at least one of the names of the battles and, by extension, to guess the others. If they don't, then of course they should be told. The words *pile* and *shovel* will also need to be dealt with – but learners should first be encouraged to try and guess what they mean. At the same time, it is important that they also focus on the words that they *do* know: there's a tendency to overemphasize unfamiliar words in texts, at the expense of the very many – often high-frequency function words – that they are already familiar with.

4   **Listening**

Read the text aloud, or play a recording of it being read.

5 **Response to text**
   Elicit statements about the poem, by providing a framework:
   I (don't) like it, because…
   It makes me feel…
   It reminds me of…
   It's saying that…
   I'm not sure I understand the bit about…

6 **Text: closer reading**
   Ask comprehending questions to help establish a clear mental schema of the poem's surface meaning and of its underlying purpose. For example:
   Whose voice is speaking in the poem? (The grass.)
   Who is being addressed?
   What do you 'see' in line 1?
   What do you 'see' in line 7? Who are the passengers? Who is the conductor?
   What is the significance of the passengers' questions?
   What has changed between the beginning and the end of the poem?
   What is the poet's feeling about the grass, do you think? How does he convey this?
   What would you change in order to 'modernize' the poem?

7 **Text: reconstruction**
   Provide a gapped version of the poem, omitting key verbs and nouns, for example, (but not the place names).

   Alternatively, ask learners to identify the most important words in the poem. That is, if they had to reduce it to just ten words, what would they be? These words could then serve as the basis for a reconstruction-from-memory exercise.

8 **Language focus: *let* + noun + verb**
   Highlight the expression *Let me work*. Elicit a paraphrase, eg *Allow me to work*. Ask learners, working together, to draw up a list of sentences following this model:

Let	me	grow,	said the grass.
Let	us	watch TV,	said the children.

9 **Writing**
   Ask learners, working individually or in pairs, to write short poems which include one of the following lines:
   I am the dust.
   I am the wind.
   I am the sand.
   I am the fire.
   I am the water.
   I am the trees.
   I am the snow.

They can choose to stick closely to the format of the Sandburg poem or to depart from it radically.

Learners read each others' poems and some of these are selected for reading aloud.

10 Listening and speaking

Describe the experience of visiting a famous historical site, your feelings about being there and how the site must have changed over time. Ask learners to share similar experiences. Alternatively, (and more riskily perhaps), introduce a discussion about the healing effect of time. For example, suggest that the poet is in two minds about the grass: that it helps heal the wounds of war, but that it also induces forgetfulness. Should, indeed, the grass be allowed to do its work?

As homework, learners could write a short appreciation of the poem.

There are many other ways that the poem could be incorporated into a lesson. For a start, no cultural-historical background has been included in the above treatment, but a short biography of Sandburg might help learners situate the text. Comparison with other texts on the same theme (such as the lawn fertilizer ad – text 7.1 above) would also be productive, especially at higher levels. Likewise, other poems on the same, or a similar, theme could be used, especially where they hint at intertextual connections. Many readers, reading Sandburg's poem, will hear echoes of Whitman's 'Leaves of Grass', for example:

> *A child said, What is the grass? fetching it to me with full hands;*
> *How could I answer the child?. . . I do not know what it is any more than he.*
> *[….]*
> *And now it seems to me the beautiful uncut hair of graves.*

Nor has much *stylistic* attention been paid to the text in the lesson outlined above. *Stylistics* is concerned with accounting for how linguistic choices determine particular textual effects. A stylistic analysis would describe the overall structure of the poem – its parallelism and use of repetition, for example – or its grammatical choices (eg imperatives) or the extreme simplicity of its vocabulary (eg apart from the proper names all the words have either one or two syllables). These choices would then be matched with the effect they create – for example, the relentless, faceless, even thankless work that the grass does by virtue of simply growing.

Ideology

We have already seen how writers use language in order to create a point of view and to position the reader vis-à-vis this point of view. In text 7.1, the lawn fertilizer ad, the writer uses the inclusive pronouns *we* and *our* to establish shared group membership and refers obliquely to *the dream*, meaning the American dream. The message is: *To be truly American, ie one of us, you should have a lawn, and the greener the better.* The connotations of greenness are very different from what you might find, say, in a Green Party election leaflet.

The choice of pronouns and articles in the advertising text are *ideological* choices. They are not neutral or accidental or value-free. They assert particular values and attempt to align the reader with these values. The study of how language is co-opted for ideological purposes is called *critical linguistics* and takes as its starting point the assumption that all texts are inherently ideological in nature. But some texts are more 'loaded' than others, especially if their function is coercive, as in the case of advertising or propaganda. And some aspects of language seem to play a particularly important role in this ideological loading.

For example, in Chapter 6 we saw how the choice of intransitive verbs with inanimate subjects can effectively disguise the agency of events:

> World War One [...] <u>broke out</u> in 1914 and <u>did not come to an end</u> until 1918. World War Two <u>broke out</u> in 1939 and lasted until 1945.

The choice of passive is also significant in the way it can avoid any mention of agency:

> World War II <u>was fought</u> in Europe, Africa and Asia…

And the transformation of actions (expressed by verbs) into things (expressed by nouns) is yet another way of disguising agency. This is called *grammatical metaphor*. In the following extract, the verbal process *drop* is nominalized into *the dropping*, thereby absolving the writer of any need to say who performed the action:

> The war against Japan ended with the dropping of the first atomic bombs on the cities of Hiroshima and Nagasaki…[95]

As an example of how language can be deliberately manipulated in the services of power, the 'sexing up' of the British government's dossier on Iraq's supposed weapons of mass destruction prior to the Iraq War in 2003, is a case in point. Note the subtle changes in the different drafts of the dossier relating to what became known as the '45-minute claim'[96]:

> Intelligence also indicates that chemical and biological munitions could be with military units and ready for firing within 20–45 minutes.
> (Joint intelligence committee report, 9th September 2002)

> … envisages the use of weapons of mass destruction in its current military planning and could deploy such weapons within 45 minutes of the order being given for their use.
> (Draft dossier, 10th–11th September 2002)

> And the document discloses that his military planning allows for some of the WMD to be ready within 45 minutes of an order to use them… The Iraqi military may be able to deploy chemical or biological weapons within 45 minutes of an order to do so.
> (Draft dossier, 16th September 2002)

> Some of these weapons are deployable within 45 minutes of an order to use them… Intelligence indicates that the Iraqi military are able to deploy chemical or biological weapons within 45 minutes of an order to do so.
> (Published dossier, 24th September 2002)

Apart from the original *munitions* becoming *weapons of mass destruction (WMD)*, all traces of modality – hence doubt – have been removed in the successive re-draftings.

Discovery activity 7.3   *Choice of vocabulary*

One of the more obvious ways that writers attempt to influence their readers ideologically is in the choice of vocabulary (such as *weapons of mass destruction*). In the following newspaper report[97], how does the writer's ideological stance show through in his choice of nouns to identify the different participants?

7.9

Ridsdale moves to ban Turks after killings

By Red Williams

Leeds are almost certain to tackle Galatasaray in the second leg of their highly-charged UEFA Cup semi-final in front of their own fans at Elland Road.

The Turkish outfit were urging UEFA to switch the explosive match to a neutral venue after two English fans were knifed to death in Istanbul on Wednesday night.

But European football's ruling body said they expected the showdown to go ahead at Leeds.

Meanwhile, grieving Leeds have told the Turks to stay away after two Leeds fans were brutally stabbed to death by Turkish thugs.

Chairman Peter Ridsdale was backed by the FA – and was calling for UEFA support – as he warned 1,500 Turkish hotheads heading for Leeds to stay at home.

The Leeds chief acted as the city mourned the horrifying killings of supporters Christopher Loftus, 37 and Kevin Speight, 40.

[...]

Leeds fans were targeted by knife-wielding Turkish thugs when a brawl spilled out onto the busy city streets, while police claim the fighting was started by English fans making obscene gestures with the Turkish flag.

Commentary ■ ■ ■

It's fairly obvious that, whereas the Leeds supporters are described as just that, *supporters*, or *fans*, the Turks are identified in pejorative terms, such as *thugs* and *hotheads*, and the Turkish football authorities are described as *the Turkish outfit*. There is no doubt in the writer's mind as to who was to blame for the incident, despite the *claim* (another loaded word) that the fighting was started by English fans. The *sub-text* is clearly visible through the surface. ■

A hidden agenda

Classroom texts are, of course, not immune to charges of ideological bias either. In fact, educational texts have a long history of ideological sub-textuality, precisely because they *are* educational. Sometimes they function as outright propaganda of the political kind, as in this text from *English for you*, the official textbook of the German Democratic Republic (G.D.R.) in the 1970s and 1980s[98]:

7.10

> **VISITING THE G.D.R.**
>
> Bob Driver, a young teacher from Oxford, got out of the train at Berlin Ostbahnhof...
>
> Bob Driver stayed two days in Berlin before he went to Erfurt. What he saw and learnt during those two days made a good impression on him. So, he thought, the 'Morning Star' had not overestimated what had been done in the G.D.R. But he had not expected to see so many new buildings, modern shops, well-dressed people, show windows full of TV-sets, refrigerators, washing machines, textiles and food. He was also surprised by the low rents and fares...

Often, though, texts simply perpetuate values through stereotypical situations, characters and behaviours, as in this example from an (admittedly fairly old) course of English for Mexican school children[99]:

7.11

> I am going to tell you what we can do.
>
> We can run and jump. We can play with our dog. We can fly our kite. We can spin our top. We can play ball. We can swing. We can not play with dolls, because we are not girls. I don't like dolls.

Apart from its not so subtle sexist message, what is curious about this text is that it seems to merge two meanings of *can: can* meaning *able to* and *can* meaning *allowed to.*

In fact, the overt language agenda of many coursebook texts may be one of the reasons why their ideological sub-texts go largely unnoticed or are condoned. In the following text[100], the language focus is firmly fixed on the past perfect. But what values does it communicate – as much by what it *doesn't* say as by what it does?

7.12

> **Admirable people**
>
> My neighbour Dien Tranh was born in 1959 in Vietnam, in the city of Hue. By the time he was 12, he had lost both his parents. Somehow he cared for himself and his younger sister. By the time he was 20 he had arrived in the United States as a refugee and he had begun working two and sometimes three jobs at a time. Within five years, he had already saved enough money to help bring many of his relatives to the United States and he had bought a small florist shop. By 1994 – 10 years after he bought that small shop – Tranh had expanded his business to include six stores and more than 30 employees.

What the text doesn't tell us is as significant as what it does. How, for example, did Dien Tranh lose his parents? Might it have had something to with the fact that Hue was the scene of one of the most bitterly contested battles of the Vietnam War? How did Dien Tranh care for himself and his little sister? How did he get to the US and why did he choose the US? How did he get work? Was he legally employed? Did his relatives enter the US legally? Who are these 30 people he employs: are *they* legal? And what values are implied by titling the text *Admirable people*?

These are all important questions and could lead to interesting speculations on the part of the learners, but the writers don't seem to think so. Having completed a time line of Dien Tranh's life, the learners' next task is to study a diagram 'about how to use the past perfect tense'.

This indifference to the content of coursebook texts has been criticized by some writers, who point out that what is *not* said, as in text 7.12, is also ideological. In actual fact, the decision to avoid confronting sensitive issues is probably less to do with either the writers' queasiness or their political affiliation and more to do with the nervousness that educational publishers feel about the possibility of causing offence to a potential market. Publishers have to tread a narrow line between the need to provide interesting, topical texts, on the one hand, and to avoid controversy, on the other. To this end, guidelines are drawn up for authors, both to ensure *inclusivity,* ie avoidance of gender or ethnic bias in the way that people in coursebooks are represented, and *appropriacy.* Topics that are considered *in*appropriate are informally known as the 'PARSNIP' topics, ie politics, alcohol, religion, sex, narcotics, *-isms* and pork. The result is what one critic[101] has called the 'soft fudginess' of most EFL materials.

But there is also a tension between the political correctness of inclusivity and the commercial expediency of appropriacy, such that some sectors of society are not represented at all. This is the case with gays and lesbians who have been glaringly invisible in coursebooks (apart from inadvertent appearances, as in the case of Roger and David!).

But even this long-standing taboo has started to yield under pressure. Witness this text from a recently published adult course[102]:

7.13

Ricardo: It was New Year's Eve and I 4＿＿＿＿＿ some people around to my house to celebrate. I planned a quiet party but my friends brought other friends and by twelve o'clock there were lots of people. I was making some drinks in the kitchen when I noticed this guy on his own. He didn't seem to know anybody, so I 5＿＿＿＿＿ over to him and 6＿＿＿＿＿ myself. He said, "So you're not Antonio, then?!" He was at the wrong party – he had made a mistake with the address! I asked him to stay and we got on really well ... and now we're together.'

The above text appears in a coursebook written primarily for a southern European market, so it is perhaps not surprising that it has been able to take liberties with its content. The problem is often that coursebooks are written for global markets and therefore cannot comfortably accommodate local interests, concerns and aspirations. John Gray, who interviewed a number of teachers about their attitudes to coursebooks, concludes that 'it is certainly the case that the teachers I spoke to about global materials clearly felt the need for what might be called a *glocal* (ie a global-plus-local) coursebook – something which could give them 'a better fit' and simultaneously connect the world of their students with the world of English.'[103] Moreover, a *glocal* focus would, in theory, be easier for local teachers to mediate, especially those whose first language was not English, and who may feel either unqualified or compromised if required to use imported materials.

Classroom applications

One approach to unmasking the ideological sub-texts of texts, whether authentic or EFL-written, is to encourage what is called *critical reading*. On the one hand, this involves *interrogating* the text, in the way that I interrogated the text about Dien Tranh (text 7.12), in order both to disclose what has been left out and to *problematize* the text. On the other, it means critically examining the language choices that the writer (or speaker) has made in order to find clues as to the ideological position that has been adopted, whether intentionally or not. The sort of questions that can be asked at the linguistic level include:

Word choice
- Are there words that have strong negative or positive connotations?
- Are euphemisms used (ie polite ways of expressing sensitive ideas)?
- What evaluative words are used?
- What idiomatic, slang or dialectic words are used?
- Are vague expressions used?
- What deictic expressions are used (such as *now, then; here, there; this, that*)?
- What metaphors are used?
- What reporting terms are used (eg *claimed, alleged, threatened*)?
- Are polarities established (eg between *fan* and *thug*)?
- Are words repeated?
- What proper nouns (names of people, places, etc) are used?

Grammar choice
- Who or what are the themes of the sentences?
- Who or what are the agents of the sentences?
- Are sentences affirmative or negative?
- Are verbs passive or active?
- Are verbs transitive or intransitive?
- Is grammatical metaphor used?
- Are modal verbs used, and, if so, which?
- Is speech direct or indirect?
- What shared knowledge is assumed, eg by the use of the definite article?
- What pronouns are used, eg first, second, or third person; singular or plural; exclusive or inclusive (in the case of *we*); masculine or feminine?

Discourse choice

- What linking devices are used to connect sentences?
- What titles, headlines, etc, are there?
- What features of layout, punctuation, type-face, etc, are there?
- Is the text illustrated?
- What larger scale structures does the text have, eg problem–solution; question–answer, etc?
- What reference is made to other texts?

Of course, it is unlikely that any one text – unless a very long one – will exhibit all these features, or even a small proportion of them. Nor is it the case that the presence or absence of these features is necessarily indicative of an ideological point of view. However, particular clusters, and more than average frequencies, of certain features are often worth examining for what they might reveal about the point of view of the writer and where the writer assumes – or wishes – the reader's sympathies lie.

Discovery activity 7.4   *Critical reading*

By way of a simple example, read the following newspaper text[104] and decide which team the writer thinks his readers support. What clues helped you decide?

7.14

> # Stratford settles for draw after top hockey start
>
> Stratford drew its Mid Central Super League top six hockey match 4–4 with Wanganui Rangers in Stratford on Saturday.
>
> In front of a sizable crowd, Stratford got off to a good start, playing some of its best hockey for several seasons. It shot to a 3–1 lead, with two goals to Grant Boyde and another from a penalty corner to Greg Bland.
>
> Going into halftime 4–2 up, it would have been expected that Stratford would try to maintain the momentum in the second half. However, positional changes and substitutions at the break had the opposite effect and Stratford lost both its shape and direction.
>
> Rangers struck back with two goals and Stratford was forced to hold out for a draw. James Newell had his best performance of the season at left half for Stratford.

Commentary ■ ■ ■

There should be no doubt that this text was written for Stratford fans, not Wanganui Rangers fans. Stratford gets eight mentions (compared to Rangers' two) and is the subject – hence *theme* – of seven of the texts' eleven finite clauses, including the headline. This foregrounding of Stratford involves using the passive in one instance (*Stratford was forced*), even though the subject of the previous clause is *Rangers*. The named players all play for Stratford; no Rangers player is named. All the words with positive connotations (*top, sizable, good, best* x2) refer to Stratford – its team's start, its crowd, its players, and so on. Moreover, Stratford's superiority is emphasized by words like *lead, up* and *momentum* and verbs with forceful connotations like *got off to* and *shot to*. On this evidence alone, you'd be forgiven for thinking that Stratford won the match comfortably.

In the second paragraph this 'accentuating of the positive' is sustained, but in order to do so the writer has to invent a hypothetical world, since in the real world there was an 'opposite effect'. The shift to unreality (called, technically, *irrealis)* is signalled by modal verbs: *it <u>would</u> have been expected that Stratford <u>would</u> try to maintain the momentum in the second half.* Compare this to the much more negative-sounding: *Stratford didn't try to maintain the momentum in the second half.* (Note, by the way, how modal verbs are always a reliable indicator of some mood, perspective, or reality, shift.) And any human agency behind Stratford's disappointing second-half performance is disguised behind grammatical metaphor: *positional changes and substitutions.* Compare this with: *The coach changed some positions and substituted some key players.*

A useful exercise aimed at sensitizing learners to the different ways in which the same facts can be very differently presented would be to ask them to re-write the text from the *Wanganui* point of view. ■

It needs to be stressed that there is nothing necessarily underhand or manipulative about the way the writer has positioned the reader in this text. To have written it with a less biased slant would have made it less appropriate for its readership. What the writer has done is exactly what all effective writers do: he or she has *kept the reader in mind.*

Conclusion

In this chapter we have extended the definition of text to include both literary texts and sub-texts. In the case of the former, we have found that literary texts share many if not all of the qualities of non-literary texts, such that it is sometimes difficult to distinguish between the two categories. Advertising texts, for instance, borrow heavily from the former in the way that they use language playfully. And some literary texts 'disguise' themselves as non-literary texts: think of novels that are written as a sequence of letters, for example. In classroom terms, the approach to literary texts need not be qualitatively different from that used for non-literary texts and a twin-pronged, TAVI and TALO, approach (see Chapter 6) is equally appropriate, although it might be more accurate to re-cast TAVI as TAVE: *text as vehicle of expression.*

As for the sub-texts of texts, the capacity of learners to identify point-of-view might usefully be developed through the study of literary texts, but also through advertising texts and the more overtly ideological text types such as journalism. But all texts, including coursebook texts, are ideological to a certain extent, in that their producers have made a considered choice out of all the many possible ways that the text *could* have been, and this choice is in part determined by the effect that they hoped to achieve on their reader or listener.

Chapter 8 **Learners' texts**

If literary texts are highly valued, *learners' texts* occupy the other end of the scale. Their purpose is primarily display (rather than, say, pleasure or information), their content is often overlooked completely in favour of niceties of grammar and punctuation, and their lifespan is typically brief and inglorious. (I had a colleague who, I'm ashamed to say, used her students' homework to stuff a pouffe.) Yet learner texts offer a rich resource for language development and it is the purpose of this last chapter to re-evaluate their usefulness.

The main benefits of learners' texts are that they can be used as

- data for diagnosis and evaluation
- data for language awareness raising
- texts in their own right.

Moreover, when students see their own texts used for analysis in the same way as, for example, a poem or a newspaper story, it can be very motivating, even flattering, and serves to break down the distinction between language *learner* and language *user*.

Diagnosis and evaluation

Texts, especially written ones, have a long history as testing instruments, especially where fluency and coherence are valued. Simply testing learners on their ability to write, or complete, isolated sentences is clearly unsatisfactory if their overall ability to communicate at the text-level is an objective. However, even when whole texts are used for testing or diagnosis, there is a tendency for many teachers not to be able to see beyond their surface grammar errors, or to appreciate their strengths irrespective of their weaknesses. To ensure a broader, fairer view, more comprehensive criteria for assessing texts are needed. Fortunately, such criteria are now available, thanks to the work of various examining bodies, and can be used not only for testing but for diagnosis.

For example, the Cambridge Advanced English examination (CAE) includes a writing paper in which candidates are set two writing tasks of approximately 250 words each. The completed tasks are assessed according to the following criteria:

- **content**
  Does the text cover a sufficient range of points, according to the specifications of the task?
- **organization and cohesion**
  Is the text appropriately organized, laid out and linked?
- **range**
  Is there a sufficiently wide range of vocabulary and grammatical structures?
- **register**
  Is the style appropriate to the topic, text type, purpose and target reader?
- **target reader**
  Has the writer kept the reader in mind? Would the text achieve the desired effect on the target reader?
- **accuracy of language**
  Is the text accurate in its use of vocabulary, grammar, discourse features, etc?

These criteria can usefully be applied to any text, at any level, in order to assess its strengths and weaknesses.

Discovery activity 8.1 *Evaluating learners' texts*

The text below was written by a pre-intermediate Spanish-speaking learner in response to the following task:

> You have answered an advertisement for a penfriend and you are writing a short description of yourself to your new friend. Include information about where you live, your work or studies, your interests and your family.

Evaluate the learner's strengths and weaknesses according to the criteria above.

8.1

Dear Luis,

I'm very pleased that we're going to be penfriends. I'll tell you a little about myself and you can do the same when you write to me.

I live in Barcelona in an area apartado of the centre, but is an area very populated and too much new.

I'm working of a taxi driver, is a profession very stressant, but the same time very distracting because I'm speaking with the people about lot of historys.

I like doing sport, overcoat running, is marvellous! because after of the run I'm perfectly.

I'm happily married with a woman very nice and we have got thre children, two soons and a daugther, my first soon, he has an arquitect and my daugther, she's going to at the University. Well, I hope you notices soon.

Best wishes,

Carlos.

Commentary ■ ■ ■

- **content**: The text covers all the areas outlined in the task, although fairly minimally, it must be admitted.
- **organization and cohesion**: The text is logically organized: there is an introductory paragraph and a rounding-off sentence, while the intervening topics have been covered in the prescribed way. New topics are separately paragraphed and the layout is appropriate to the kind of letter it represents. There are few connecting devices, but on the whole the organization of the text is transparent enough not to require overt signposting. Some topic signalling devices – such as *As for my job…, Regarding my free time…* – might provide a bit more variety, however.
- **range**: The range is fairly limited, as might be expected in a learner of this level. Core vocabulary words, such as *very, because, like, nice* and *and* are used where a more advanced learner might have chosen *extremely, since, love, charming* and *also,* for example. Where attempts have been made to use less general terms, they usually fail, either because direct or indirect borrowing from Spanish is

used (*apartado, stressant*), or because the word chosen is a false friend (*distracting* rather than *entertaining, historys* rather than *stories, notices* rather than *news*). Grammatical range, too, is fairly limited, although some sentences – especially in the first paragraph – achieve a relatively sophisticated degree of complexity, with subordinate clauses and a variety of verb phrase constructions.

- **register**: On the whole the style is appropriate to the kind of letter this is – neither too chatty nor too formal. The greeting and final salutation are well judged.

- **target reader**: Inasmuch as this is an 'invented' task, and therefore the target reader is imaginary, the writer does take the reader into account, addressing him directly, at least in the opening and closing. But, apart from this, at the interpersonal level the letter is a bit flat. More expressions of the type *as you know* and *I'm sure you know what I mean,* or direct questions, such as *Do you also run?* would have ensured a more positive, engaged reader response. Likewise, giving his family members' names would have made the text more intimate as well as more informative.

- **accuracy of language**: Despite the (suspiciously?) promising beginning, there are a number of basic problems with grammar and lexis, one of the most persistent being the tendency to place adjective phrases after, rather than before, nouns: *an area very populated, a woman very nice,* etc. Most errors, apart from those Spanish borrowings mentioned above, don't seriously threaten intelligibility. However, there is one that only English teachers working in Spanish-speaking countries will be able to explain and that is the use of the word *overcoat* (*overcoat running*) – a problem due to flawed dictionary use, where the learner has looked up *sobretodo* (overcoat) instead of *sobre todo* (above all).

On balance, however, the text rates passably in many of the criteria outlined earlier, especially for a learner at this basic level. It is worth underscoring the point that simply working on grammatical accuracy is no guarantee that the learner will improve on this kind of task and that remedial work might be more usefully spent on extending and refining vocabulary and on developing ways of engaging the reader more directly. ■

Language awareness raising

Just as real texts and coursebook texts provide data for language study, so too can learners' texts be exploited for the same ends. In fact, there's a good case for learners' texts being the *best* resources for a focus on language. After all, learner-produced texts are more likely to be *closer* to the developmental stage that other learners are going through (their *interlanguage*). One disadvantage of using literary texts as models for language instruction is that most literature (especially of the capital L variety) is at such a far remove from what learners can realistically achieve that it may in fact be de-motivating. And the sophisticated, often subtle, use of language in literary texts will either be lost on learners, or be of little relevance in terms of their immediate language needs. On the other hand, learner texts are more likely to include features that other learners can appropriate, given the current state of their interlanguage.

Of course, learner texts have an image problem, being neither 'genuine' nor native-speaker productions and most learners will be justifiably suspicious of a diet of unmediated other-learner input. For a start, how will they know what is acceptable usage (ie standard usage) as opposed to 'error' (ie non-standard usage)? To meet this concern there are a number of strategies available to teachers:

pre-editing

The learner text is 'tidied up' before being made available to other learners. For example, errors are corrected and awkward wordings are reformulated. Yet the content – and ideally the flavour – of the original remains the same. This is analogous to the way that teachers (and coursebook writers) simplify, or adapt, authentic texts, both to make them easier to process, but also so as to maximize their language learning spin-off. What can be particularly revealing for learners is to see the two versions, the original and the edited, side-by-side and to make comparisons and notice differences. In other words, the awareness-raising process is self-initiated, rather than teacher-directed, although, of course, a certain amount of 'nudging' on the part of the teacher is perfectly legitimate.

guided self-editing

This strategy requires learners to do their own editing, but with teacher guidance. Traditionally, this takes the form of the teacher flagging errors in the text, using codes, such as *Sp* (spelling), *Gr* (grammar), *MW* (missing word), etc, and the learner then re-writes the text, incorporating the teacher's corrections. A more time-consuming, but ultimately more helpful approach is *conferencing*, where individual learners meet with the teacher and talk through the text that the learner has produced. In this way, the editing process is both more personalized and more interactive. The learner then re-drafts the text, taking into account the suggestions that came out of the 'conference'.

Self-editing need not involve written texts only. Recordings of spoken texts can also be subjected to similar scrutiny. Here, a teacher describes how he uses recordings to prepare groups of Japanese learners to make joint oral presentations[105]:

> Two weeks before the scheduled final presentation, each group of three students performed a private rehearsal, with me as the only listener. The rehearsals lasted approximately 20 minutes and were tape-recorded. These rehearsals, like the final presentations, were given without the use of scripts, though students were allowed to use small cue cards. I asked the students to transcribe a five-minute segment, which included equal contributions from each of them. They first of all transcribed the extract 'warts and all', including any errors that they made. They produced a typed transcript with double-spacing and made their own corrections in red pen. When they were finished, I took the copy and indicated any corrections or improvements that they had missed. This completed the task and the paper was returned to them one week before they were due to give the final presentation.

In the final presentations, the teacher noted that there was marked improvement in a number of language features, particularly in the use of articles and prepositions, as well as in the overall organization of the content.

4 Text work
  4.1 Text
  4.2 Vocabulary items
  4.3 Words and definitions
  4.4 True/false statements
  4.5 Matching ideas
  4.6 Translation drills
  4.7 Literary translation
5 Communication Activities
  5.1 Discussion
  5.2 What's the difference?
  5.3 Role playing
  5.4 Essay writing

Commenting on the experience, one of the students said, 'Working on the Alternative Textbook gives us the opportunity to choose themes which are more important and useful than those in the textbook. Besides, it makes us read a lot of authentic texts.'

A similar initiative, but one which also incorporates learner-produced texts as well as learner-chosen ones, is described by David Hall, who was working with a group of students of technology in Thailand on what was called the 'Talkbase' course[108].

> On the first morning of the course, the only teacher-provided 'material' of the first week is given to students. This consists of a slip of paper, on which are written the words:

> 'Welcome to the Talkbase course. We would now like you to leave the classroom and to come back again this afternoon ready to talk for a few minutes about X.'

> 'X' is a single word or a phrase chosen by the teacher. Examples are: Drying; Unexpected Outcomes; Autonomy; Water; Technology; Saving.

> First presentations by students are normally short and not particularly coherent, but they are discussed by the teacher and all the other students, normally in groups. At the end of this, students have to plan again, informed now by feedback from others and by their experience of what others have done. They then go off and report back a second time. On the third occasion, they report in writing and writing is passed around among the group for comments. As the first week develops, students begin to find personal meanings in their 'word' and gradually the very wide area covered by the original word is delimited to a topic which is of personal interest to the student.

> As the course develops and students begin to analyse published and unpublished academic discourse produced by others, both form of presentation and organization of content improve markedly and communication within the classroom, as well as outside it, becomes committed and almost totally student-dominated. Except at a very few places, such as the example from their first day of the first week, texts (recorded interviews, journal articles, etc) are found and brought to class by the students themselves, so that the course content is generated by students, not by teachers.

Conclusion

Texts – authentic, genuine, invented, simplified, adapted, spoken, written, literary, found, jointly constructed or learner created – they all have a place in the language classroom. Language learning, I have argued, should both begin and end in texts. The starting point is whole texts, whether the learners', the teacher's, or the coursebook's. These are subject to study and analysis. Individual features of these texts are extracted, manipulated and practised. And then, using these features and with reference to the original texts, new texts are constructed. The process looks like this:

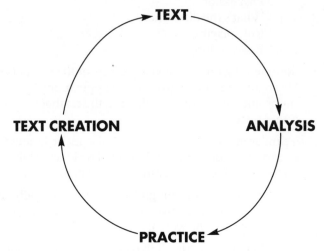

The cycle can continue – as we saw in the Talkbase example – as long as is necessary, as texts are progressively fine-tuned, elaborated, reformulated, critiqued, corrected, responded to and personalized. But always texts.

Photocopiable tasks

Introduction

The following photocopiable tasks are designed to demonstrate some of the key principles in each chapter of the book. Most of them are based on existing authentic or coursebook texts, but there is no reason why the teacher shouldn't replace these texts with texts that may be more relevant or more appropriate to the needs and abilities of a particular group of learners. The following tasks, then, are offered as templates that can be adapted to accommodate the texts of your choice.

Note also that the tasks have been designed with language students in mind, but many, if not all, of them would also be suitable for use with trainee teachers. In this case, the task – rather than the text – might need to be adapted, to include a question such as: 'What does this task suggest about the use of texts in the classroom?'

In Chapter 1 we saw how much grammar is 'locked up' in a text, however short the text is. Task 1 is designed to draw attention to the grammar locked up in a short (50-word) text, with a special focus on word classes, and the distribution of function and content words.

In Chapter 2 we looked at those features of a text that bind it together as text (ie that make it *cohesive*). In Chapter 3 we looked at those features that contribute to its capacity to make sense (ie to be *coherent*). Tasks 2–6 are designed to raise learners' awareness about these features.

In Chapter 4 we looked at the way spoken texts are both cohesive and coherent. We also noted how naturally occurring spoken language not only differs from written language in many significant ways, but also differs from the way it is typically represented in ELT materials. Tasks 7 and 8 look at characteristic features of spoken texts.

In Chapter 5 we saw how context factors impact on the register of texts, and how certain frequently occurring constellations of these variables have become institutionalised over time and form genres. Task 9 takes a specific genre and subjects it to analysis.

In Chapter 6 we saw how texts for classroom use are sometimes under-exploited in terms of their linguistic features. Quite a lot of attention is devoted to unfamiliar vocabulary, but less time spent on exploring the potential of the words the learners *already know*. Task 10 focuses on the familiar words in a text, and subjects them to close scrutiny.

In Chapter 7 it was noted that one characteristic of literary texts is that writers can adopt a *point of view* that is not necessarily their own, and how the point of view, in turn, determines the reader's interpretation of the events, and is probably the most significant factor in determining the text's style. Task 11 focuses on the linguistic features that shape the point of view.

Finally, learner texts, as was argued in Chapter 8, provide a rich source of material both for diagnostic purposes and also as texts in their own right. Too often, diagnosis focuses on what learners *haven't achieved* in their texts, drawing attention to such things as errors in grammar and vocabulary. A more balanced view of learner texts should take into account their achievements, especially in terms of the effect they create on the reader. This is the focus of Task 12.

Task 1: Unlocking Texts

Below is a mini-saga – that is, a story told in exactly 50 words.

1 **Read the text and find an example of each part of speech: noun, verb, adjective, adverb, pronoun, determiner, preposition, conjunction.**

2 **Identify the grammar words and the content words (that is, words that carry the main information).**
   - How many functional words are there?
   - How many content words are there?

3 **Are any words repeated? Which? Why?**

4 **Identify the noun phrases (groups of words with a noun or pronoun as the main component). What different ways of making noun phrases are there?**

   For example, *his sleep* = determiner + noun

5 **Identify the verb phrases, and classify them in as many ways as you can think of. Are they main/auxiliary; transitive/intransitive; finite/non finite; passive/active; regular/irregular; what tense and person are used?**

   For example, *staying* = intransitive, non-finite, participle, present

6 **Identify who or what the pronouns (*he*) and possessive adjectives (*his*) refer to. Are there any referents (the person or thing referred to) that are not actually in the text?**

7 **Explain the use of any articles in the text, including the 'zero article'.**

8 **Identify the preposition phrases in the text – that is groups of words that consist of a preposition plus noun phrase. For example, *with friends* and describe their function (for example, *accompanying, time, place*).**

A Dream So Real

Staying overnight with friends, his sleep was disturbed by a vivid dream: a thief broke in, stole everything in the flat – then carefully replaced every single item with an exact replica.

'It felt so real,' he told his friends in the morning.

Horrified, uncomprehending, they replied, 'But who are you?'

By Patrick Forsyth, in *Mini-Sagas from the Daily Telegraph Competition, 2001* (Enitharmon Press)

PHOTOCOPIABLE

164

Task 2: Lexical cohesion

1 Read the text[1] and decide how the underlined words are related.

For example:

wrinkles, creases = synonyms

> **WRINKLE FREE**
>
> Wrinkle <u>Free</u> is an <u>amazing</u> new formula <u>aerosol</u> that will actually <u>remove</u> <u>wrinkles</u> and <u>creases</u> from all sorts of <u>fabrics</u>, leaving them looking <u>neat</u> and <u>super</u> <u>smart</u>. Fast and convenient to <u>use</u>, Wrinkle Free is <u>ideal</u> for busy people and travellers, and can be <u>used</u> with complete safety on all <u>fabrics</u> and <u>garments</u>, and won't leave a build-up on <u>clothes</u>. It costs only pennies a <u>spray</u>! 3oz <u>can</u>.

2 Read the text[2] and find examples of the following.

- direct repetition of content words
- synonyms, and near synonyms
- hyponyms (general term versus specific word)
- antonyms (opposites)
- words that belong to the same lexical set

> ### EASY SHOE SHINE
>
> The Shoe Valet will deal with the family's footwear in record time, with no mess and no grubby hands. Four interchangeable wheels will give your leather shoes the full valet treatment. One removes mud and dirt, another applies neutral shoe cream to the leather, and the two soft brushes will polish your light or dark shoes to a deep shine. Shoe Valet operates quickly and efficiently at the touch of a button.

[1] advert from *Kleeneze* Catalogue, Solutions, 69 Campus Rd, Listerhills Science Park, Bradford BD7 1HR
[2] ibid.

Task 3: Reference

Reference using articles

1　**Read the text and explain why the definite article (*the*) is used. Why do we know what is being referred to?**

　1　*the youth = a young man (line 1).*

> A certain girl was given by her parents to a young man in marriage. She did not care for the[1] youth, so she refused and said that she would choose a husband for herself. Shortly after there came to the[2] village a fine young man of great strength and beauty. The[3] girl fell in love with him at first sight and told her parents that she had found the[4] man she wished to marry, and as the[5] latter was not unwilling the[6] marriage soon took place. Now it happened that the[7] young man was not a man at all, but a hyena, for although as a rule women change into hyenas and men into hawks, the[8] hyena can change itself into either man or woman as it may please. [...]

Reference using pronouns

2　**Read the text and identify the underlined words. Find the following.**

- a subject personal pronoun　*she*
- an object personal pronoun
- a relative pronoun
- an indefinite pronoun
- a reflexive pronoun
- a demonstrative pronoun

> This[1] is what a woman did.
>
> She[2] was then living in the bush, never showing herself[3] to anyone[4]. She[5] had living with her[6] just one daughter, who[7] used to pass the day in the fork of a tree making baskets.
>
> One day there appeared a man just when the mother had gone to kill game. He[8] found the girl making baskets as usual. 'Here now!' he[9] said. 'There are people here in the bush! And that girl, what a beauty! Yet they[10] leave her[11] alone. If the king were to marry her[12], would not all the other queens leave the place?' [...]

3　**Now identify the referent (the person or thing being referred to) of each of the underlined pronouns.**

From Carter, A. (Ed.) 1990, 1991. *The Virago Book of Fairy Tales*. London: Virago, p. 64.

Task 4: Cohesion

Read the text and identify the ways that it is joined together (or made cohesive). Find examples of the following.

1 lexical cohesion:
- direct repetition *bad breath* (lines 1, 2, 5, 7)
- synonyms
- antonyms
- words from the same semantic field; lists

2 grammatical cohesion
- reference: pronouns
- reference: articles
- ellipsis of clause elements
- conjuncts (also called linkers)
- tense

3 rhetorical cohesion
- question–answer

Bad Breath: Why you're always the last to know.

A simple question: when someone you know or work with has bad breath, do you tell them?

•

If you're like most people, the answer is probably "No." Which means that nobody is going to tell *you* when *you* have bad breath.

•

So to be sure you don't, use RetarDEX® products.

•

They're guaranteed to ban bad breath, because they actually get rid of something dentists call Volatile Sulphur Compounds, or VSCs.

These are the end products of bacteria feeding off dead cell tissue and debris in the mouth that, hardly surprising, smell terrible.

•

Ordinary mouthwashes, toothpastes and sprays only mask the odour with a nicer smell which soon wears off. But the clinically proven RetarDEX range of 24-hour oral care products has a patented active ingredient called CloSYS II® which eliminates these VCSs and rapidly restores fresh breath.

•

So don't wait for someone to tell you. Because they won't.

Task 5: Coherence

Read the text and explain how each sentence connects with the one before it and/or the one after it. For example, does it 'gather up' the previous sentence, or set up an expectation about the sentence that follows?

COMPUTER	
(1) Computers are electronic machines like calculators.	repeats topic from title of article
(2) But computers do more than work out mathematical problems.	*but:* logical contrast; repeat of *computers; work out mathematical problems* is a re-phrasing of *calculate,* gathering up *calculators* from sentence 1; *do more* sets up the expectation that this will be elaborated in sentence 3.
(3) They can *process* information.	
(4) This means that they can be given information, store it and sort through it in order to carry out a task.	
(5) What is more they can work at incredible speeds.	
(6) Computers cannot think.	
(7) They have to have instructions called *programs* to tell them what to do with the information they are given.	
(8) These programs can be changed so that computers can do an enormous number of different things.	
(9) They can send spacecraft to outer planets, help forecast the weather, run machines and play exciting games.	
(10) Every computer has four main parts.	
(11) The *input* is where the computer receives instructions and information; the *central processing unit* (CPU) is where calculations are carried out; the memory is where information and instructions are stored and the *output* is where the result is displayed.	

From *Pocket Encyclopedia* (Kingfisher Books)

Task 6: Textualising

Put these facts together and write a cohesive, coherent text of eight sentences or fewer.

George Orwell

He was born in India.
He was born in 1903.
His real name was Eric Blair.
His father worked in the Bengal
  Civil Service.
He went to Eton.
He left Eton in 1921.
He joined the Imperial Police
  in Burma.
He spent five years working in the
  police force.
He returned to Europe.
He worked in a number of
  menial jobs.
He wrote a book about these
  experiences.

The book was called *Down and Out in Paris and London*.
He fought on the republican side in the Spanish Civil War.
He wrote a book about this experience.
The book was called *Homage to Catalonia*.
It was published in 1938.
He also wrote novels.
His best known novels are *Animal Farm* and *Nineteen Eighty-Four*.
Animal Farm was published in 1945.
Nineteen Eighty-Four was published in 1949.
Animal Farm is a satire on communism.
Nineteen Eighty-Four describes a nightmare future world.
He died in 1950.
He died from tuberculosis.
He was 47.

Task 7: Spoken texts

Read these transcriptions of recorded speech. Decide which is scripted dialogue, and which is spontaneous. Say what clues helped you decide.

(Note: speech transcription conventions – including minimal punctuation – have been used in both extracts. The sign ∟ indicates an overlap, ie where one speaker starts speaking before another has finished.)

<S1> = Tourist guide <S2> = Visitor

1

1 <S1> Hello can I help you?

2 <S2> Yes I'm staying in Plymouth for a few days for a conference can I ask you a few questions about the town?

3 <S1> Yes of course

4 <S2> Well first about the sports facilities is there a swimming pool in Plymouth?

5 <S1> Yes there is there's one near the sea on the other side of the Hoe and another at the sports centre but most visitors prefer to swim in the sea

6 <S2> I see are there any good beaches?

7 <S1> Yes there are there's one on the other side of the Hoe it's called Pebbleside Beach

8 <S2> Mm good what about old buildings has Plymouth got a castle?

9 <S1> No I'm afraid it hasn't [...]

2

1 <S1> Can I help?

2 <S2> Yes erm I'm gonna stay in Plymouth for a couple of days erm I was wondering if I could get some information off you erm is is there a swimming pool or in Plymouth

3 <S1> Yes erm the one in the city centre where are you staying first of all?

4 <S2> Er I haven't decided yet but somewhere in the city

5 <S1>   ∟You'll be central [<S2> Yeah] OK well there's a fun pool in the city centre that's The Pavillions but if you want some serious sort of exercise swimming then the [<S2> Yeah] it's Central Park that you need that has 33 metre pool that has lane swimming early in the morning [<S2> Right] and there's a separate diving pit as well there

6 <S2>   ∟Right and where where's that?

7 <S1> It's at Central Park (6 seconds) right you're here at the moment [<S2> Yes] and Central Park is up here the swimming pool's [<S2> Oh right] up here
                                     ∟Lovely thanks erm

8 <S2> there are any good beaches (1 second) around here?

9 <S1> Sandy beaches do you mean?

10<S2> Yeah yeah

11<S1> Sandiest beaches are erm either Whitesand Bay which is over to the right vaguely as you're looking out of Plymouth Sound it's around sort of the corner and out along the bay there

12 <S2>   Yeah [...]

Task 8: Spoken texts

Re-write this dialogue including some of the features of unscripted speech that you identified in Task 7.

A Where are you from?

B I'm from Turkey.

A Have you been to Edinburgh before?

B No, this is my first visit to Scotland.

A How long did it take?

B Only six hours from London.

A And where are you staying?

B In a hotel near the centre.

A How far away is it?

B Not far.

A What's it like?

B It's quiet, but my room's a little small.

A How did you come?

B I got a taxi.

A Whose drink is that?

B I don't know. It's not mine. I haven't had anything to drink yet.

A Would you like me to get you something?

B Yes, please. A lemonade.

A How do you like it?

B With a little ice, please.

A How many languages do you speak?

B Turkish, of course, as well as Arabic and a little English.

From Bell, J and Gower, R. 1992 *Upper Intermediate Matters, Student's Book.* (Longman)

PHOTOCOPIABLE

171

Task 9: Genre analysis

1 Read these four texts and identify the features they have in common. Describe the similarities in their overall organisation, grammar, and vocabulary.

2 The texts are all abstracts for conference presentations as printed in a conference programme. Explain how this context determines the features of the texts. Think about the following.

- Function
- Relationship of writer and reader
- Topic
- Mode

1

Hugh Dellar
The empty whiteboard: problems and possibilities when teaching skills
Talk

The idea of teaching receptive skills is widely accepted, yet neither research, classroom experience, nor student needs offer much support to the concept of skills training. I will argue that we need to reconsider the content of texts as materials for the classroom and reconnect them more explicitly to the teaching of language. I will suggest that students come to class as skilful readers and that second language acquisition research shows that the route to better skills in L2 is learning more language. I will give practical examples of language-focused tasks and of texts and questions that generate student talking.

2

Gillian Lazar
Food for thought: metaphors in the ELT classroom
Workshop

We use metaphorical language all the time when we speak or write in English, yet it is often neglected in the teaching of English. This workshop will begin by considering some of the features of metaphorical language relevant to the classroom teacher. We will then focus on a range of practical activities and materials that enable learners of English to explore metaphors in the classroom. These activities can be used to improve students' vocabulary, particularly their knowledge of idioms and collocations, and to develop creativity and cross-cultural awareness.

3

Sheelagh Deller
Self-esteem
Workshop

Many learners suffer from low self-esteem and a consequent feeling of guilt and inadequacy. This is also true for many teachers. Low self-esteem leads to low motivation. In this workshop we will be working on our own confidence and self-esteem, using techniques that could easily be transferred to use with our students. We will also consider how to create a classroom atmosphere where students respect and understand each other.

4

Pete Sharma
The Internet in Business English
Publisher's presentation

Many teachers underuse both the Internet and the World Wide Web, sometimes due to under-confidence with technology. However, many Business English learners expect technology to be integrated into their course work. This presentation will explore a range of activities involving the use of the Web in Business English to enhance:

Learner training
Listening and reading skills
Vocabulary: collocations
Grammar: noticing and
  consciousness-raising
Business skills: presentations
English for Special Purposes

While offering a pedagogical rationale for the tasks described, the session aims to be of practical value to Business English teachers.

PHOTOCOPIABLE

Task 10: Classroom texts

Read this authentic text and make a concordance for each of these words:
been, also, for, you, as, to, get (+ getting), at

For example:

I've	**been**	working as a chef
I've	**been**	doing this for four months
it's	**been**	very challenging
I've	**been**	involved in some TV work

Now identify some patterns in the examples.

For example:

have + *been* + present participle
have + *been* + adjective

Top of the food chain

Name:	Ben O'Donoghue
Career:	Chef
Age:	33
Lives:	London
From:	English-born, Australian-raised

"I've been working as a chef for 15 years, and I'm currently head chef at the Atlantic Bar and Grill in Piccadilly. I've been doing this for four months and it's been very challenging. My role is to manage the kitchen and oversee such things as ordering and sourcing new produce, stock control, menu and recipe design and staff training, as well as financial control like gross profit, wages and food cost and, not to forget, staff discipline. Previously I worked for a private members' club in Knightsbridge called Monte's.

While also doing the day job, I've been involved in some TV work, namely a BBC programme called *The Best*. It ran for over 10 weeks and was broadcast in England, Australia and on other international channels. I've just completed filming *Surfing the Menu* for the ABC, which was an amazing experience. I'm also writing a column for *Olive*, a food magazine published by BBC Worldwide, and I've also co-written two cookbooks, the second of which was out last month.

The most important thing I'm involved with at the moment, though, is the Atlantic Bar and Grill. My main goal is to create a young, fresh and innovative menu with a balance of internationalism and a dedication to good cooking and distinctive flavours while, at the same time, remaining price competitive.

I ended up as a chef quite by accident. A part-time summer job led to a full-time job as a kitchenhand and, from there, I developed a talent for cooking and started to look for an apprenticeship. If you want to become a chef, I couldn't recommend getting actual experience more highly, because it's the only way you'll be able to tell if you have the right qualities to get on in the kitchen. You'll need a balance of theory and practical education, though, so look for an employer who will let you do day release at college.

I like the feeling you get when you put together a dish and it smells fantastic, looks amazing, tastes awesome and is cooked to perfection. It's great when you try it for the first time and the other chefs dig in with their fingers and love it, and then the diners love it too. I also get a kick out of the energy and buzz you get from doing a very busy service and drinking that first beer afterwards.

The perks of the job include access to good food, cheap drinks if you feed the barman (this is very important) and getting looked after at other restaurants."

Emily Colston, *TNT Magazine*, March 2004, p. 75.

PHOTOCOPIABLE

173

Task 11: Point of view

1 **Read these texts, which are all the openings of novels, and identify the writer's point of view. Through whose eyes, where, and when, are we seeing the events, and with what kind of attitude?**

2 **Explain how the point of view affects the choice of verbs, verb tense and person, proper nouns, articles and pronouns.**

3 **Explain any other language choices that might influence the reader's interpretation of the writer's point of view.**

1

In these times of ours, though concerning the exact year there is no need to be precise, a boat of dirty and disreputable appearance, with two figures in it, floated on the Thames, between Southwark Bridge which is of iron, and London Bridge which is of stone, as an autumn evening was closing in.

The figures in this boat were those of a strong man with ragged grizzled hair and a sun-browned face, and a dark girl of nineteen or twenty, sufficiently like him to be recognizable as his daughter. The girl rowed, pulling a pair of sculls very easily; the man, with the rudder-lines slack in his hands, and his hands loose in his waistband, kept an eager look out. He had no net, hook, or line, and he could not be a fisherman; his boat had no cushion for a sitter, no paint, no inscription, no appliance beyond a rusty boathook and a coil of rope, and he could not be a waterman; his boat was too crazy and too small to take in cargo for delivery, and he could not be a lighterman or river-carrier; there was no clue to what he looked for, but he looked for something, with a most intent and searching gaze.

2

They are watching me, thought Rupert Stonebird, as he saw the two women walking rather too slowly down the road. But no doubt I am watching them too he decided, for as an anthropologist he knew that men and women may observe each other as warily as wild animals hidden in long grass.

The situation had nothing particularly unusual about it – an unmarried man visiting the house he had just bought and wondering where he should put his furniture, and two women – sisters, perhaps – betraying a very natural interest in the man or the house or both. One day, he thought, we shall probably know each other, and for that reason he turned away from the window, not feeling quite equal to meeting the unashamed curiosity of their glances as they came nearer.

3

I am in a car park in Leeds when I tell my husband I don't want to be married to him any more. David isn't even in the car park with me. He's at home, looking after the kids, and I have only called him to remind him that he should write a note for Molly's class teacher. The other bit just sort of … slips out. This is a mistake, obviously. Even though I am, apparently, and to my immense surprise, the kind of person who tells her husband that she doesn't want to be married to him any more, I really didn't think I was the kind of person to say so in a car park, on a mobile phone.

4

I suppose that if this story has a beginning it is with Kahu. After all, it was Kahu who was there at the end, and it was Kahu's intervention which perhaps saved us all. We always knew that there would be such a child, but when Kahu was born, well, we were looking the other way, really. We were over at our Koro's place, me and the boys, having a korero and a party, when the phone rang.

'A *girl*', Koho Apirana said, disgusted. 'I will have nothing to do with her. She has broken the male line of descent in our whanau. Aue'.

Task 12: Learner texts

Below are two learner texts written in response to the following task:

Write a letter to a friend explaining that you have recently moved house. Describe your new place, its advantages over your last place, and invite your friend to the party that you will be having to celebrate this event.

1 Read the texts and evaluate them according to the following criteria.

· **content**: does the text cover a sufficient range of points, according to the task instructions?
· **organization and cohesion**: is the text appropriately organized, laid out, and linked?
· **range**: is there a range of vocabulary and grammatical structures?
· **register**: is the style appropriate to the topic, text type, purpose, and intended reader?
· **target reader**: has the writer kept the reader in mind?; would the text achieve the desired effect on the reader?
· **accuracy of language**: is the text accurate in its use of vocabulary, grammar, discourse features, etc?

2 How do the two texts compare?

1

Dear Paul,

I'm writting to you for telling that I've recently moved house, now I live in 23 Street Road near the post office, do you know?

I'm very happy because for me this house has been my dream during all my live, the main advantage, it's new and the other hand, there is a garden where we can play, eat and stay in our free time. For me there are a lot of advantages than my first house. My neighbours are very kind with me and the area is very quite.

I would like that you'll come to my house next month to celebrate the new house, with my parents and friends, please come in, I'll wait you. If you couldn't come, tell me, my telephone number is 309524.

I'm looking forward to seeing you next month,

love,

Núria

2

Dear Steve,

I'm writting to you as I have just finished moving to a new house, it was very tiring days. I left my old house because there were some things I didn't like, such as it had quite so little rooms. Not only were there little and dark rooms but there were also little sunlight, it was always in the shade. Moreover, I asked to the owner of the house to paint it, as it was very dirty, but he turned down what I had asked. So I decided to leave the house.

I have moved to a brand-new building so there are no problems with the painting and other things at all. That house is very comfortable and it also has large windows to pass through the sunlight. By the way, my new neighbours are very nice, they helped me with moving my furniture and all my things.

I have moved to an area near lots of parks, it is a beautiful place.

Well, to sum up I'd like you to come to my house-warming party to open that pretty place I've got. So wishing to hear from you soon.

Yours sincerely,

Pilar

Photocopiable tasks: Commentary

Task 1: Unlocking texts

1 Parts of speech
Nouns: *friends* (x 2), *sleep, dream, thief, flat, item, replica, morning*
Verbs: *staying, was disturbed, broke [in], stole, replaced, felt, told, replied, are*
Adjectives: *vivid, single, exact, real, horrified, uncomprehending*
Adverbs: *overnight, in* (as in *broke in*), *carefully, so*
Pronouns: *everything, it, he, they, who, you*
Determiners: *his* (x 2), *a* (x 2), *the* (x 2), *every, an*
Prepositions: *with* (x 2), *by, in* (x 2)
Conjunctions: *then, but*

2 Functional words: *was, are, in* (x 3), *so, everything, it, he, they, who, you, his* (x 2), *a* (x 2), *the* (x 2), *every, an, with* (x 2), *by, then, but* (= 25).
Content words: the rest (= 25). The proportion is thus 1:1.

3 Repetition
Six words are repeated (see above). One of these is a content word representing a key player in the story (*friends*); the others are function words which tend to occur frequently in any text because of their important grammatical functions.

4 Noun phrases and their patterns
determiner + noun: *his sleep, a thief, the flat, his friends, the morning*
determiner + adjective + noun: *a vivid dream, every single item, an exact replica*
noun/pronoun + prepositional phrase: *everything in the flat*

5 Verb phrases
staying: intransitive, non-finite, participle, present
was disturbed: (auxiliary + past participle) transitive, passive, finite, third person, past simple, regular
broke in: (verb + adverb particle) intransitive, finite, third person, past simple, irregular
stole: transitive, active, finite, third person, past simple, irregular
replaced: transitive, active, finite, third person, past simple, regular
felt: intransitive, finite, third person, past simple, irregular
told: transitive, active, finite, third person, past simple, irregular
replied: intransitive, finite, third person, past simple, regular
are: intransitive, finite, second person, present, irregular

6 Reference
his (sleep): reference not explicit in text, but to implied subject of *staying*
it: back reference to the *dream*
he: as *his*, above, reference is inferred as being the subject of the story (the person staying, dreaming, etc)
his: as above
they: back reference to *friends*
you: reference outside text to person in real world

7 Articles

[zero] *friends:* indefinite, plural
a vivid dream, a thief, an exact replica: indefinite (first mention); singular
the flat: definite (inferred from *staying overnight with friends*)
the morning: definite, ie *the morning after the night just described*

8 Prepositional phrases

with friends: adverbial (accompaniment)
by a vivid dream: adverbial (agent)
in the flat: part of noun phrase, post-modifying everything (place)
with an exact replica: adverbial (material)
in the morning: adverbial (time)

Task 2: Lexical cohesion

1 **direct repetition:** *fabrics, fabrics*
partial repetition: *use, used*
synonyms: *free, remove; garments, clothes*
partial synonyms with positive connotation: *neat, smart; fast, convenient; amazing, super, ideal*
antonyms: *remove, leave*
same lexical set: *aerosol, spray, can*

2 **direct repetition of content words:** *shoe/shoes* (x 6); *leather* (x 2); *shine* (x 2)
synonyms and near synonyms: *mess, grubby; mud, dirt; quickly, record time, efficiently*
hyponyms (general term versus specific word): *footwear, shoes*
antonyms (opposites): *light, dark; removes, applies*
words that belong to the same lexical set: *footwear, shoe(s), leather; shoe cream, brushes, polish, shine; wheels, button*

Task 3: Reference

1 **Reference using articles**
the youth: back reference to *a young man*
the village: unique reference outside text – the village in which the family presumably live
the girl: back reference to *a certain girl*
the man: forward reference – which man? The one *she wished to marry*
the latter: unique reference – there is only one of two preceding referents that is the latter one. The *latter* itself is back reference to *the man she wished to marry.*
the marriage: reference outside the text – by implication, the marriage to which the preceding events have been leading up to
the young man: as before
the hyena: unique reference – not any particular hyena, but the class of hyenas in general, in the world outside the text (this is sometimes called *generic* reference)

2 **Reference using pronouns**
a subject personal pronoun: *she, he, they*
an object personal pronoun: *her*
a relative pronoun: *who*

an indefinite pronoun: *anyone*
a reflexive pronoun: *herself*
a demonstrative pronoun: *this*

Referents

This: the whole story that follows; cataphoric (forward) reference
She: anaphoric (back) reference to *a woman*
herself: ditto
anyone: no referent in text
She: as before
her: anaphoric (back) reference to *she*
who: anaphoric reference to *one daughter*
He: anaphoric reference to *a man*
he: ditto
they: anaphoric reference to *people*
her: as before

Task 4: Cohesion

1 lexical cohesion

- direct repetition: *bad, breath, smell, someone, know, products, tell, you*
- synonyms: *ban, get rid of, eliminate(s); odour, smell; rapidly, soon*
- antonyms: *bad breath, fresh breath; terrible, nice(r)*
- words from the same semantic field: *dentists, oral care, mouth; bacteria, cell tissue, debris, sulphur compounds; lists: mouthwashes, toothpastes and sprays*

2 grammatical cohesion

- reference: pronouns: *someone* → <u>*them*</u>; *the answer is probably "No"* → <u>*Which*</u> *means; products* → <u>*they*</u>; *VSCs* → <u>*these*</u>
- reference: articles: *a question* → *the answer*
- ellipsis of clause elements: *to be sure you don't [have bad breath]; Because they won't [tell you]*
- conjuncts (also called linkers): *So, But, Because*
- tense: present tense throughout

3 rhetorical cohesion

- question–answer: first two sentences

Task 5: Coherence

COMPUTER	
(1) Computers are electronic machines like calculators.	repeats topic from title of article
(2) But computers do more than work out mathematical problems.	*but*: logical contrast; repeat of *computers; work out mathematical problems* is a re-phrasing of *calculate*, gathering up *calculators* from sentence 1; *do more* sets up the expectation that this will be elaborated in sentence 3.

(3) They can *process* information.	Expectation satisfied; *They = computers*
(4) This means that they can be given information, store it and sort through it in order to carry out a task.	*This* gathers up all of the last sentence; repeat of *they* (ie *computers*)
(5) What is more they can work at incredible speeds.	*What is more* builds on the last sentence; repeat of *they*
(6) Computers cannot think.	*Computers* continues as the theme; negative statement sets up the expectation of affirmative elaboration.
(7) They have to have instructions called *programs* to tell them what to do with the information they are given.	*They = computers*
(8) These programs can be changed so that computers can do an enormous number of different things.	*These programs* gathers up new information from the last sentence and makes it the topic. *Different things* is very general, implying that these things will be specified.
(9) They can send spacecraft to outer planets, help forecast the weather, run machines and play exciting games.	Expectation met: *different things* are specified.
(10) Every computer has four main parts.	*Four main parts* sets up the expectation that these parts will be specified.
(11) The *input* is where the computer receives instructions and information; the *central processing unit* (CPU) is where calculations are carried out; the *memory* is where information and instructions are stored and the *output* is where the result is displayed.	Expectation met.

Task 6: Textualising

Here is a possible way that the facts could be textualised:

George Orwell, whose real name was Eric Blair, was born in India in 1903, where his father worked in the Bengal Civil Service. After leaving Eton in 1921, Orwell spent five years working for the Imperial Police in Burma, before returning to Europe, where he worked in a number of menial jobs. The book he wrote about these experiences was called *Down and Out in Paris and London.* He fought on the republican side in the Spanish Civil War and wrote a book about this experience, called *Homage to Catalonia,* which was published in 1938. He also wrote novels, the best known of which are *Animal Farm,* published in 1945, and *Nineteen Eighty-Four,* published in 1949. The former is a satire on communism, while the latter describes a nightmare future world. He died from tuberculosis in 1950, at the age of 47.

(7 sentences)

Task 7: Spoken texts

Transcript 1 is the coursebook dialogue; transcript 2 the authentic one[109].
Significant differences are that, in the coursebook dialogue:

- there are no overlapping turns
- there are no marked pauses
- there is no backchannelling (cf *Yeah; right*)
- only one participant asks questions; there are no attempts at clarifying (cf *where are you staying first of all?*)
- there are no hesitations (cf *erm*)
- there is no repetition (cf *where where's that?*)
- there are no false starts (cf *then the [<S2> Yeah] it's Central Park that you need*)
- there is a narrow range of discourse markers (*well* is used once, compared to *OK, well, right*)
- there is no vague language (cf *some serious sort of exercise*)
- there are no 'tails' added to utterances, (cf *Sandy beaches do you mean?*)
- there are no grammatically 'incorrect' constructions (cf *there are any good beaches around here?*)
- there is less detail provided, and so it is shorter
- there is little or no evaluative language (cf *a fun pool; Lovely*)

Task 8: Spoken texts

Here is a one way of adapting the dialogue:

A So where where are you from?
B Erm I'm from Turkey [**A** Right] erm from Istanbul actually
A Oh great. Did you erm have you been to Edinburgh before?
B No, this is sort of my first visit to Scotland in fact.
A Oh really.
B What about you, have you…
A No, actually I live here, I mean I was born here [**B** Oh, right, I see]. How long did it take, you know, to get here?
B From London, do you mean? [**A** Yeah] Only six hours or so.
etc.

Task 9: Genre analysis

Macrostructure (i.e. overall organisation)

Heading: name of speaker, title of presentation, type of presentation (*talk, workshop*). The title of the presentation has a two-part structure in the case of texts 1 and 2.

Abstract: problem–solution organisation, the latter consisting of at least two stages (*we will…we will also…*) with the promise of practical answers in the second stage.

Grammatical features

The problem is presented in the present tense, as a general truth; the solution uses future *will*.

The discourse markers *yet* or *however* are used to signal the problem in three of the texts (1, 2 and 4).

The problem is qualified by the use of *many, much, often, sometimes, as in many teachers/learners, [not] much support, often neglected, sometimes due to…* This serves to 'modalise' the general truth: *Many learners suffer from low self-esteem* is like saying *Learners may suffer from low self-esteem.*

Two of the texts (2 and 3) modalise the solutions as well, using *can/could* to express possibility: *These activities can be used…; techniques that could easily be transferred…*

Personal pronouns: first person (in 1, 2 and 3), and plural (in 2 and 3), ie inclusive *we*. In 4, on the other hand, the agent in the solution part is *this presentation, the session* – not *I/we*. There appears to be some flexibility in terms of establishing the *tenor*, 2 and 3 being more inclusive, 4 being the most detached.

Vocabulary

Lexical chains of words associated with learning and language (the *field*). Note that texts 2, 3 and 4 use the term *learners*, while text 1 prefers *students*.

The use of words with negative connotations in the problem section: *neglected, suffer, low (self-esteem), underuse, under-confidence*

In the solutions, the use of verbs of mental and verbal processes: *consider, reconsider, explore, focus on, argue, suggest*

Also in the solution section, the use of verbs emphasising developmental processes: *generate, develop, create, improve, enhance*

And the use of words emphasising practice: *practical (value), relevant, examples, activities, techniques, tasks;* and words with a facilitative meaning, such as *enable, easily, skilful, use.*

Note that all these features are context-sensitive, in that they are consistent with

- the function of the text: ie to inform, but at the same time to attract by emphasising the usefulness of the session it is advertising
- the relationship between writer and reader (the tenor), which is one of more or less equal status (practising professionals, rather than academics, theoreticians, etc) and minimal social distance – or at least that is the relationship the writers are seeking to project
- the topic, or field, of the conference – language and language teaching
- the written mode, in the form of a conference programme, which must reflect the professional aspirations of the discourse community that is hosting and attending the conference, plus practical constraints such as the need for brevity and transparency.

Task 10: Classroom texts

Patterns

also:	*also* + present participle
	auxiliary + *also* + participle
	also + finite verb
for:	*for* + period of time (*15 years, four months*)
	for + name of sponsoring organisation (*the ABC, Olive*)
	look + *for*
	noun + *for* (*a talent for*)
	for + *the first time*

you:	*you* + finite verb
as:	*as* + a job (*a chef, a kitchenhand*)
	such things + *as* + *-ing*
	as + *well* + *as*
to:	noun + *is* + *to* + verb (*my role is to manage, my goal is to create*)
	verb + *to* + verb (*started to look, want to become*)
	adjective + *to* + verb (*able to tell*)
	noun + *to* + verb (*qualities to get on*)
	not + *to* + verb (*not to forget*)
	noun + *to* + noun (*dedication to good cooking; access to good food*)
	verb + *to* + noun (*led to a full-time job; cooked to perfection*)
get:	*get* + noun (*experience, feeling, a kick, buzz*)
	get + *on*
	get + past participle
at:	*at* + place (*the Atlantic Bar, college…*)
	at + time (*the moment, the same time*)

Task 11: Point of view

Extract 1: (from *Our Mutual Friend* by Charles Dickens) The point of view is that of a detached observer who is neither physically nor psychologically involved in what is being described: he or she is not privy to the thoughts or even the perceptions of the participants. Instead, he or she identifies with the reader (*In these times of ours*), and, for the time being at least, provides no more information than that which the reader might also deduce from the description. This detachment is realised through the use of action and state verbs only (*rowed, looked for; were, had*) rather than verbs of cognition or perception (e.g. *thought, saw*) and the exclusive use of third person past tense forms, as well as the absence of proper names (*the girl, the man*). The use of modal verbs (*could*) to express the observer's speculations, and the repeated use of negatives, situate the writer as completely outside the situation.

Extract 2: (from *An Unsuitable Attachment* by Barbara Pym, Grafton Books) By contrast, the point of view in this extract is that of one of the participants in the action. Not only do we see what Rupert Stonebird sees (*he saw*), but we are privy to his – and no one else's – thoughts (note the preponderance of verbs of cognition: *thought, knew, decided, wondering*) and to his – rather than the writer's – speculations (*no doubt, probably*). The use of *they* and *the women* in the first sentence, marking as *given* what is in fact *new* information, plunges the reader straight into – not just the action – but the mind of the protagonist (compare the very deliberate scene-setting in Extract 1). But, despite our exclusive access to his point of view, Rupert is *not* the writer: the events are narrated in the third person, and the past tense provides further distance. The author is sufficiently detached to be able to comment on the situation (*The situation had nothing particularly unusual about it*) and to slip some key information to the reader, e.g. Rupert is an anthropologist, he is unmarried, he has just bought a house…

Extract 3: (from *How to be Good* by Nick Hornby, Penguin Books) Here the author's voice is the protagonist's, and their points of view coincide. The use of the first person and the present tense provides an immediacy, and an exclusive perspective on the situation as it unfolds in the protagonist's thoughts, realised mainly through state verbs (*am, is*), and verbs of mental and verbal processes (*think, want; tell, remind, say*). The use of proper names (*David, Molly*) reinforces the illusion that we know what the protagonist knows, and the use of features of spoken language, such as pausing and vagueness, as in *The other bit just sort of …* *slips out*, conveys the effect of hearing her thinking aloud, as does the use of informal language, such as *the kids*.

Extract 4: (from *Whale Rider* by Witi Ihimaera, Reed Books) The narrator's point of view is that of a participant in the story (witness the use of the first person), but perhaps not the main one. Instead, a character called Kahu is mentioned constantly. Moreover, the first person pronoun, at first singular, becomes plural: the narrator's point of view merges to become a kind of chorus figure (*me and the boys*). Nor does the narrator do anything except be present: it is not him but Koho, for example, who answers the phone. There is also a lack of assertiveness that is conveyed through the modalised uncertainty of *I suppose* and *perhaps*, and the conditional *if*, in the first two sentences, and which becomes explicit with *we were looking the other way*. Nevertheless, the point of view assumes a degree of complicity on the part of the reader: the reader is positioned as an intimate, and quite a lot goes unexplained as if it were shared knowledge, such as the untranslated Maori words, the identity of Kahu and of Koro, the assumption that at least some of the facts of the story, such as its ending, are known. This sense of being talked to by an intimate insider is reinforced through the use of conventions of informal spoken language – *well; really; me and the boys*. This in turn underscores the narrators' lack of assertion, and sharply contrasts with Koho's unequivocal rejection of his newly-born daughter.

Task 12: Learner texts

Text 1

content: The writer has fulfilled the brief, although minimally, as when itemizing the advantages of the new house, for example.

organization and cohesion: The text is appropriately organized and laid out; the paragraphs, and the sentences which comprise them, are logically ordered. An over-reliance on commas, instead of full stops, means that, at times, sentences run on. Cohesion is achieved mainly through logical sequencing of sentences and lexical means (such as repetition, lexical sets) and not by use of conjuncts (apart from *and* and *because*) or more sophisticated devices. One attempt to use a logical linker (*[on] the other hand*) is inaccurate.

range: There is a narrow range of fairly simple vocabulary used throughout; evaluative language is basic (*happy, kind*) and the intensifier *very* is over-used. The writer over-relies on the verb *to be* in her description, and the sentences are generally not complex. The most complex sentence (*I would like that you'll come…*) is flawed.

register: The style is fairly neutral but sufficiently informal to be appropriate, and the salutations, etc are suitable.

target reader: There is one attempt to engage the reader (*do you know [it]?*), but on the whole any shared knowledge that reader and writer might have is not mentioned. The rather abrupt *If you couldn't come, tell me…* may have a rather negative effect on the reader, not least because no time or date for the party has been given!

accuracy of language: There are relatively few spelling errors (*writting, live, quite*), nor errors of tense (apart from *couldn't*) and agreement. The bulk of errors are either lexical or syntactic. The former are due mainly to the wrong choice of word, as in *during, stay, come in, wait,* and the latter to wrong choice of syntax following verbs, as in *I'm writing…for telling you* and *I would like that you'll come.* The comparative structure (*a lot of advantages than…*) is incorrect. Perhaps unusually, the sentence *I'm looking forward to seeing you is* accurate.

Text 2

content: The writer fulfils the task prescription satisfactorily.

organization and cohesion: The letter is logically organized and appropriately laid out. But the third paragraph is under-elaborated and could perhaps have been included in the preceding one. At times commas are used instead of full-stops, so that sentences run on. There is a varied range of linking devices, both within and across sentences, and these are generally accurate, although *moreover* is rather formal for this kind of text, and the use of *by the way* is inaccurate here, and *to sum up* in the last paragraph doesn't work, as it is not the right register, nor is what follows a summary . But the text is highly cohesive overall.

range: There is a wider range of vocabulary and sentence structure than in Text 1, although it is still rather limited (apart from one or two well chosen low-frequency words like *brand-new* and *housewarming*), and the evaluative language consists of common adjectives like *comfortable, nice, beautiful* and *pretty,* and the over-worked intensifier *very.* Some sentences are quite adventurous in terms of complexity, as in *Not only were there little and dark rooms but…*

register: Apart from some of the linkers already mentioned (*moreover, to sum up*) the style is generally appropriate and is neither too formal nor informal, although *Yours sincerely* is a little too formal a way of signing off for a friendly letter.

target reader: There is no reference to shared knowledge, nor any real attempt to engage the reader, and even the invitation lacks sincerity (and, like Text 1, fails to provide any details as to when the party will be).

accuracy of language: The writer has taken greater risks than the writer of Text 1, but has made more errors as a consequence. These consist mainly of awkward syntactic constructions, many involving complex noun phrases, such as *it was very tiring days, quite so little rooms, little and dark rooms, large windows to pass through the sunlight, and that pretty place I've got.* There are some wrongly chosen words, eg *turned down, to open.* However, at the level of tense, agreement, and surface features such as spelling, it is generally accurate.

Extract 1.1: Transcription

ḥtp-di-nsw   *Gb* *psḏt*

An offering which the king gives (to) Geb [and to the Ennead of the]

itrt *mḥwt*   *ḥ3* *m* *t* *ḥ3* *m* *ḥnkt*

shrines of Lower Egypt : a thousand of bread, a thousand of beer,

ḥ3 *m* *k3w 3pdw*   *ḥ3* *m* *ḥnkt nbt*

a thousand of oxen and geese, a thousand of every offering and

rnpt   *snṯr* *nb*

growing thing and all (kinds of) incense, (that he may give it to)

s3,f *mr.f* *sš* *imn-m-ḥ3t* *m3'-ḥrw* [damaged]

his son, beloved of him, the scribe Amenemhat, [justified].

Extract 5.2

Reading list

Cook, G. 1989 *Discourse*. Oxford: Oxford University Press

Derewianka, B. 1990 *Exploring How Texts Work*. Primary English Teaching Association (Australia)

Hillier, H. 2004 *Analysing Real Texts: Research Studies in Modern English Language*. Palgrave Macmillan

Hoey, M. 2001 *Textual Interaction: An Introduction to Written Discourse Analysis*. London: Routledge

McCarthy, M. 1991 *Discourse Analysis for Language Teachers*. Cambridge: Cambridge University Press

Sinclair, J. 2004 *Trust the Text: Language, Corpus, and Discourse*. London: Routledge

Useful websites

http://www.onestopenglish.com/
http://www.hltmag.co.uk/
http://www.developingteachers.com/
http://www.bbc.co.uk/worldservice/learningenglish/
http://www.etprofessional.com/
http://www.iatefl.org

References

1 Trask, R. 1999 *Key Concepts in Language and Linguistics*. London: Routledge, p 312

2 Shenk, D. 1997 *Data Smog*. London: HarperCollins

3 Kress, G. 1985 *Linguistic processes in sociocultural practice*. Victoria, Australia: Deakin University Press, p 18

4 Watterson, B. 1993 *Introducing Egyptian Hieroglyphs*. Edinburgh: Scottish Academic Press, p 114,

5 Watterson, B. ibid. p 16

6 from www.ananova.com, Story filed: 11:23 Tuesday 16th September 2003

7 Sweet, H. 1899, 1964 *The Practical Study of Languages*. Oxford: Oxford University Press, p 163

8 Stevens, J. (trans.) 1977 *One Robe, One Bowl: The Zen Poetry of Ryokān*. New York: Weatherhill, p 76

9 ibid. p 63

10 Greenall, S. 1994 *Reward, Pre-Intermediate Student's Book*. Oxford: Heinemann, p 23

11 Oxenden, C. and Seligson, P. 1996 *English File Student's Book 1*. Oxford: Oxford University Press, p 125

12 Edmond, M. 1994 *The Switch*. Auckland: Auckland University Press, p 40

13 *The Observer Magazine*, 7 Sept 2003, p 16

14 http://www.newscientist.com/opinion/opbooks.jsp

15 Jack, A. 1983 *Pocket Encyclopedia*. London: Kingfisher, p 199

16 Langley, A., Macdonald, F. and Walker, J. 2000, 2003 *500 things you should know about history*. Great Bardfield: Miles Kelly Publishing, p 85

17 Bushnaq, I. 1986 *Arab Folktales*. Harmondsworth: Penguin Books, p 19

18 Langewiesche, W. 1997 *Sahara unveiled: A journey across the desert.* London: Vintage Books, p 98

19 Carter, A. (ed.) 1991 *The Virago Book of Fairy Tales.* London: Virago, p 192

20 French, N. 'How we write.' In *The Author,* Winter 2003, p 163

21 Adams, P. and Newell, P. (eds.) 1994 *The Penguin Book of Australian Jokes.* Harmondsworth: Penguin Books, p 292

22 http://www.ethnic.bc.ca/sampledurak.html

23 Widdowson, H. 2003 *Defining Issues in English Language Teaching.* Oxford: Oxford University Press, p 40

24 Marshall (ed.) 2003, *Great Little Encyclopedia.* Great Bardfield: Miles Kelly Publishing, p. 110

25 ibid, p 184

26 ibid, p 166

27 ibid, p 128

28 ibid, p 198

29 Raimes, A. 1983 'Anguish as a second language? Remedies for composition teachers.' In Freedman, A., Pringle, I. and Yalden, J. (eds.) 1983 *Learning to write: First language/second language.* Harlow: Longman

30 Jack, A. 1983 *Pocket Encyclopedia.* London: Kingfisher, p 152

31 Advert for holiday property

32 *Guardian Weekly,* 18–24 December, 2003, p 12

33 Advert for Scholl flight socks

34 McCarthy, M. 1991 *Discourse analysis for language teachers.* Cambridge: Cambridge University Press, pp 55–56

35 Jack, A. 1983 *Pocket Encyclopedia.* London: Kingfisher, p 102

36 Sinclair, J. 2004 *Trust the Text.* London: Routledge, p 15

37 ibid, p 97

38 Spufford, F. 'The Habit.' In *Granta, 77,* 2002

39 Jack, A. 1983 *Pocket Encyclopedia.* London: Kingfisher, p 213 (adapted)

40 Widdowson, H. 1978 *Teaching Language as Communication.* Oxford: Oxford University Press, p. 1

41 from Thornbury, S. 2004 *Natural Grammar.* Oxford: Oxford University Press

42 Porter, D. 'Death of the Poet.' In *Heat,* 3, 1991, p 88

43 Pilcher, H.R. 'Honey bee genome sequenced.' © Nature News Service / Macmillan Magazines Ltd, 9 January 2004

44 Hoey, M. 1991 *Patterns of Lexis in Text.* Oxford: Oxford University Press

45 Hoey, M. 2001 *Textual interaction.* London: Routledge, p 5

46 Jackson, A. and Day, D. 1993 *Collins Complete DIY Manual.* London: HarperCollins, p 79

47 McDevitt, D. 'How to cope with spaghetti writing.' In *English Language Teaching Journal,* 43/1, January 1989

48 *Aussietalk*: Macquarie/UTS Australian English Corpus

49 Aherne, C. and Cash, C. 2002 *The Royle Family: The complete scripts.* London: Granada Media, p 85

50 Laffal, J. 1965 *Pathology and Normal Language.* New York: Atherton. Cited in Duranti, A. and Goodwin, C. (eds.) 1992 *Rethinking context.* Cambridge: Cambridge University Press

51 www.fury.com/AOLiza

52 Ochs, E. and Schieffelin, B. 1983 *Acquiring conversational competence.* London: Routledge & Kegan Paul, p 22

53 Tannen, D. 1989 *Talking voices: Repetition, dialogue and imagery in conversational discourse.* Cambridge: Cambridge University Press, p 97

54 Oxenden, C. and Seligson, P. 1996 *English File Student's Book 1.* Oxford: Oxford University Press, p 125

55 Kuiper, K. and Flindall, M. 2000 'Social rituals, formulaic speech and small talk at the supermarket checkout.' In Coupland, J. (ed.) *Small Talk.* Harlow: Pearson, p 201

56 cited in Channell, J. 1997 "I just called to say I love you': Love and desire on the telephone.' In Harvey, K. and Shalom, C. (eds.) *Language and desire.* London: Routledge

57 *Aussietalk*: Macquarie/UTS Australian English Corpus

58 Jack, A. 1983 *Pocket Encyclopedia.* London: Kingfisher

59 Freud, E. 1992 *Hideous Kinky.* Harmondsworth: Penguin Books, p 8

60 from 'Sweet love rules!' In *Sugar*, March 2000

61 Halliday, M. and Hasan, R. 1989 *Language, context and text: aspects of language in a social-semiotic perspective.* Oxford: Oxford University Press, p 10

62 Jack, A. 1983 *Pocket Encyclopedia.* London: Kingfisher

63 Naipaul, V.S. 1988 *The Enigma of Arrival.* Harmondsworth: Penguin Books, p 115

64 Coates, J. 2003 *Men Talk: Stories in the making of masculinities.* Oxford: Blackwell, pp 125–126

65 Ionesco, E. 1958 (trans. by D. Watson) *The Bald Prima Donna: A Pseudo-Play in One Act.* London: John Calder Publishers, p 1

66 Hornby, A.S. 1954 *Oxford Progressive English Course for Adult Learners, Book One.* Oxford: Oxford University Press, p 52

67 Alexander, L. 1967 *First Things First.* Harlow: Longman, p 29

68 Garton-Sprenger, J., Jupp, T., Milne, J., Prowse, P. 1979 *Encounters.* Oxford: Heinemann

69 Abbs, B. and Freebairn, I. 1982 *Opening Strategies, Students' Book.* Harlow: Longman 1982, p 40

70 Palencia, R. and Thornbury, S. 1998 *Over to Us, 4, Workbook.* Harlow: Addison Wesley Longman, p 42

71 Viney, P. 1985 *Streamline English: Directions.* Oxford: Oxford University Press, Unit 5

72 Abbs, B. and Freebairn, I. 1989 *Blueprint Intermediate, Student's Book.* Harlow: Longman, p 45

73 From 'Sidelines', Europe Times, February 1995

74 Nabokov, V. *Speak Memory.* Cited in Cook, G. 2001 "The philosopher pulled the lower jaw of the hen.' Ludicrous invented sentences in language teaching.' In *Applied Linguistics*, 22:3, p 384

75 Soars, J. and Soars, L. 2000 *New Headway English Course.* Oxford: Oxford University Press, p 58

76 *New Scientist*, 22 July 2000

77 *Sugar*, March 2000, p 15

78 Sydney Morning Herald Sept 8, 1992, p. 1

79 Scott, M. 1999 *WordSmith Tools, Version 3.* Oxford: Oxford University Press

80 Kay, S. and Jones, V. 2000 *Inside Out, Intermediate Student's Book*. Oxford: Macmillan Heinemann, p9

81 *Glamour*, May 2004

82 Noble et al (ed) 2000 *Mexico*. Lonely Planet Publications, p 923

83 *Great Little Encyclopedia*. Great Bardfield: Miles Kelly Publishing 2003

84 *Great Little Encyclopedia*. Great Bardfield: Miles Kelly Publishing 2003

85 Kress, G. 1985 *Linguistic processes in sociocultural practice*. Victoria, Australia: Deakin University Press, p 18

86 Bowler, B. 'Magazine looks lose their gloss.' In *Guardian Weekly*, 18 March 2004

87 *How to recycle a goat* (Christian Aid brochure)

88 Cook, G. 1992 *The Discourse of Advertising*. London: Routledge, p 143

89 Sandburg, C. 1918 'Grass.' In *Cornhuskers*. New York: Henry Holt and Company

90 Ginsberg, A. 'America.' In *Journals Mid-Fifties 1954-1958,* Penguin Books 1996, p 207

91 Bamworth, S. 'Leave-taking.' In Aldiss, B. (ed.) 2001 *Mini-Sagas*. London: Enitharmon Press

92 Eagleton, T. In *London Review of Books, 26/3,* February, 2004, p 16

93 Nabokov, V. 1957 *Pnin*. London: Doubleday p 7

94 Aherne, C. and Cash, C. 2002 *The Royle Family: The complete scripts*. London: Granada Media, pp 499–500

95 Jack, A. 1983 *Pocket Encyclopedia*. London: Kingfisher

96 source: *The Independent on Sunday,* 21 September 2003, p 8

97 *The Sun*.

98 cited in Byram, M. (ed.) 2003 *Intercultural Competence*. Council of Europe, p 26

99 *Método de Inglés, Segundo Libro*. Colección F.T.D. Mexico 1923, p 17

100 Ellis, R. and Gaies, S. 1999 *Impact Grammar*. Harlow: Longman, p 42

101 Rinvolucri, M. 1999 'The UK, EFLese subculture and dialect.' In *Folio*, 5/2, p 14

102 Goldstein, B. 2003 *Framework 2*. Madrid: Richmond Publishing

103 Gray, J. 2002 'The global coursebook in English Language Teaching.' In Block, D. and Cameron, D. (eds.) *Globalization and language teaching*. London: Routledge, p 166

104 http://www.stuff.co.nz/stuff/dailynews/0,2106,2955760a6404,00.html

105 Mennin, P. 2003 'Rehearsed oral L2 output and reactive focus on form.' In *English Language Teaching Journal, 57/2,* pp 133–4

106 George Cooper (1820–1876) 'Only One.' In Edmund Clarence Stedman (ed.) 1900 *An American Anthology, 1787–1900*. Boston: Houghton Mifflin

107 Kulchytska, O. 2000 'The Alternate Textbook and teaching English in Ukraine.' In *The Journal of the Imagination in Language Learning and Teaching*, Vol 5: http://www.njcu.edu/CILL/vol5/kulchytska.html

108 Hall, D. 2001 'Materials production: Theory and practice.' In Hall, D. and Hewings, A. (eds.) *Innovation in English Language Teaching*. London: Routledge, pp 229–239

109 Gilmore, A. 2004 'A comparison of textbook and authentic interactions.' In *ELT Journal*, 58/4 October 2004, pp 363–374

Index

adapting texts for classroom use 14–16, 28–9, 32–4, 47–51, 60–62, 82, 97–102, 116–21, 121–4, 129–31, 136, 142–5, 156–8

alternative textbooks (see *learner-chosen texts*)

authentic texts 17–19, 62, 98, 103–7, 109–13, 116, 132, 142
  choosing 124–6
  exploiting 129–31
  vs semi-authentic texts 106–7

brainstorming 52, 60–61, 118, 120, 143

CAE (Cambridge Advanced Examination) 153–4

CEF (Common European Framework of Reference for Languages) 127–8

chunks (multi-word units) 65, 76

CLL (Community Language Learning) 157–8

cleft sentences 49–50

coherence
  at macro-level 36, 51–62
  at micro-level 36–51
  in spoken texts 68–9, 77, 83
  in written texts 18–19, 35–62
  vs cohesion 35–6, 53–4

cohesion 19–34, 84, 141, 167

cohesive devices 20–27, 47

communicative approach 104–5

conjunctions (see **conjuncts**)

conjuncts 22–3, 29–34, 59, 61–2, 64–5, 71, 141

connectors (see **conjuncts**)

content words 15, 55

contexts 84–102
  in classroom 97–101
  and coursebook texts 97–9
  and register 91–4
  and use 84–91

contextual clues 8–9, 84–5

continuing a text 47–8

conversations 63–83 (see also **spoken texts**)

conversational skills 80–82

corpuses 51, 104, 158

co-textualising (text adaptation strategy) 117

critical reading 150–2

coursebooks
  and agenda (text content) 147–52
  and contexts 97–9
  and dialogues 72–3, 77–9, 104–5
  and genre 79, 109
  and text types 126–8

definite article 25–7, 166

dialogues (see **conversations**)

discourse markers 66, 71, 76, 104, 105, 141

e-mails
  and genre/register 92, 94–5

exams 6–7, 46, 153–4

field, tenor and mode 91–4, 97, 100–102

function words 15–16

gap-fill 15–16, 29, 144

genre 94–7, 101–2, 124, 172
  and coursebooks 79, 109
  vs text type 97

glossing 117

grammar (in texts) 12–16

grammar words 15–16, 55

grammatical cohesion 21–34

grid-filling 119

guided collaborative editing 157

guided collaborative production 157–8

ideology (see **loaded texts**)

incoherence (in spoken texts) 68–9

interactivity
  and spoken texts 65–6, 76, 78, 80, 83
  and written texts 58–62

Internet use 160

interpersonality 66–7, 76, 78, 80, 83

IRF (Initiate, Respond, Follow up) 72, 79

jigsaw technique   116–17

key words   40, 51–5, 118

learner-chosen texts   160–61
learner corpuses   158
learners' texts   10–11, 31–4, 60–62,
    100–102
    adapting for classroom use   155–8
    advantages of   153–62
    and language awareness raising   155–8
    as texts in their own right   159–60
    evaluating/testing   153–5, 175
lesson plans   128–31, 143–5
lexical chains   20–22, 52–5, 62, 71, 77, 141
linkers (see conjuncts)
listening skills   131
literary texts
    advantages of   142
    characteristics of   141
    cultural-historical backgrounds   145
    exploiting   136, 138, 139
loaded texts   145–52
logical relations   41–5
logical relationships
    additive   37, 45
    adversative   37
    causal   37, 44–5
    temporal   37, 44–5

nominalization   27, 40, 146

parallelism   22–3, 32, 135, 141
passive constructions   48–9
poetry   12–14, 159–60
pragmatics   84–5, 90
predicting   112, 118–19, 120
pre-editing (of learners' texts)   156
pre-teaching   117–18, 120, 121
    and key words   118
process writing   101

question tags   65, 67

reference   23–9, 166
    back-reference (anaphoric)   23, 24, 25,
    27–8, 44, 96
    forward-reference (cataphoric)   24, 25, 28
    outside-reference (exophoric)   24–7

referents   21, 23, 28–9, 166
register (see also **field, tenor and mode**)
    and text types   91–4
relevance
    in spoken texts   70–71
repetition   62, 70–71

schemas (mental maps)   10, 23, 26, 98–9,
    143
    and scripts   55–62
scripts   55–62, 69, 72–4
segmenting   116–17
self-contained texts   17–19
self-editing (of learners' texts)   156
sentence deletion and insertion   46–7
sentences
    vs texts   6–7, 11–12, 28, 32–4, 37–8, 43–4,
    47, 48–51, 126, 153
sequencing tasks   119
shortening   116
simplifying   117, 120
skimming   98, 112, 119, 120
spaghetti writing   61
speaking skills   131, 156
speech-in-action   75
spoken texts (see also **conversations**)
    and self-editing   156
    in ELT materials   65, 68, 72–3, 77–9,
    104–5
    vs written texts   63–77, 83, 93–4
spontaneity   64–5, 76, 80, 83
    and coursebook dialogues   65, 78
story sequences (in spoken texts)   74–5
stylistics   145
syllabuses   126–8, 132

TALO (text-as-linguistic-object)   121–32,
    152
task types (see individual entries:
    brainstorming, gap-fill, etc)
TAVI (text-as-vehicle-of-information)
    121–32, 152
teacher–learner interaction   72, 79–80, 83
text-based syllabuses   126–8, 132
text difficulties   9–12, 113–16
text messages
    and register   93–4
text types   10, 17–19, 85–98, 101–2, 112,
    126–8

texts (see also **learners' texts, literary texts, text types**)
    adapting for classroom use   14–16, 28–9, 32–4, 47–51, 60–62, 82, 97–102, 116–21, 121–4 129–31, 136, 142–5, 156–8
    and grammar   12–16
    and skills development   112–13, 121–6, 128
    difficulties in interpreting   9–10, 97–8
    unlocking/unpacking   8–16, 136, 164
    vs non-texts   17–20
    vs sentences   6–7, 11–12, 28, 32–4, 37–8, 43–4, 47, 48–51, 126, 153
textualizing   50–51, 169
topic
    of sentence   38–45
    of spoken texts   70–71
    of text   51–4, 62

written texts
    vs spoken texts   63–4, 83, 93–4